NATIONAL INSTITUTE SOCIAL SERVICES LIBRARY
NO. 46

———◆———

THE SUPPORTIVE NETWORK

National Institute Social Services Library

THE SUPPORTIVE NETWORK

Coping with old age

G. Clare Wenger

London
GEORGE ALLEN & UNWIN
Boston   Sydney

George Allen & Unwin (Publishers) Ltd,
40 Museum Street, London WC1A 1LU, UK

George Allen & Unwin (Publishers) Ltd,
Park Lane, Hemel Hempstead, Herts HP2 4TE, UK

Allen & Unwin, Inc.,
9 Winchester Terrace, Winchester, Mass. 01890, USA

George Allen & Unwin Australia Pty Ltd,
8 Napier Street, North Sydney, NSW 2060, Australia

First published in 1984.

British Library Cataloguing in Publication Data

Wenger, G. Clare
 The supportive network.—(National Institute
social services library; no. 46)
1. Aged—Wales, North—Social conditions—
Case studies 2. Wales, North—Rural
conditions—Case studies
I. Title   II. Series
305.2′6′0926   HQ1064.G7
ISBN 0–04–362056–6
ISBN 0–04–362057–4 Pbk

Library of Congress Cataloging in Publication Data

Wenger, G. Clare.
 The supportive network.
(National Institute social services library; no. 46)
Bibliography: p.
Includes index.
1. Aged—Services for—Wales—Case studies. 2. Social
work with the aged—Wales—Case studies. 3. Aged—
Wales—Family relationships—Case studies. I. Title.
II. Series.
HV1481.G54W35 1984   362.6′09429   84–6298
ISBN 0–04–362056–6
ISBN 0–04–362057–4 (pbk.)

Set in 10 on 11 point Times by Preface Ltd, Salisbury, Wilts.
and printed in Great Britain by Billing and Sons Ltd, London and Worcester

In memory of

MARY LEWIS BAXTER

and

TINA MAE WENGER

whose spirited independence well into their
nineties first made me conscious of what old
age can offer

and for

Alex, Max and Matthew Wenger

their great-grandsons, who formed the link
between them.

CONTENTS

———◆———

ACKNOWLEDGEMENTS

The research on which this book is based was funded by a grant from the DHSS as part of a larger programme of work conducted by the Social Services in Rural Areas Project at the University College of North Wales, Bangor. During the conduct of the study I have been lucky to have had the support, advice and encouragement of other members of the team: Dr Gordon Grant, Mr Jim Black and Miss Elizabeth Tarran and, early in the project, Mr John Turner, whose death in a road accident was a great shock to all of us. I would like to express my thanks to these colleagues for their help and friendship and to also thank Mrs Angie Rowlands and Mrs Angie Martin, without whose assistance and tolerance in all the practical matters involved, the task would have been overwhelming. Angie Martin in particular has borne the brunt of typing and retyping the manuscript with commendable cheerfulness and efficiency. I am also grateful to other friends and colleagues who also read, advised and/or commented on parts or all of the manuscript, including Miss Tilda Goldberg, Professor Roger Hadley, Mr Robin Huws Jones, Professor Roy King and Mr Bob Woodward.

The interviewers who worked on this project had to contend with extremes of weather, a scattered rural population and on occasions the unwelcome attentions of proprietary dogs! Their performance under these conditions and the ability of most of them to interview in English or Welsh as the situation demanded won my respect and lasting gratitude. I would like to take this opportunity to thank personally: Mrs Ann ap Iorwerth, Mrs Beryl Davies, Mrs Gwenda Edwards, Miss Janet Edwards, Mrs Menna Edwards, Mrs Peggy Griffiths, Miss Winifred Griffiths, Mrs Barbara Jones, Mrs Megan Jones, Mrs Pat Jones, Mrs Llinos Kilfoil, Miss Mary Lloyd-Davies, Mrs Ann Malin, Mrs Pat Martindale, Mrs Eurwen Owen, Mrs Blodwen Parry, Mrs Dilys Richards, Mrs Eirlys Roberts, Mrs May Roberts and Mrs Evelyn Williams. I am also indebted to many others in the study communities, particularly doctors, district nurses and clergymen, who freely gave of their time to talk to me about their roles in the lives of the elderly and their perceptions of the problems faced.

My deepest gratitude, however, is felt towards all those old people who shared their lives and opened their homes to us. Their trust, willingness to help and interest made the task an enjoyable one and I remember them not only with thanks but with affection. They gave not only the information desired but also a more positive image of old age. This book is a testimony to their confidence, courage and resourcefulness.

Part One

BACKGROUND

Chapter 1

THE RESEARCH CONTEXT

INTRODUCTION

This is a study of how a sample of the elderly manage their day-to-day lives. It looks at how they gain access to a range of services, what problems they face and how they overcome them. It is an optimistic book which demonstrates that the majority of the elderly are able people who, together with help from their families and friends, find solutions to most of the difficulties they encounter as they get older.

THE QUESTION OF COMMUNITY

When we hear about old people we are usually told about their difficulties. This is because much research has focused on the problems of the elderly. This book is different in that it takes as its subject retired people living in their own homes in the community and for the most part coping capably and competently with their daily lives. It presents a picture of a well-supported elderly population and describes the informal help and support which is available to them. It seeks to encourage readers to stand back and look at the *whole* elderly population; to become aware of the majority who are well, happy, participating and contributing citizens. In this way, it hopes to challenge the negative stereotype of old age and while not denying that problems exist for some old people, to see these in the context of the broader range of experience. It is also hoped that by putting the problems in perspective their solution will be seen as more attainable.

The research, which was conducted in North Wales, was conceived originally as a first study of the United Kingdom rural elderly. The urban elderly in England had already been the subject of studies by Hunt (1978) and M. Abrams (1978, 1980) and it was felt that ageing in rural areas might present particular difficulties for old people, especially in terms of access to services. It also sought to test the hypothesis that rural communities provide a more supportive environment for the elderly.

The rural community tends to be perceived as an altogether more benign environment, seen by many as a coveted haven of stability and intimacy in an increasingly urbanised and unstable world (Russell, 1975; White, 1974). This view originally was given substance by the writings of: Tönnies (1957) who characterised the rural 'community' as *gemeinschaft* as opposed to the urban 'society' *gesellschaft*; and Redfield (1956), who characterised these two ideal types as the *sacred* and the *secular*. The popular view has clung to the idealisation of the rural village, and many of the functionalist community studies reinforced the image of the stability and timelessness of rural communities (e.g. Rees, 1950; Williams, 1956). Later writers on rural areas in the United Kingdom have pointed out that some rural villages display characteristics which approximate *gesellschaft* (Brody, 1974; Frankenberg, 1957; Littlejohn, 1964; Pahl, 1965), while the *gemeinschaftlich* aspects of urban villages have also been noted (Young and Wilmott, 1957; Townsend, 1957; Rosser and Harris, 1965). Whether these findings represented a dilution of the intimacy and interdependence in rural communities as a result of urbanisation and increased mobility (both migration and commuting) and the levelling of cultural distinctions between town and country is not clear, but at least one writer has suggested that the benign image of rural life is nostalgia for an imagined past (Laslett, 1965).

Studies conducted in urban areas do not seem to support the thesis that cities are less caring environments. The findings of Isaacs *et al.* (1972), in a study in the city of Glasgow, found that admissions to geriatric units occurred only after the family had struggled to care in increasingly difficult situations and that amongst those elderly who died at home a significant proportion were bedfast for a year or more before death, cared for by relatives. Although now dated, Townsend's (1957) study demonstrated the comparable integration of elderly people in London into networks of support. While one limited study indicates that less effective networks exist in the decaying inner city of London (Knight and Hayes, 1981), studies in the United States have pointed to the development of relationships of concern even among the most alienated elderly in single occupancy rooming houses (Shapiro, 1969). In other words, the indications are that commitment to caring is the norm, whether in an urban or rural environment, although there may be some variation according to the stability of the neighbourhood (Warren, 1980). There is some indication, however, that urban residents are more dependent on family resources, as opposed to other informal sources of care, than rural residents (Wenger, 1982). However, differences are more likely in terms of degree and style, rather than in terms of presence or absence.

In studies of rural communities, there is much evidence to support the widespread existence of neighbourliness (Arensberg, 1937; Jenkins, 1971; Rees, 1950). However, it has also been suggested that social relations also reflect not so much settlement type as stability (Gans, 1968), hence the findings of Young and Wilmott in Bethnal Green

(1957) which demonstrate the importance of neighbourliness in the city. The increased mobility of the 1960s and 1970s may have changed this situation considerably. This also has particular relevance for the elderly, who demonstrate a desire to move from urban to rural (or seaside) areas thus adding to the social change of the host community (Golant, 1979; Karn, 1977). Underlying much of the concern expressed about the position of the elderly in today's society is the implicit assumption that many of their problems tend to be urban problems: traffic, fear of crime, isolation, poor housing, and so on. On the other hand, in the field of rural deprivation, the elderly are pointed out as those most disadvantaged by problems of transport, access and inadequate services.

The current study contrasts with earlier studies in two significant dimensions. Previous studies of the elderly in the community have not paid specific attention to the various types and sources of help received, while studies of help have focused on dependent groups within the population. This research looks at help received and the sources of such help within the elderly population as a whole, including those who are dependent on such help and those where help is primarily expressive. Such expressive help of course is important in the context of increasing dependency.

METHODOLOGY

The data on which the book is based were collected in a cross-section of eight rural communities in North Wales, covering settlement types ranging from small nucleated towns (under 3,000), including two small seaside resorts with high proportions of retirement migrants, to a highly dispersed sheep-rearing area. The communities, on a wide range of outcome variables, demonstrate a high degree of similarity, the main differences being between incomers and long-term residents.

The research was conducted in two major phases. In Phase I a door-to-door census of occupied households, using rating assessors' lists, was conducted. This method was chosen because experience had shown that electoral registers and family practitioner records are frequently out of date or, in the case of the former, do not always include all the resident elderly. Phase I made it possible to collect basic background data on *all the elderly* so that any subsequent sample could be checked for sampling error. Data were elicited on age, sex, marital status, household composition, place of birth, length of community residence and whether or not Welsh speaking. This last was important so that steps could be taken to ensure that all those who spoke Welsh would subsequently be approached by a bilingual interviewer and the interview conducted in the language of the respondent's choice. Nearly three-fifths of respondents were Welsh speakers and 82 per cent of Welsh speakers were interviewed either wholly in Welsh (74 per cent) or at least half in Welsh (8 per cent) as they chose.

A Phase II sample was selected from the Phase I data. In this case, *one person from each elderly household* was selected in all communities except the three largest where half the elderly households were included. The sample was randomised for sex and household composition and the resultant sample and responding sample checked for representativeness against the Phase I data. Phase II consisted primarily of interviews in the respondent's own home, following a questionnaire schedule (Appendix 1).

Both Phase I and Phase II data were elicited by interviewers recruited and trained by the research team. Before each phase a day's training session was conducted for interviewers in an effort to standardise as far as possible interpretation and recording techniques. Interviewers were paid hourly, including travel and clerical time, plus a mileage allowance, since it was felt that the nature of the terrain and the characteristics of the sample population were such that this method of payment would ensure both equity and quality of returns. The performance of interviewers as reflected in the high standard of returns and the high response rate (87 per cent), it was felt, fully justified this decision.

In addition to objective and attitudinal data, interviewers in Phase II were requested to report verbatim comments of respondents and to write a full interviewer's report upon completion of the interviews. In only 2 per cent of interviews were respondents unco-operative and in eight out of ten instances no problems were encountered. However, with an elderly subject group some physical impairments are to be expected. In approximately one in ten instances hearing was a problem and in another one in ten interviews confusion, illness, speech, or other impediment caused some difficulty, but in spite of this 94 per cent of interviews were completed. A short form of the questionnaire (indicated in the Appendix by asterisks) was used in cases where the health or concentration of respondents made the full form impractical. Of the 534 (unweighted) interviews conducted, only 6 per cent were either short form or uncompleted.

The questionnaire covers data on residence and migration; accommodation and heating; household composition; contact with community services; morale; family, friends and neighbours; loneliness and isolation; health; mobility and dependency; access to services; help with common problems and crises; voluntary association; ethnicity; employment history and income. Where appropriate, effort was made to replicate questions used in comparable studies of the elderly (cf. Hunt, 1978; M. Abrams, 1978, 1980). In addition, composite measures of morale, loneliness, isolation and support network were included. These measures will be discussed in the context of the relevant data analysis.

Phase I was conducted in November and December 1978 and Phase

II interviews were completed between May and August 1979. In addition to interviews with respondents, open-ended interviews were conducted with clergymen, doctors, social workers and other community leaders about the elderly and their needs. Feedback meetings with interviewers were also held to glean further impressions of the elderly and their communities.

A triangulated approach to data collection was adopted in an attempt to overcome some of the shortcomings of both the positivist and participant-observer approaches. In order to cover a representative sample and to satisfy customer needs for numerical validity, it was necessary to adopt a questionnaire method both to cover a large enough population and to systematically collect a broad range of objective data on the background, current situation and demographic details of the subjects and their families. At the same time, it was felt important that the elderly people should have the opportunity to express themselves more fully and idiosyncratically without their responses being forced into precoded categories. For this reason, allowances were made for extensive verbatim comments to be recorded, particularly in those areas where more subjective responses were called for. Interviewers were also asked for their own perceptions of the subjects' situation and notes of any other incidents or information of which they became aware in the course of interview. Interviewers were made fully aware of the aims and interests of the study so that they could better assess the relevance of their observational data. The feedback meetings conducted with interviewers in groups provided opportunity for exchange and assessment of opinion and experience. In this way it was hoped to gain not only access to objective facts about the old people but also some idea of their feelings and subjective responses to their situation. Interviewers' reports also gave information, in many cases, on the process involved in the development of respondents' current situation. Thus, it was hoped to combine the quantitative validity of a survey with some of the insight of an interpretative approach.

THE STUDY POPULATION

Compared with most urban areas, the rural areas studied have a higher proportion of their population in the elderly category, but within the elderly population itself the age and sex distributions are comparable with the general English population (Hunt, 1978). However, there does appear to be some relationship between population sparsity and the incidence of singleness. Approximately twice as many in the general sample have remained unmarried; three times as many males and twice as many females as in Hunt's study (1978). Bachelorhood appears to be closely related to low population density; however, this does not hold for spinsterhood, perhaps because females are more likely to move into larger settlements at all stages of the life cycle.

Singleness is less frequent among the young elderly, but is still almost twice as common as in Hunt's sample (Hunt, 1978, p. 12). The number of divorced persons in the study is minimal. However, in both the current study and Hunt's survey, these are concentrated at the younger end of the age distribution and, given the overall increase in the rate of divorce, may be expected to increase further in subsequent cohorts.

As in Hunt's survey, a third of the rural elderly are living alone, three-quarters of whom are women. However, fewer live only with their spouse or in households with young relatives, while more live with other elderly relatives (Hunt, 1978), related to the higher incidence of singleness. In the more dispersed areas, more live in households with younger relatives than in the small towns and villages. With increasing age, more live alone or with younger relatives, but overall three-quarters of the elderly are either alone or living with other elderly persons. One-tenth have members of their households who are physically dependent on them.

Despite retirement migration, the rural population in Wales remains predominantly of local provenance, with more than three-fifths living within 50 miles of where they were born. Three-fifths think of themselves as Welsh and almost as many are Welsh speakers, although there is a wide range of variation reflecting migration trends. Based on the numbers who have moved within the previous ten years, most of the communities are more stable than Hunt's areas of comparable population density; but speculative building of retirement bungalows can completely distort this stability in particular communities.

Incomers to the region arrived at all stages of their lives. Those who moved into the area in their youth and middle age came mainly from other parts of rural Wales while retirement migrants came mainly from the midlands and north-west of England. There is some indication that retirement migration reflects the national economy and is currently reduced. Those who came to their present communities before retirement moved primarily because of their jobs or available housing or because of prior connections with the area. Of those who moved after 60, short moves were based on available housing, to be nearer relatives and to move into town from the countryside, while 'migrations' were stimulated predominantly by the attraction of the environment supplemented by connections with the area, available housing and proximity to relatives.

Compared with Hunt, slightly more of the elderly are owner-occupiers (59 as opposed to 50 per cent) and fewer are either council or private tenants. Retirement migrants are more likely to be owner-occupiers. Despite the greater average age of housing, household amenity provision appears to be better than in Hunt's more urban sample. It seems that poor housing may be related to population density since it is known that in rural Wales itself, pockets of bad housing exist in the larger towns not included in this study. In terms of general housing conditions, the rural elderly appear to be better situated than the urban elderly both in terms of amenities and convenience.

On the other hand, many of the elderly live in fairly remote places. A quarter have no year-round next-door neighbour and for nearly a fifth their nearest neighbour is more than 50 yards away. However, few of those living in remote situations live alone.

As a result of the occupational structure of the region and selective mortality amongst males, the class distribution of the elderly is skewed towards social classes I and II, comparable with Hunt (1978). Interestingly, while retirement migrants are concentrated in social class III (skilled workers), short-distance retirement moves appear to be a primarily middle-class phenomenon.

More men than women work after retirement age in both Hunt's study and the current study. Although more men were working in the rural area, fewer work full time. Fewer women were working in the rural area, reflecting the fact that fewer women have actually been in the work force.

Because of generally depressed regional incomes during their working lives and lower proportions eligible for contributory pensions the rural elderly are worse off financially than their urban counterparts. This is reflected in the fact that half as many again receive supplementary pensions. Their weaker financial position is, however, exacerbated by higher regional food prices; the need for many to run a car due to inadequate public transport, coupled with higher petrol prices; higher average fares per mile; absence of piped gas in most communities forcing the use of more expensive fuels; and, in many cases, delivery charges for small orders. On the other hand these problems are offset to some extent by higher proportions of owner-occupation and available firewood and garden produce.

The position of the rural elderly and their needs for social services can be described as a swings and roundabouts situation in comparison with their urban peers. While a higher proportion of the population is elderly, amongst whom more are single and thus potential isolates, and while fewer have younger household members and their financial position is less favourable, these demographic disadvantages are offset by generally better housing conditions, a slightly greater proportion of owner-occupiers and, as data analysed elsewhere will demonstrate, a greater level of social integration and local adaptations to solve problems of the rural milieu. However, as subsequent discussion will show, the similarities between the elderly in rural communities and urban settings are more significant than the differences.

PLAN OF THE BOOK

The aim of this book is to explore the hypothesis that the elderly and others in their social network negotiate help and adapt to the demands of ageing in a flexible, creative and mutually supportive way. It attempts to evaluate the availability of potential help; to identify and describe the types and sources of support which old people receive and to look in the broader context at the coping strategies which they develop in order to maintain themselves in their own homes. The book looks at the patterns of help developed through such negotiations. While it was not possible within the constraints of the research remit to study in detail *how* such patterns emerge, the data show clearly the existence and prevalence of competent adaptations where help is needed.

Part One of the book discusses some of the relevant literature, the methodology and the basic demographic characteristics of the rural elderly studied. Comparison with Hunt's (1978) study shows that the rural elderly in Wales are comparable in most instances with the elderly population of England as a whole. Before considering the nature of informal help, it is of course necessary to know something about the levels of dependency of the elderly and their access to and reliance on formal services. Part Two, therefore, describes the health, mobility and dependency levels of the rural elderly. It looks at communication systems available to them and the adaptations they make to gain access to needed goods and formal services.

Part Three of the book covers sources of potential informal help by looking at the social context of the elderly and contacts with family, friends and neighbours, their participation in voluntary organisations and community. In Part Four the nature, extent and sources of various forms of help given and received by the elderly are discussed and overall objective and subjective measures of their social environments considered. The presentation of data in an aggregate form can distance the reader from a fuller appreciation of the lives and experiences of the old people upon whom the study depended and so several detailed studies of the coping strategies of real respondents are presented. Part Five considers the implications of the findings with particular emphasis on the nature of coping as a phenomenon and their significance for future social services policy.

Chapter 2

THE SOCIAL CONTEXT OF CARE

INFORMAL CARE

The paradox of old age is that while we all hope to achieve it, the success of Western society in making this possible for more and more people is seen as a growing social problem. The sociology of ageing in the United Kingdom has tended to ignore the contributions and self-reliance of most elderly people. And yet it is the self-sufficiency of the elderly and their families which social policy seeks to promote. The normal lives of ordinary old people may not stand out as extraordinary but they may nevertheless be remarkable in their own way. Perhaps because they are so much a day-to-day part of living, such aspects of social life have received little attention; but it is the minutiae of life which form the major component of experience and play the central role in determining for the individual life's character and quality.

The nature and importance of the adaptations we make in coping with the problems of life and the informal support and help we expect from family, friends and neighbours are two such areas which have not received the attention they deserve. Adapting to changing experience is frequently made possible only by the informal help available. For most of us such help is given and accepted as an integral part of daily life taken for granted as unremarkable and only noticed when it becomes unavailable. It is perhaps for this reason that interest has more recently turned to considerations of sources and reliability of informal help.

Each one of us is embedded in a web or network of social relationships. The last decade has witnessed a growth of interest in these social networks and in self-help against a background of concern for the decline of natural support. Anxiety has been expressed about the impact of increased geographic mobility, the expansion of the female labour market, the decline of the inner city neighbourhood, the increase in the elderly proportion of the population, and the increasingly individualistic emphasis of life in late twentieth-century Western civilisation. At the same time, economic difficulties have resulted in the recognition that welfare interventions cannot keep pace with growing expectations and there has been a shift in policy towards greater reliance on the resources of the community. This chapter looks at the available literature in an endeavour to answer questions about the availability of relatives, friends and neighbours and other potential sources of help and the types of problems that may exist. It also considers what has been written about adaptations to old age.

A shift towards community social work has been advocated by the Barclay Report (NISW, 1982): 'to work in close understanding with informal care networks' (para. 13.13). However, the authors of the report admit that more information about the nature of such networks is needed. In urging more study of non-problem behaviour it has been suggested that 'We may never know how many helping hands are extended and reached out for every day' (Smith, 1978).

Because social workers and health care professionals deal primarily with instances where informal care networks cannot cope with the demands, they frequently underestimate the prevalence and persistence of informal patterns of support. Writers in the social policy field have questioned both the existence of informal support networks (Parsloe, 1981) and their prevalence and reliability (P. Abrams, 1980). Often misgivings about available informal support have been predicated solely on the proximity of immediate kin (M. Abrams, 1980). Philip Abrams, whose earlier writing on neighbourhood support took the view that informal networks were weak and ineffective, admitted later that subsequent research had changed his mind and that the strength of informal networks was greater than he had initially thought. In this climate of uncertainty and discovery, recent shifts in policy emphasis towards greater reliance on informal community support have received mixed reactions. If government policy is to concentrate ameliorative measures on the community, however, we need to know more about the extent, nature and sources of informal helping behaviours. On the one hand, social changes are perceived as weakening the system of informal care, and on the other, governments are increasingly pointing to informal care as a basis for statutory interventions.

For no one group are these two conflicting states of affairs more germane than for the elderly. As the largest client group of health and social services, care for the old has traditionally come from the family. Now, with increased longevity, not only are the aged an expanding part of the population but their adult children, as the most likely potential carers, are also an ageing group. Since more people are living into their eighties and nineties, the problem of providing care to the frail elderly is becoming more prevalent. This has meant more pressure on local authorities to provide support. Current policy aims to maintain the elderly in their own homes as long as possible and more emphasis is being placed on domiciliary services. However, the statutory services provide help for only a small proportion of the elderly in the community. Most help comes from family, friends and/or neighbours. It will, therefore, become increasingly important for social services to reinforce and bolster such informal support as exists.

Like all members of society, the elderly fill many roles. They are parents, brothers, sisters, grandparents, friends, neighbours and members of voluntary organisations and communities and it is from this social network that many of their satisfactions and most help and support comes. Considerable attention has been given to the study of family life, friendship patterns and voluntary associations of the elderly, and this research, in spite of some differences of opinion, gives a good picture of the social milieu in which different old people live.

THE FAMILY

Policy-makers in urging a shift of emphasis back to community care are placing great importance on the family: 'One of the major findings of social research in ageing in all western countries has been the rediscovery of the important role of the family in old age. Research evidence indicates that family help and exchange of services are widespread between both old people and their children and relatives. . . . The continued reports of the family as a major caretaker for the sick elderly . . . reflect not only the inherent strength of the family as primary support group but also the fact that family members are available who can fill the role of unpaid nurses and home helpers' (Shanas, 1977). However, in spite of the weight of evidence of family support, M. Abrams (1980) claims that 'for a large minority of the elderly in this country family members are certainly not available and [that] even where they are available the family bonds are sometimes so fragile as to be almost non-existent' (p. 34). Although he bases this statement on the nearby availability of children and siblings only, geographical separation, female employment and the tensions inherent in the frequent role conflicts of adult children result in a high level of pressure on family bonds. However robust these may be and because of the trend towards smaller families, subsequent cohorts of the elderly will have fewer available relatives.

Much that is written about the family in industrialised nations is often based on the explicit assumption that the pre-industrial family, sometimes thought to survive in remote rural regions, consisted of three-generational households providing care and security for the elderly based on commitment and the pressures of social norms. This idealised family structure is thought to have been disturbed or even destroyed by the accelerating rate of social change which followed the industrial revolution. Research, however, shows that this form of family has not been typical in Britain. Discussing the agricultural community at the turn of the century, Jenkins (1971) notes that 'children set up their own homes on marriage' (p. 157). Two decades earlier Rees (1950) commented that 'three generation households occur only under exceptional circumstances' (p. 70). Laslett (1965) has demonstrated convincingly that the nuclear family was the norm in pre-industrial British society, both as a result of life expectancy and custom. Few could hope to live long enough to see their grandchildren and old age was not taken for granted. Even where parents lived to be old, filial responsibility was no more guaranteed than it is today. Shanas and Streib (1965) have pointed out that as a result of enhanced life expectancy the statistical incidence of the 'multigenerational' family is increasing as higher proportions achieve three score years and ten. They suggest that in a rapidly changing world, the family becomes more important rather than less important to the individual. Research from a wide cross-section of developed countries demonstrates that not only does most care come from the family (Maede, 1981; Cibulski, 1981) but that most people think that this is where the responsibility should lie.

The importance of the extended family in the lives of elderly people, and vice versa, has been well documented (e.g. Adams, 1967; Blau, 1973; Bott, 1957; Lebowitz, 1980; Rosenmayr, 1968; Rosow, 1965; Rosser and Harris, 1965; Shanas, 1968; Townsend, 1957; Young and Wilmott, 1957). Although the family in the lives of the elderly has been exhaustively explored, primary attention has focused on the role of children. The childless and their relationships have received less study. However, those without children and/or siblings form primary links with available kin or non-kin in the form of close family substitutes (Kivett and Maxheamver, 1980; Townsend, 1957). Indeed, Stephens et al. (1978) found that social support systems of the childless are more extensive than those of people with only one or two children, although this does not imply that they are more effective.

Other research has investigated the *relationship* between parents and their adult children, and while cultural expectations of care exist, the result of the pressures these place on the relationship depends on previous patterns of behaviour (Sussman, 1965) and may not be conflict free (Kivett and Maxheamver, 1980). While Blenkner (1965) found that children 'voluntarily and willingly' assume caring responsibilities, she suggests that social work is not equipped to help middle-aged children of ageing parents because training is oriented towards the individual and the nuclear family. However, Isaacs et al. (1972) found that in many instances children tried to help even alienated or rejecting parents when they were in trouble, although in some cases such help was refused. With increased longevity, caring children are now frequently themselves grandparents and suffer problems of role conflict, while the relationship of the frail elderly to adult grandchildren is less well understood (Shanas, 1981; Stevenson, 1980).

Statements about the availability of family, while empirically valid, tend to overlook the importance of the psychological relationship between the aged and their helpers. Relationships with carers tend to be ignored in social work assessments (Luders, 1981). Luders found that lack of help for carers and interpersonal tensions were extensive, with disability causing more physical strain and confusion more psychological tension. More than fifteen years ago, Townsend (1965) identified the breakdown of caring relationships (either physical, emotional, or interactional) as one of the primary precipitating causes of admission into old people's homes, and others have stressed the need for the support of family carers (Fengler and Goodrich, 1979; Gross-Andrew and Zimmer, 1980; Hobman, 1981; Hörl and Rosenmayr, 1981; Savitsky and Sharkey, 1972; Treas, 1977). However, it is daughters and daughters-in-law who are usually the care-givers (Hunt, 1978; Sussman, 1965), and Finch and Groves (1980) have recently pointed out that present policies tend to presume the availability of women. This may not be in harmony with ideas about equal employment opportunities.

By the same token the present elderly generation, freed of inevitable economic dependency on working children by the welfare state, value their physical independence and find pride in their continued autonomy. Blau (1973) has shown that while the elderly may turn to their children for help, this is not without reluctance, for being dependent on children can lead to loneliness and demoralisation. However, she also found that the elderly are reluctant to talk about the negative aspects of dependency on children. The nature of the adult child–parent relationship is, perhaps for this reason, not a well researched field despite being a frequent fictional topic. It is discussed here in detail in view of current trends in social policy.

Recent research in the United States, Japan and Western Europe has shown that similarly large majorities of respondents (approximately 80 per cent) in each country studied felt that the dependent elderly should be cared for in a child's household. Only in Japan, however, where legislation provides tax and service incentives for the family, is this happening on a large scale (Maede, 1981).

It has also been shown that the family's position as care agency demonstrates variations according to class (Hellebrandt, 1980; Leyton, 1975). An earlier US study (Jandetti and Gelfand, 1976) found that independent living was favoured by the middle class while immigrant families were more inclined to the three-generation household. It is important, therefore, not to ignore cultural factors of preference or tradition. Back (1965) has suggested that while today's elderly parents were socialised when taking care of aged parents was normative, successive generations may feel differently. In a more recent cross-cultural study, Weihl (1981) found that *most* aged parents said that they preferred living apart from children. The dynamics of this relationship, the practical and emotional needs of the care-giver and the types of problems involved warrant further research and greater understanding if social services are to adapt domiciliary services to provide support for old people and their carers, which the present policy climate indicates will be necessary.

FRIENDS AND NEIGHBOURS

Although the family has been the central focus of research on the elderly, attention has also been given to the importance of friends and neighbours. Friendship has been shown to be more important than family interaction for high morale and life satisfaction (Blau, 1973; Spakes, 1979; Wood and Robertson, 1978). However, certain structural constraints appear to affect friendship patterns. Allan (1977) has demonstrated systematic class differences, showing that middle-class persons do not limit friendship interactions to one activity, whereas working-class relationships tend to be more activity specific and family assumes a more central role. A recent study of the middle class elderly by Hellebrandt (1980) reinforces his findings, demonstrating that high value is placed on friends, friendship and independence from children. Commenting on the importance of age homogeneity in social relationships, Rosow (1967) found that the elderly find it easier to make friends where there is a high proportion of old people in the local population. This view is supported by Karn's (1977) findings. Bennett and Despres (1960) have described how friendship groups may 'simulate consanguinal ties and obligations' in the absence of proximate kin.

Many of the elderly make little distinction between friends and neighbours, the distinction appearing to be a mainly middle-class construct. The proximity of neighbours is a present safeguard for the elderly who spend many hours each day at home. The importance of neighbourly support has been considered by Hadley et al. (1975), Power (1980) and Robinson and Abrams (1978), and neighbours and friends appear to have a high substitution potential in the absence of family (Bytheway, 1979). The importance of neighbourhood support has led to attempts to create such involvement where it is absent (Hadley et al., 1975; Power, 1980), although this trend appears to have a longer history in the United States where it was already identified in 1964 (Harp and Gagan, 1969).

Migration also affects social networks. Walker (1975) found that the size of visiting networks was proportional to the length of residence in a locality, although it seems this may be related to the nature of the neighbourhood since migrants to retirement destinations stress the ease of involvement (Karn, 1977; Spakes, 1979). Homogeneity may be more critical. Fairly rapid integration of rural migrants in the United States has been reported by Rieger and Beegle (1974), although there are indications that this is less likely in larger receiving communities or where migrants belong to lower socio-economic groups. Class homogeneity seems to be important for assimilation, since Pahl (1965) found comparable problems for middle-class migrants into working-class villages (see also Karn, 1977; and Law and Warnes, 1973).

Retirement migration has received considerable attention (Karn, 1977; Law and Warnes, 1973; Lemon, 1973; Mellor, 1962; Whittington, 1977). Pull factors are generally seen as more important than push factors with the environment being the greatest attraction. However, proximity to friends or relations is a significant minority motive for retirement moves (Hunt, 1978; Karn, 1977; Law and Warnes, 1973) so loss of social support must not be overestimated. On the other hand, the usual retirement migratory household consists of a man and wife and bereavement soon after such a move can result in extreme social isolation. In a small sample study of widows in a seaside resort, Whittington (1977) found migrant widows to be more isolated than more local widows, although local widows were equally lonely. This seems to suggest a lower level of social integration among the migrant group.

The indications are that friends or neighbours are likely to be more important than family to some sub-groups, such as the childless, those who have never married, the middle class and those who have moved away from family or whose family have left an area, for instance in search of employment. At the same time it may be that length of residence in a community has a significant effect on the strength of affectual bonds and recent incomers may find themselves less well supported than long-term residents.

VOLUNTARY ORGANISATIONS AND COMMUNITY INVOLVEMENT

Jerrome (1981) has illustrated the close relationship between friendship patterns and voluntary association. Participation in voluntary associations has been shown to be highly correlated with life satisfaction (Cutler, 1973; Knapp, 1977; Kutner, 1962), although this in turn is related to the better health and socio-economic status of participants (M. Abrams, 1980; Bollman *et al.*, 1975; Bull and Aucoin, 1975; Cutler, 1977; Karn, 1977). Social participation decreases as health deteriorates, and Stephens *et al.* (1978) find that informal social support also declines with age. There are *some* indications that for certain groups involvement in voluntary associations may be sought to compensate for the absence of closer social ties.

ISOLATION AND LONELINESS

Some of the elderly either fail to develop or lose contact with social networks so isolation and loneliness have received considerable attention (Aughney, 1963; Hadley and Webb, 1974; Harris, 1975; Help the Aged, 1977; Kivett, 1979; Lebowitz, 1980; Mulligan and Bennett,

1977; Palmore, 1976; Shanas, 1968; Whittington, 1977; Wilkes, 1978). It has been repeatedly shown that there is no direct relationship between isolation and loneliness. There seems to be no one cause of loneliness and for any sub-group the majority are not lonely. Other research shows that loneliness and isolation are frequent presenting problems among elderly social services clients (Black *et al*., 1983), though there appear to be discontinuities between the existence of such needs and the degree to which the personal social services can meet or ameliorate them. Shanas (1968) has pointed out that loneliness is more related to loss than to isolation and that old age brings multiple losses such as job, spouse, friends and health. Even those living with others may be lonely.

Both isolation (Palmore, 1976) and loneliness (Hazan, 1980) have been linked with demand for institutional provision. In contrast with social isolation, which is an objective state, loneliness as a subjective state is less apparent to the observer. Perhaps for this reason, ameliorative effort has tended more to recommendations for self-help (Help the Aged, 1977; Lake 1980). The understanding of loneliness has remained elusive, partly due to problems in definition of such an abstract and subjective concept and partly due to the reluctance of sufferers to discuss it. The difficulties of measurement of subjective states are well documented and the problem with loneliness is exacerbated by denial amongst those who experience it because of the stigma involved. While loneliness amongst the aged appears to be no higher than among other vulnerable groups, certain categories are more prone to it than others: those living alone, the recently widowed, the single, the very old and those in poor health.

INFORMAL SUPPORT NETWORKS

It is recognised that most help and support for the elderly comes from the family, with friends and neighbours stepping in where needed. Recent research has stressed a need for interweaving family, friends, neighbours and volunteers with the statutory services and charitable organisations (Black *et al*., 1983; Hadley and McGrath, 1980; Tinker, 1981), and some experimental projects aimed at promoting enhanced care-giving for the dependent elderly have been initiated (Challis and Davies, 1980; Tarran, 1981). It has been said that the extent of informal social support is an important variable in understanding the social needs of the elderly (Stephens *et al*., 1978) and the usefulness of knowledge of social networks has been demonstrated in planning services for the elderly in the United States (Snow and Gordon, 1980). Unfortunately, the nature and functioning of informal support networks is still inadequately understood. Collins and Pancoast (1976) suggest that 'Social workers are trained to notice instances when people fail to receive help or support from those in their normal circle of acquaintance', and therefore functioning helping networks receive little attention. It is this gap that this book seeks to narrow by using a population rather than a client sample.

What we do know about networks has more to do with their structure and form than the dynamics of how they work. Warren (1980) describes different types of neighbourhoods and finds that support systems also differ. He identifies a continuum of support styles from the 'parochial' to the 'anomic' neighbourhood. In the parochial setting there is a high level of mutual aid and 'taking care of one's own', while in contrast the anomic setting refers all problems to outside agencies and resists any involvement. Stable rural communities, in Warren's scheme, would in most instances be considered parochial. Presumably the inner city studied by Knight and Hayes (1981) is at the anomic end of the continuum. However, the key discriminator appears to be stability rather than the urban–rural distinction. Stable urban neighbourhoods are no less likely to be parochial than rural parishes.

Urban networks are found to have a kinship core with peripheral friendships while rural networks include more friends and neighbours (Walker, 1975). Collins and Pancoast (1976) also report differences between urban and rural networks and state that rural networks are more likely to be of the small, dense variety. Craven and Wellman (1973) found that dense networks are generally small with strong linkages while loosely knit networks tend to be large with less involvement. Loose networks provide better access to tangible resources but dense networks better access to emotional resources. Cibulski (1981) has hypothesised that a person's personal resources are related to his or her social support network. She distinguishes between expressive and instrumental support and finds that informal supporters of the elderly are, in order of importance, spouses, children and neighbours. Social and geographic proximity are found to be important for network formation and Collins and Pancoast (1976) also found spatial proximity important. Stephens *et al*. (1978) found that religious activity and organisational membership were also linked to greater support but that the level of support declines as community size increases. However, they found that very few had a social support network of less than four persons.

In the United States the network approach to social and health service provision has received considerable attention over the past decade (Garrison and Howe, 1976; Collins and Pancoast, 1976; Froland *et al*., 1979; Kent, 1976; Rueveni, 1979). Approaches have covered the full range of working with and through networks to attempts to develop artificial networks. Others have studied 'natural' and paid helpers. Patterson (1977) found that these two types differed. Paid helpers concentrated on specific people and problems while natural helpers directed efforts to any form of need as and when required.

The elderly are more frequently the providers rather than the recipients of help (Worach-Karolas, 1979). The involvement of the elderly as natural helpers has been recognised and formalised in some instances and the elderly have been involved in peer counselling (Bolton and Dignum-Scott, 1979) and in self-help groups (Butler *et al.*, 1979–80). The dynamics of informal help are complex, however, and P. Abrams (1978) stresses that 'individuals use different informal networks for meeting different kinds of needs', reiterating the observation of Litwak and Szelenyi (1969).

LIFE SATISFACTION AND ADAPTATION

Many of the same social factors which contribute to social integration and availability of support are also related to overall life satisfaction. Considerable attention has been placed on the quality of life experienced by the elderly and various attempts to measure and describe life satisfaction have been made (Szalai and Andrews, 1980). Toseland and Rosch (1979–80) find that among those over 55 there are nine main predictors: (1) family life satisfaction; (2) personal health satisfaction; (3) satisfaction with dwelling; (4) number of close friends; (5) community integration; (6) age; (7) satisfaction with health facilities; (8) homogeneity of neighbourhood; and (9) satisfaction with community. However, among these over 65, health and adequate income obviously affect several other factors. Adequacy of income as a significant factor in life satisfaction among the elderly has been discussed by several writers (Bull and Aucoin, 1975; Chatfield, 1977; Scott and Kivett, 1981). These findings suggest a broad area of overlap between adequate support and satisfaction with life in general, although so far the findings remain often contradictory.

Creecy (1976) and Kutner (1962) have found that morale also demonstrates a high correlation with social and community involvement. However, Scott and Kivett (1981) maintain that neither health nor social participation explains differences in subjective well-being among widows and find adequacy of income most diagnostic. Lawton (1980), discussing the fact that the rural elderly are objectively more disadvantaged than the urban elderly, wonders why life satisfaction measures are not more depressed. He suggests the presence of intervening variables, particularly the informal social network. Fengler *et al.* (1981) have reported similar findings.

Bell (1974) claims that satisfaction with life is less concerned with external factors but reflects the degree to which expectations are met. For instance, all older persons expect some contact with their family; some expect frequent contact, others do not, and either way if the expectation is disappointed life satisfaction is likely to be reduced. He stresses therefore that the amount of contact with family is not a reliable indicator. The importance of expectations has also been discussed by Maclean (1976) who finds that personality, age and confirmed expectations are more indicative of a positive reaction to retirement and life satisfaction than either health or adequacy of income. In what might be considered a related field, Andrews and Withey (1974) found that feelings of self-efficacy were an essential component of life satisfaction, while Gifford and Golde (1978) found that effective coping styles leading to a feeling of control over one's life are two important dimensions of self-esteem among the elderly.

Recent trends in research directed to a better understanding of ageing have shifted from the quantitative to the qualitative, notably in the University of Bonn's longitudinal study of ageing. Lehr (1981) has suggested that styles in ageing adaptations can only be effectively studied through consideration of the life history of the individual. She identifies two basic adaptations which are affected by the events of the life history: an intra-familial adaptation (where family activity increases and there is withdrawal from community) and an extra-familial adaptation. Those adopting the extra-familial response have generally higher IQ; higher social activity; feel more needed; have less conflict with children and co-operate more with children. Fooken (1981), studying older women, describes a variety of life-styles and adaptations related to life experience and marital status and stresses that it is impossible to speak of a typical elderly woman or a typical or optimal adaptation. Her positive adaptations indicate a high salience of positive self-image supportive of Gifford and Golde's (1978) findings. Maas and Kuypers (1974), using a similar approach, also point to continuities in the life cycle, although they find that personality is more stable for women than for men but women's adaptations are more dependent on their social context. They also stress the importance of extra-familial activity and involvement.

Elder and Rockwell (1979) also urge a life course perspective of adaptations among the elderly. They suggest that adaptation and the stressfulness of change depends on (1) the nature of the change, that is how drastic; (2) life experience, expectations and flexibility; and (3) the temporal context of change, that is, its position in the life course. Death of a spouse is seen as the highest magnitude of life change. Some changes, however, may be stress reducing. The life course perspective has an interesting parallel in the normal experience of reminiscence, the reviewing of one's life in old age. Butler (1964) has commented on the therapeutic effect of the life review for the individual in understanding and coming to terms with his or her own life.

Life satisfaction is an all-embracing concept in which the social and physical environment and one's adaptation to it play a large part. It is evident that a broad overlap exists between support from family and friends, which reinforces self-esteem and self-image, and one's outlook on life in general. At the same time, intervening variables of income, health, age, marital status and personality also play an important part. As the individual moves through life, experience and personality interact to produce varying styles of adaptation and coping strategies. These individual approaches to life can be seen to shape one's expectations and responses to the problems of old age and presumably affect patterns of interaction and reciprocity which develop.

CONCLUSIONS

British research on the elderly has, in the words of Todd and Taylor (1981), 'been always obsessed with old age as a social problem'. As a result, most of this work has been problem oriented or concerned with the functioning of the welfare state. The result has been that we know far more about the problems of the elderly than we do about their successes and competences.

The foregoing discussion of the literature indicates that the elderly are well supported by their families and friends. While children are the most likely supporters of the frail elderly, those who are childless or separated by distance or estrangement from children form similar relationships with more distant kin or with friends or neighbours. In fact, the importance of peer group friendship appears to be more important for the morale of the elderly than family contacts. Today's well elderly value their independence and participate in a wide range of extra-familial activities. While loneliness in old age is feared, it appears to be no more common than amongst other groups and the majority of the elderly are enmeshed in functioning social networks. Frequently, the elderly themselves are the givers rather than the receivers of care. Both the social integration and the community contributions of the elderly are important in terms of their overall morale and satisfaction with life. Depending on the social milieu in which they find themselves, they make appropriate adaptations to deal with the problems of ageing flexibly and competently.

While the literature reviewed in this chapter does indicate the existence of support for the elderly, much of it is narrow in scope. Studies tend to look at particular aspects of old age in isolation: for example, contacts with children, the importance of friendship, or attitudes to community. What this book attempts to do is to present a composite picture of the total social environment of old people and the types and sources of informal help available to them. By attempting to consider total support networks, variations between the sources of support for various sub-groups of the elderly and how different crises are approached, the author hopes to be able to make specific policy recommendations in terms of how, why and where informal networks may be bolstered, reinforced, or supported. At the same time, the book seeks to identify where weaknesses in informal systems may occur and need to be addressed in face of the increasing burden that enhanced longevity, coupled with smaller family size, may incur.

Part Two

ACCESS

Chapter 3

———◆———

MOBILITY AND COMMUNICATIONS SYSTEMS

To gain a clear picture of how elderly people deal with the day-to-day practicalities of life, it is necessary to know something about, first, their general health and mobility and the extent to which their own physical limitations may create difficulties; and, secondly, the use and availability of communication systems (telephones, transport). Subsequently, Chapter 4 will look at how the elderly get to various services or how services are brought to them – both frequently needed services such as shopping, post office and library and infrequently used services such as those provided by the health, social services and other commercial and voluntary bodies. It is intended to look at by what means access to various services is achieved and what adaptations are made to counteract problems of sparsity, particularly by those without cars or those unable to go out alone.

In reporting on the data, the historic present tense is used throughout. This of course refers to the situation at the time of the survey.

HEALTH, MOBILITY AND PHYSICAL DEPENDENCY

Health and Mobility
Only about 2 per cent of those over 65 live in residential care accommodation (OPCS, 1980) and a similar proportion in long-stay hospitals, so that those living in the community comprise more than 95 per cent of the elderly population, although those in residential institutions represent higher proportions of the older age categories.

The most striking aspect of the health of the elderly is their generally positive attitudes and the overall high level of mobility: striking because it is in contrast with the generally negative stereotype of old people as suffering poor health. More than 90 per cent in the study are able to go out unassisted; a further 7 per cent go out with help and less than 3 per cent are bedfast or housebound, figures which are close to Hunt's findings (1978, p. 70). Only one-fifth claim to be in poor health (2 per cent) or say their health is only fair (18 per cent); all others say either that their health is good or excellent (44 per cent), or that it is all right for their age (37 per cent). However, in most medical surveys it has been noted that differences of opinion between doctors and the elderly are likely to exist on the subject of their own health (Anderson, Ferguson and Judge, 1974), and a random check of questionnaires found that the rural elderly appear to consistently estimate their state of health as better than an objective assessment might indicate. This factor was also commented on by clergymen in the area, who frequently found themselves either contacting doctors or persuading their members to do so. It has been suggested that because the negative stereotype of old age promotes expectations of ill health, old people refuse for as long as possible to accept the label and continue to profess that they are well (Tinker, 1981).

More than half, on the other hand, admit that their activities are limited in some way by their physical condition, and this goes some way to explaining the difference between those who claim their health is good and those who claim it is all right for their age. (Two-thirds of those who say that their health is all right for their age suffer from limitations.) But not all those who suffer from limitations claim their health is other than good. There seems to be a high level of acceptance of physical restriction as a natural consequence of the ageing process, a fact which has been documented elsewhere (Williamson *et al.*, 1964).

Health is obviously affected by ageing. The proportions of those stating that their health is all right for their age increases steadily with age, suggesting acceptance of increasing limitations, with the majority of those over 90 claiming that their health is all right for their age! Since any evaluation of this type includes a measure of subjectivity on the part of the respondent, the fact that such high proportions in all age groups report that their health is at least all right for their age suggests a high level of psychological as well as physical well-being, which is borne out by generally high morale as measured on the Philadelphia Geriatric Center Morale Scale and discussed in Chapter 8 (Lawton, 1975).

Physical Limitations on Activity

Those who said that their activities were limited in some way were asked what the limiting condition was. By far the most common limiting factor is arthritis or rheumatism, restricting activity for a fifth of all respondents. This figure, of course, does not represent the true proportion of sufferers since many others suffer from the complaint but do not feel that it hampers their mobility. Heart and respiratory problems are the other main constraints. Women are more likely to suffer from arthritis, rheumatism and other physical handicaps, while men are more prone to respiratory complaints. (This is supported by Hunt's findings, 1978, Table 10 5.1, p. 71.)

Those who are housebound suffer predominantly from arthritis/

rheumatism or other physical handicaps and heart problems, although almost half cite 'other ailments'. Those who can go out only with help are primarily limited by arthritis/rheumatism, impaired vision and other physical handicaps. Arthritis/rheumatism is the greatest threat to mobility for the elderly and raises questions with respect to its prevention, treatment and management if more elderly are to be encouraged to remain longer in their own homes.

Personal Care and Dependency
As the foregoing indicates the majority are well able to care for themselves in spite of their limitations, but for a minority physical deterioration can make even the simplest tasks of personal care impossible. Respondents were asked how they managed on a modification of the list of personal care items used by Hunt (1978). On most items more than 90 per cent manage on their own without difficulty. The item most have difficulty with is cutting their own toenails. Whilst most can manage to do this task for themselves, nearly a fifth need help.

The other tasks where 5 per cent or more need help are: taking a bath or all-over wash (7 per cent); getting out of the house alone (7 per cent); and getting up and down steps (5 per cent). For all other areas of personal care – washing hands and face, putting on shoes and socks, doing up buttons and zips, dressing, getting to and using the toilet, getting in and out of bed, eating, brushing hair or shaving, and getting around the house – 3 per cent or less are in need of help and most have no difficulty at all. As one would expect, limitations on activity increase with age. While 98 per cent of those under 75 are able to go out alone this is true for only 80 per cent of the over-75s.

Loss of mobility brings more problems for those who live alone than for those who live with others, and just as many living alone suffer from limitations on their activities. In spite of this, 95 per cent are able to go out without help compared with only 82 per cent of those living with relatives. Those living alone are less dependent than those living with others, even given the average lower age of those who are married. However, those living with younger relatives or other elderly relatives form the most dependent group. Family support is very evident here.

The majority of those needing help receive assistance from other members of their household or relatives living in another nearby household (Table 3.1). In some cases, where facilities are limited, baths are taken in relatives' homes. As in Hunt's study, significantly low proportions are helped by friends or neighbours; it appears that personal care falls into the family domain with support when necessary from health services.

Professional help is prevalent only for chiropody services and for help with bathing, that is, longer-interval needs. All short-interval needs are met by relatives, usually in the same household but in some cases from

Table 3.1   *Sources of Help (Where Received) Given with Personal Care Tasks to Those Who Can Do Only with Help or Not at All (percentages)*

	Taking a bath	Cutting toenails	Getting up and down steps	Getting out of the house
N =	(48)	(110)	(26)	(45)
Person in household	48	35	77	69
Relative outside household	10	6	19	29
Friend/neighbour	0	2	4	2
District nurse	42	9	0	0
Home help	0	0	0	0
Chiropodist	0	47	0	0
Not enough help	12	3	0	0

another household. Of those receiving help, more than half receive professional help with cutting toenails and two-fifths with bathing. Compared with Hunt's findings, higher proportions of the dependent elderly receive help with bathing from the district nurse and fewer get help with cutting toenails from chiropodists. But in both studies the majority of help comes from the family, mainly those within the household.

Compared with Hunt's survey (Table 10.8.1, p. 73) the rural elderly appear to be slightly less dependent, although the same four long-interval items present greatest difficulty:

Can do only with help:	Wales	Hunt
Cutting toenails	17	27
Taking a bath	7	15
Getting out alone	7	12
Up/down stairs	5	6

This difference is difficult to explain, particularly since Hunt states that regional differences are not significant. Unfortunately she gives no breakdown by region or population density. The fact that 2 per cent more were housebound in her total sample would not account for the degree of difference measured. Since the level of domiciliary services received in the study areas is comparable or higher than in Hunt's study, it would appear that a similar level of domiciliary services is available, albeit to a population with an apparently lower level of dependence! Unfortunately, Hunt's study gave no comparable self-perceptions of the state of health so a comparison cannot be made, but similar proportions of limiting conditions and of mobilitiy restrictions indicate similar levels of impaired health. Another possible explanation might be a higher ratio of available geriatric or Part III beds, thus removing the more dependent from the population, but this also would not explain the similar proportions of housebound and those whose activities are limited.

In both the current study and Hunt's study it was found that levels of dependency are higher amongst those elderly living with younger members of the household. While it is reasonable to imagine that increasing dependency increases the likelihood of moving in with younger relatives, it is also possible that this may subjectively increase perceived dependency. Since fewer of the rural elderly have younger relatives in the household (19 per cent compared with Hunt's 33 per cent), and since twice as many are single, it is possible that these figures reflect the greater independence of those who continue to do things for themselves. Obviously, if a task is repeatedly done by someone else it is easier to accept that one needs that help, that is, figures may reflect available help rather than need. It is interesting to note that Schooler's (1975) study of 4,000 elderly in the United States found that although the urban elderly perceived their health to be better, the rural elderly scored higher on questions relating to functional performance on a variety of personal tasks. It seems likely, then, that what this difference measures is greater determination to be self-sufficient among the rural elderly. The fact that they place a high value on independence has been noted (Goldstein and Eichhorn, 1961; Britton et al., 1961a), as has the expectation of acquiescence of elderly parents towards children (Britton et al., 1961b). Thus regional or rural–urban variations may be cultural rather than epidemiological (see Collier, 1977).

The epitome of such independence was encountered by one of the interviewers. Having found the potential interviewee out on two occasions, she returned and met an old man with one leg hobbling home on crutches carrying what she described as 'an enormous log', which he planned to saw up for the fireplace. He explained that he had declined an offer of home help because he felt the neighbours – none of whom could be seen from his remote cottage – might 'talk' if he had a woman in the house!

Summary

In summary, the vast majority of the rural elderly are sufficiently mobile to be able to go out alone, and although half have some physical problem which places limitations on their activities, few consider their health to be only fair or poor. Their general level of health and mobility compares with that of the urban elderly, but the rural elderly appear to be more independent in terms of personal care tasks and it is suggested that this may reflect household composition and rural norms of greater determination to maintain self-sufficiency and independence.

AVAILABILITY AND USE OF COMMUNICATION SYSTEMS

A quarter of the elderly surveyed have no year-round next-door neighbour. The problems of remoteness can of course be mitigated by adequate communications systems. If efficient linkages can be made between people and the services they require, then sparsity becomes less of a problem. Either people must be able to get to the services or the services must be able to come to the people, which requires that the person needing the service can communicate that need. Transport and telephones are therefore very important to the rural community, not only in emergencies but for many essential requirements of day-to-day life.

Transport

Transport is the most serious problem facing rural populations, and where community services are concerned the elderly expressed serious dissatisfaction only in this area. Of the study communities, only two small towns have rail service. Most communities have some sort of bus service but in many cases it is rudimentary. In some communities, while services are less frequent than one would expect in an urban area, there is more than one bus a day. Others have one bus a day but frequently buses run less than daily. In one community with two buses a week hospital visiting is impossible. However, many of the elderly people interviewed live more than 2 miles from a bus route and even where buses exist timetables present difficulties. Voluntary car schemes have been introduced in a few communities, designed particularly to help the elderly and for journeys which cannot be made by existing bus services. In most outlying hamlets there is no bus service and thus there is heavy reliance on private cars. Those elderly people who do drive frequently express anxiety about the need to retain their cars and admit that although they are loath to move, the expense of running a car or the failure to get licences renewed would force them to move into town. Several people have given up their cars because of the expense. A few, however, use bicycles, including one woman of 90, and one or two admit to hitch-hiking!

Private cars

As a reflection of the demands of the rural area, 50 per cent of the elderly live in households with a car, compared with 32 per cent in Hunt's study. This figure is higher than Hunt's low population density areas (39 per cent), medium density areas (41 per cent) and retirement areas (41 per cent). But half of the elderly households surveyed are without a car; in one-third of households the elderly person has a car and in the rest another member of the household owns a car. Although a higher proportion of the elderly are living in households with cars, the difference between the elderly and the non-elderly remains. A recent mid-Wales study indicated that approximately

Table 3.2 *Access to Car and Telephone (percentages)*

| | Has | | |
	Car in household	Telephone	N
Total	51	65	(702)
Hunt (1978)	32	44	
By household composition			
Living alone	18	49	(228)
With spouse only	64	71	(275)
With younger members of household	75	71	(134)
With other elderly relatives	60	63	(60)

three-quarters of households have at least one car, that is, half as many again as the households of the elderly (Wenger, 1980). Car ownership is highest in the least densely settled communities as a direct reflection of lack of public transport; and in the most scattered and remote community studied where fewer live alone, more than three-quarters of the elderly live in households with cars (see Table 3.2).

Since rural incomes are low relative to urban areas (Thomas and Winyard, 1979; Wenger, 1980), the necessity of car ownership, referred to by Coles (1978) as 'forced car ownership', can place an acute financial burden on households which in an urban context would not take on this expense. This, of course, is additionally burdensome for the elderly, whose incomes are further depressed. National data (CSO, 1978) indicate that those with the lowest incomes spend most on food, housing and heating. As incomes rise, additional money goes to the expenses of car ownership. Obviously, if rural car-owners have lower incomes, savings must be made on food, housing and heating, all of which, given the longer hours spent at home per day, are likely to cause greater hardship for the elderly. Those with their own cars frequently comment on the high cost (overall and regional) of petrol, and express anxieties about keeping their car in the face of increasing costs.

Car ownership declines with age, and married persons are more likely to have a car, both as a reflection of age and income. Widowhood can result in the loss of private transport, not only as a result of reduced household income but because many women of this generation have never driven. This can also mean a forced move in from the countryside to a service centre. It is those who live alone who are most likely to be in a household with no car. All other types of household are more than three times as likely to have a car (see Table 3.2).

The overall proportion of households with cars, however, is important not only to those who live in such households but also to those who live in households without a car. As subsequent discussions will show, lifts with others are an important mode of access in some communities, and while most may use other means in the normal course of events, in emergencies a lift is frequently the only possible way of transport. Respondents were asked about lifts in the context of necessity, so that even those with cars were asked where they would turn in the event of their own car being unavailable. The fact that only one in ten would not ask for a lift or is unable to name a potential driver is indicative of the high level of acceptance that this demand on others has in the rural context. Very few would call a taxi.

Sources of lifts are slightly more likely to be a neighbour or friend than a relative, and for those without a car, a neighbour or friend would be the most usual source. Overall, two-thirds would turn to someone outside the household, two-fifths to a neighbour or friend. Reliance on friends and neighbours, as might be expected, is highest in those communities with high proportions of incomers. Most of those who would not turn to anyone were car-owners, who would presumably call out the garage!

One significant difference is that those who need help to go out alone rely overwhelmingly on family members; hardly any mentioned friends or neighbours. As with personal care it seems that a constraint exists on making demands on friends and neighbours which could perhaps be construed as 'above and beyond the call of duty'. This area of what demands various persons might feel free to make or accept from others standing in different degrees of relationship and different roles, and under what circumstances, is one which warrants further exploration.

Public transport   The availability of public transport is reflected in the fact that half of the respondents never use any form of public transport whatsoever, compared with approximately one-tenth in Hunt's survey. As already noted, bus services in all the communities are at best rudimentary and fares are generally high. The small towns of the region tend to be approximately 20 miles apart so most of the elderly use buses mainly to go into town and home again rather than from one town to another. Less than two-fifths overall use a bus, and it is interesting to note that where the train service does exist, more use the train than the bus.

Although car ownership compensates for lack of public transport, this does not necessarily mean that those in households with cars never use public transport. Some use the bus or train for specific journeys, particularly over longer distances. Those who do not have their own cars but live in households where someone else has a car cannot always count on the availability of a lift and use public transport occasionally. However, 75 per cent of bus-users, 61 per cent of train-users and 100 per cent of regular taxi-users live in households with no car, and only 28 per cent of those with no car never use public transport, compared with approximately 70 per cent of those where cars are available.

With increasing age and widowhood fewer of the elderly drive, so that higher proportions of the older elderly and those whose health is impaired use buses and taxis. Trains and longer journeys are taken *less* frequently by these sub-groups.

More use the bus than other forms of public transport and in most communities concessionary fares are offered to pensioners. At the time the survey was conducted, these generally meant an annual concession of £5 which has since been increased. For most journeys this means five free trips a year into the nearest shopping centre. For comparison, 87 per cent of the elderly living in the Greater London area are able to get a *free* pass, 65 per cent in Yorkshire and Humberside, and 49 per cent in the West Midlands where most of the migrants to the area came from, but in retirement areas only 9 per cent are eligible for free passes (Hunt, 1978).

Significantly public transport users comment on fares as a problem as common as physical mobility. Nearly a quarter find fares a problem and almost a fifth of users find that timetables are difficult. In instances where there is only one bus on a day this means the elderly have to spend far longer away from home than they would wish. Often this means additional expense on a cup of tea or a meal out in order to pass the time and have somewhere warm to sit down. Sometimes timetabling causes more severe problems. One elderly woman has to leave her husband, who is in his nineties and chairbound, alone in the house while she takes the bus to do the weekly shopping. She lives in a small village with no real shop and so has to make this trip almost every week. The bus schedule means that she is away from home for more than five hours and she worries all the time about her husband.

In other cases, it is impossible to use the bus to visit a town further away than the next nearest town, because it is impossible to return the same day. Also mentioned is the fact that buses and trains operate independently, meaning long waits of an hour or more at the station. Many have long walks to reach bus stops, which are without seat or shelter, and although rural traffic is not excessive, lanes are frequently narrow, outside the small towns there are no pavements and often what traffic there is is heavy or agricultural. Roads are more likely to be uneven, muddy, or in bad weather strewn with debris from surface water, all of which can make walking more difficult, and in the winter months schedules may make it difficult to return before dark. On the plus side, most local motorists will stop to offer a lift to anyone they recognise. One old lady in an extremely isolated cottage walks 2 miles to the bus stop with a wheeled shopping basket and comments ruefully that the difficult part is coming back uphill since hardly anyone ever goes that way! Another admits unashamedly that she hitch-hikes.

More than two-fifths of those who use public transport have mobility problems. The most commonly mentioned is difficulty with the step up or down into the train or bus. Frequently this is not merely a problem of stiff joints but of physical mobility coupled with the difficulties of carrying shopping, coping with a walking stick and needing one or both hands free to pull oneself into the vehicle. Getting out presents equally difficult problems. Respondents comment on the kindness of bus-drivers/conductors who are helpful. One small private firm was singled out for praise: the driver carries a small portable step and one old lady tells how 'when I have a lot of shopping he helps me out and carries my bags right up to the front door for me', adding 'so I always go to X rather than Y because then I can go on his bus'. Overall, more than two-thirds of users are satisfied with the service and dissatisfaction is highest among those who are occasional users, mostly where the household car belongs to someone else.

Several rural communities have now introduced community bus services and in others a rural car service has been established to supplement the ordinary bus service. The service is for people who 'have no public transport, cannot use a private car' or 'because of age or infirmity can't use public transport'. One service is provided by the county council and run by the local WRVS. It is a local service within a 20-mile radius, and although users may make a donation, there is no obligation to pay. The service has been very well received by the elderly in the area. However, a private individual in another community who wished to provide a mini-bus and start a similar more local service for the elderly was unable to get support from the local authority and found that the costs involved in insurance made the venture impossible without such support. Another county council which has introduced a number of innovatory schemes (Davies, 1978) runs voluntary essential car schemes. The most common use to which such cars are put is to visit relatives in hospital.

When asked for suggestions of things that might help the elderly in general in their community, two-thirds are able to suggest changes. The most frequently mentioned overall is improved transport (15 per cent). Also mentioned is the need for better travel concessions (6 per cent).

In summary, car ownership is high in the region and public transport limited. Of those who do use the buses, a significant minority have problems with fares, mobility, or timetables. The whole area of public transport is one which offers scope for innovation and flexibility. Supplementary schemes are now appearing and it is felt that integration of various forms of transport could provide a more flexible service. For instance, the rural car schemes provide transport to visit hospital patients for those unable to get there otherwise, while out-patients in most cases are transported by ambulance. Currently, indications are that rural bus services will be cut further as local authorities find themselves unable to maintain or increase subsidies to regional bus companies. It is hoped and anticipated that local innovations in transport will be the outcome.

Telephones

While the problems of population dispersal are tempered by high car ownership, they are also offset by a higher proportion of households with telephones (see Table 3.2). Two-thirds of the elderly are on the telephone compared with just over two-fifths (44 per cent) in Hunt's study (Hunt, 1978, p. 105). Of those without a telephone only 3 per cent have tried to get one through social services and most without say that they do not need one. Several old people state that they have never used a telephone and that when needed neighbours telephone for them. On the other hand, several say that the telephone has been installed and is paid for by their children as a present so that they can telephone to reassure themselves that their parents are well. In some cases, this occurred after refusal by social services. It therefore seems significant that telephones are more common in those communities where the highest proportions are more than 50 miles from their nearest child.

While 65 per cent have a telephone in their home, another 24 per cent use the telephone in a neighbour's house and only the remaining 11 per cent use a kiosk. For most of those who do use a kiosk, the nearest one is more than 100 yards from the house. Several respondents comment that kiosks are frequently out of order or vandalised, or that the coin box is over-full so that calls cannot be made. Whilst the proportion using kiosks is small, the fact that unprofitable rural kiosks are being removed is a source of some concern. One might consider their significance as an emergency service – how profitable, for instance, are motorway emergency telephones?

Many give the impression that telephones are only for emergencies. This is particularly so for those without telephones in the home, but several with telephones comment that they rarely make outgoing calls although their children regularly 'check up' on them, especially those who live outside the area.

For those who live alone the telephone provides a sense of security and/or a link with their children. It is also the most commonly mentioned source of *help* in an emergency. However, fewer of the elderly living alone have telephones than those living with others. Less than half have a telephone, compared with 71 per cent of those living with their spouses or with younger relatives and 63 per cent of those with other elderly relatives. Again this reflects the low incomes of single-person households. Telephone calls on average are more expensive in rural areas because the spread of population and services means a higher proportion of calls incur long distance charges.

Other research conducted as part of the same programme has shown that the telephone is the major means of contact (and referral) with social services and becomes more significant the further away one moves from the area office (Grant, 1981a). It is also the main form of communication with the doctor when illness strikes. Many of those who have groceries delivered and those few who use taxis also rely on the telephone. It is perhaps not putting it too strongly to suggest that for the rural elderly the telephone is both literally and figuratively a lifeline.

Overall only 5 per cent are dissatisfied with their access to a telephone. However, fewer telephones are supplied to persons of pensionable age by the social services departments in Wales than in any region in England. The discrepancy is such that Yorkshire and Humberside – the English region providing the fewest SSD telephones – provide almost twice as many as Wales, and in the West Midlands, which is the main 'sending' region for retirement migrants to rural Wales, more than five times as many telephones are provided per 1,000 households (Regional Statistics, No. 12, 1976, p. 67, Table 4.15). Those who applied to social services for a telephone are turned down mainly because they are not considered to be 'disabled' or because it is felt a kiosk is within walking distance. In one instance, such a decision involved a woman over 80 with no nearby relatives, who was waiting for a hip replacement and walked with two sticks.

Summary

Both the car and telephone offset the problems of remoteness, isolation and poor public transport. Some elderly households have both car and telephone, some one or the other, but more than a quarter of elderly households have neither. What is particularly perturbing is that nearly half of those who are living alone have no car and no telephone – more than twice as many as those living with others – and only 14 per cent have both compared with approximately half of those living with others.

Households are more likely to have a telephone than a car. Telephones are more common in those communities with high proportions of retirement migrants. Cars are related to sparsity with most in the low density communities and fewest in the high density communities.

In summary, although car ownership is higher and telephone installation more frequent in the rural areas, significant minorities are without either and thus reliant on help from friends and neighbours or, for a small minority, the use of public transport and telephone kiosks. Those who live alone are twice as likely to be without a car or telephone as other groups. While car ownership is related to population sparsity, telephone installation appears to be related to retirement migration.

Chapter 4

ACCESS TO BASIC GOODS AND SERVICES

Given the fact that distances and transport present rural people with greater problems than urban residents, how do elderly people manage to acquire necessary goods and services? It is possible to divide services into those which are needed on an average weekly basis, such as food shopping, post office and perhaps library; and those which are needed less frequently, such as medical attention, social services and chemist. Access to those services needed weekly is obviously more critical, needing more patterned adaptations than longer-interval needs, where solutions can be on a more *ad hoc* basis. For instance, someone might be prepared to ask for or offer a lift on occasions but might hesitate to make regular demands or to commit themselves on a regular basis. Data were collected on where and how people have access to various goods and services, when they last used the service and how satisfied they are (see Tables 4.1, 4.2, 4.3 and 4.4). The results indicate a high level of adaptation to and satisfaction with the rural situation.

SERVICES NEEDED ON A WEEK-TO-WEEK BASIS

Shopping for Food

The majority of respondents get their groceries, greengroceries and fresh meat from their local village. This of course varies by community, and the local village for someone living in a small town may be designated as a nearby town by someone in an outlying hamlet; by the same token, some are not within walking distance even of their local village. However, 'local village' is interpreted to mean the nearest settlement where there is likely to be a shop. In some of the communities the village shop is the only commercial enterprise. Nearly three-quarters of respondents obtain their groceries from their local village, while a fifth go to a nearby town. Greengroceries and fresh meat are less likely to be available in the smallest villages and this is reflected by the fact that slightly fewer obtain these supplies locally. A high proportion grow at least some vegetables. Some choose to go to the nearest town rather than the village to take advantage of greater variety, faster turnover of goods (which are therefore more likely to be fresh) and often lower

Table 4.1 *Sources of Goods and Services (%)*

	N =[1]	Local village	Nearby town	Mobile service	Delivered/ house calls	Other	Not available	Not[2] needed
Groceries	(666)	73	20	2	4	3	0	1
Greengroceries	(666)	67	21	4	4	2	0	3
Fresh meat	(664)	58	31	5	3	1	0	3
Post office	(667)	86	13	-[3]	-	-	0	1
Library	(665)	26	10	12	1	0	-	51
Prescription	(667)	62	31	1	1	-	0	4
Doctor's surgery	(668)	65	31	0	2	-	0	3
Chiropodist	(666)	12	17	0	4	-	1	65
Optician	(666)	23	63	0	1	2	-	12

[1] Missing values fluctuate slightly for various items.

[2] Either living in child's household or catered accommodation for groceries etc., also including home produce and vegetarians for greengroceries and meat.

[3] Hyphen indicates less than 0.5%.

Table 4.2 *Access to Local Services (%)*

	N =[1]	No need/ never use	Someone else goes	Delivered/ house call	Walk	Drive	Lift	Public transport (or taxi)	More than one/others
Groceries	(647)	0	20	9	36	20	6	4	5
Greengroceries	(642)	3	19	9	35	20	5	3	5
Fresh meat	(647)	3	19	10	30	22	7	5	5
Post office	(647)	2	17	-	47	19	7	4	4
Library	(640)	54	5	5	20	10	4	1	2
Prescriptions	(645)	5	19	2	33	21	10	7	4
Doctor's surgery	(645)	4	5	4	36	25	16	8	3
Chiropodist	(643)	63	0	5	6	11	5	5	1
Optician	(631)	14	1	0	17	29	19	18	2

[1] Missing values fluctuate for various items.

Table 4.3 *Access to Services by Car Ownership*[1] *(%)*

		No need/ never uses	Someone else goes	Delivered/ house call	Walks	Drives	Lift	Public transport (or taxi)	More than one
Groceries:	No car	1	22	12	(49)	1	5	7	4
	Own car	-	11	4	31	(43)	4	-	7
	Car in HH	5	(30)	7	11	26	17	0	4
Greengroceries:	No car	2	21	15	(47)	1	5	7	5
	Own car	1	10	4	31	(44)	3	-	5
	Car in HH	11	(30)	3	9	27	15	0	4
Meat:	No car	4	22	16	(40)	0	5	9	5
	Own car	-	10	4	26	(51)	4	1	5
	Car in HH	5	(33)	6	9	26	19	0	4
Chemist:	No car	5	25	3	(42)	0	9	14	3
	Own car	7	7	1	27	(46)	5	1	6
	Car in HH	4	(25)	1	19	24	24	0	3
Doctor's surgery:	No car	5	8	6	(49)	0	14	16	3
	Own car	4	1	-	27	(54)	9	0	4
	Car in HH	2	2	7	18	31	(39)	0	1

Chiropodist:	No car	70	-	7	8	0	4	(9)	1
	Own car	66	0	3	5	(23)	4	-	1
	Car in HH	66	0	6	0	(16)	10	2	1
Optician:	No car	18	2	0	22	0	21	(35)	2
	Own car	9	0	0	16	(63)	10	1	2
	Car in HH	15	2	0	2	31	(42)	8	0
Post office:	No car	2	24	-	(59)	0	5	8	3
	Own car	1	7	0	40	(43)	4	-	5
	Car in HH	4	21	1	(26)	20	25	0	4
Library:	No car	58	6	5	(24)	0	3	3	1
	Own car	49	3	4	18	(20)	3	0	3
	Car in HH	53	4	7	9	(16)	11	0	0

[1] Modal form of access is circled.

Table 4.4 *Last Use of Local Services (%)*

	N =[1]	Within last week	Within last month	Within last 6 months	Up to a year ago	More than year ago	Never use
Grocer	(627)	96	2	0	0	0	2
Greengrocer	(626)	93	2	-	0	0	4
Fresh meat	(626)	92	3	1	0	0	4
Post office	(622)	91	6	1	0	0	2
Library	(636)	21	14	4	1	2	57
Prescriptions	(623)	25	31	22	8	8	6
Doctor's surgery	(628)	14	31	28	10	12	5
Chiropodist	(648)	1	7	11	4	5	72
Optician	(636)	2	1	11	21	50	15

[1] Missing values fluctuate for various items.

prices. Small village shops are more expensive and carry a narrower range and limited fresh foods. However, even in the small towns prices are higher regionally than those in the conurbations.

While more than a third walk to fetch their groceries, an equal proportion rely on others to deliver their groceries to them. A quarter go by car, mostly their own, with a small proportion depending on lifts. Public transport is used by very few.

The low figure for mobile services reflects their rarity rather than choice. Mobile grocers serve only some of the more outlying areas. Mobile greengrocers and mobile butchers are more common, serving more communities. Since the figures reflect only the most usual source, the proportion who *use* mobile services is probably higher, with others using them occasionally, in bad weather, or when ill. Those over 75 are more than twice as likely to use the mobile services, and the fact that they are also twice as likely to have goods delivered or to have someone else doing their shopping for them is indicative of the real need mobile services meet. Recent economic developments have resulted in cutbacks or higher charges for mobile services and deliveries, and it may be that the situation has deteriorated since the data were collected. Almost 40 per cent of those over 75 rely on someone else to bring their groceries – twice as many as those in the 65–74 age group. And twice as many in the older age group use public transport while fewer drive. Shopping for food is not merely a question of access to shops, it also involves carrying bags back home, so that even if the shop is within walking distance, those with available transport are likely to take advantage of the use of a car and others will have goods delivered.

There were very few housebound in the survey, but half relied on someone else to do their shopping and the other half have goods delivered to the door (not mobile services). Of those who can only go out with help, more than two-thirds have their goods brought to them by someone else and most of the remainder have goods delivered to the door. Four people only in this category went themselves (with help), two walked and one each had a lift or went by bus.

The main form of access for food shopping is related to both availability of a car and household composition which, as has been shown above, are not independent of each other. Among those without cars, walking is the most common form of access; otherwise someone else goes or goods are delivered. Where the elderly person owns a car they usually drive but a substantial minority still walk. Where the car belongs to another member of the household it is apparently they who shop; usually someone other than the elderly person does the shopping. Most of those living alone walk; most of those living with their spouse only drive; and in the majority of other cases someone else does the shopping. Public transport is used only by households with no car and the very elderly. Those with their own car are most independent of others getting their food, but those without cars are more independent than those who live in households where someone else has a car – independent in this context taken to mean they gain access without help from others, that is, they walk, drive, or use public transport. Almost three-fifths of those without a car either walk (the vast majority) or use public transport.

More than 90 per cent had obtained groceries, greengroceries and fresh meat within the week preceding the interview, so there does not appear to be any problem in getting provisions, and satisfaction with the services is very high, 93–95 per cent being satisfied with their sources of food.

Post Office

Eighty-six per cent have access to a post office in their local village and nearly half walk there; however, fewer walk to the post office in rural than in urban areas. Hunt (1978, p. 121) found that nearly three-quarters were able to walk to the post office. However, more of the elderly walk to the post office than walk anywhere else because even some small hamlets without a shop may have a post office. Because post offices are more locally based, even those with cars walk to the post office almost as frequently as they drive. The local village post office is used by the majority in every community and a very high level of satisfaction exists.

Nine out of ten had been in contact with the post office within the week before the interview, either in person or by someone going for them. The most common reason for going to the post office is, of course, to collect their pension, which is due on a particular day. The role played by the local post office in the monitoring of old people will probably never be entirely known, but the interviewers found rural post offices helpful and informative about finding the sample. They knew if people were at home, were ill, were away, or in hospital and unlikely to return. The threatened closure of small rural post offices would obviously reduce potential community contact for the elderly and destroy an important network link through which informal monitoring now takes place.

Library

Just over half of the respondents never use a library. The proportions not using the library are highest in those communities with the highest proportions of Welsh-speakers. It is dangerous to draw any conclusions from this, but it is tempting to speculate. Many of the elderly were educated in Wales when the emphasis was on learning to read and write English, while Welsh was neglected. Subsequently while living their lives in Welsh, many found that they could read and write fluently only in English. Could this discourage the habit of reading books?

This is one area where mobile services are well provided. Most of the outlying areas are served by mobile libraries and 12 per cent overall use them. However, as a percentage of library-users 26 per cent use a mobile service (36 per cent of users over 75). Again, access to libraries is by car where this is available, but the majority go on foot. Readers who use the mobile service must be at a specific place on a specific day irrespective of weather or needs. However, the mobile library service generally provides an excellent service and for the housebound will, in extreme cases, take books to a house during their visit to the village and willingly find books and bring them in for readers. Most users use the library regularly and here again a very high level of satisfaction exists with the service.

Getting out and using these services is of course far more than merely instrumental behaviour. Visits to the village shop or post office (which may be the same establishment) are more than role interactions. The shop frequently serves as an informal centre for the area during the working day. It serves as an information exchange where one may inquire whether the road to X is snowbound or clear, what has been decided on an issue by the community council, or when Mrs Jones is coming out of hospital. A visit to the shop is a social exchange for the elderly as well as an access to services. Some elderly people who live nearby may make more than one trip in a day, often it is felt by shop-keepers for a 'little chat'; two-thirds of respondents report that they talk regularly to people in the local shop(s).

Mail and milk are delivered to all but the most remote dwellings, often on a daily basis. Whether or not residents meet postmen and milkmen depends in part on the timing of deliveries, but more than half talk regularly with the postman and almost half with the milkman. Conversations in shops are more prevalent in the three small towns because more people can get to the shops themselves. These contacts are perhaps more important to the well-being of the elderly for the validation they provide – most will know and use the elderly person's name – but they also demonstrate contact with essential services.

HEALTH SERVICES

As Moseley *et al.* (1977) have noted, primary health care in rural areas has increasingly been organised on the basis of group practices covering larger catchment areas than previously. Hospital services have also been increasingly centralised so that distances between hospital and home have been increased. In the study area, for instance, there are no district general hospitals. There are, however, cottage hospitals in some of the small towns. Only two small towns of our eight study settlements have

Part III accommodation for the elderly. One psychiatric hospital in Denbigh serves all North Wales.

Only one community studied is large enough to have its own thirty-bed hospital. Ten of those beds are geriatric beds in a new wing built recently by public subscription. However, because of the high proportions of elderly persons in the community, doctors told us that at least half the acute beds are regularly filled with long-stay geriatric patients. Recent trends in migration concern doctors in this community who anticipate a rising demand for geriatric beds over the next decade. In two communities, geriatric patients are sent to hospitals well outside the local area.

Hospital visiting is one of the most difficult aspects of rural life and in-patient care for a spouse is perhaps one of the more stressful aspects of ageing which many people have to face. While many of the elderly face the prospect of their own death with equanimity, the loss or threatened loss of a life's partner is a real anxiety.

The anguish which the long distances to hospitals cause was well illustrated in a conversation with a tearful old man. He explained that he was very upset because his wife was in hospital approximately 40 miles away. (She died of cancer within a week of the conversation.) He had tried to nurse her at home as long as possible but she had been in hospital for about a month, and since there was no feasible public transport beyond the next nearest town 25 miles away he had hired a taxi twice to go and see her. Because of the distance, he had to ask the taxi to wait for him. It had cost him, he said, £15 a trip. Subsequently, he had been offered help through social services to pay the cost of transport. 'But', he said, with tears running down his face, 'she's so far away!' He felt he could not go as often as he wished and although it remained unspoken he obviously knew his visits were limited by time as well as access. The natural anxieties experienced by the elderly faced with hospital treatment are, therefore, exacerbated because of the separation from friends and relatives that this will mean, and in many of the smaller settlements this also applies to old people's homes. The importance of the survival of small cottage hospitals in rural areas cannot be overestimated in this regard. In all study communities, hospital visiting by bus was out of the question, except for the one local cottage hospital.

Out-patients without their own transport are taken to hospital by ambulance. For some of the elderly this may be preferable to using a car if the distance is long or if their ailment makes driving difficult. Such visits to hospital can amount to an ordeal since other patients must be picked up on the way and dropped off on the return trip. It is probably no exaggeration to state that an out-patient visit takes up a full day, much of it spent waiting – for an ambulance to arrive, picking up other patients, for the doctor, for the ambulance to return and dropping off other patients. The distances involved coupled with the sparsity of population again maximise the inconveniences suffered. In a few outlying areas there is no ambulance service for out-patients and many are forced to use taxis.

Ambulance services in the region have also been centralised and this has serious effects for some communities. In the study communities, provision ranges from one with an ambulance station in the town itself to another which straddles the county line between Clwyd and Powys. The nearest Clwyd ambulance station takes approximately an hour to reach the village. Ambulances from the Powys side can be there in fifteen minutes. The Clwyd service, therefore, tries to insist on the Powys ambulance being used! The hazards of this aspect of remoteness are evident, particularly in cases of cardiac arrest and life-threatening emergencies. Often retirement migrants, finding themselves in a town or village with no hospital, no ambulance station and the nearest intensive care unit more than 50 miles away, are shocked at the contrast with their former urban environment.

Most medical practices in the study area are group practices of two to four doctors, serving populations of approximately 5,000 with offices in the small towns of the region. However, 'country calling stations' are held in outlying villages for non-acute cases. In one community the doctor sees an average of twenty to thirty patients in front of the fire in the sitting room of one of the pensioners' bungalows. In another, ten to fifteen patients are seen in the old village hall where the caretaker acts as 'liaison officer'.

The country doctor has higher visibility for his patients than his urban colleague. Most of them know where he lives, as in many cases this is also where he sees his patients. Because of the small scale of communities, his children or grandchildren may go to school with the grandchildren of his elderly patients. He may belong to the same church and his wife to the Women's Institute. The doctor's car is recognised on its rounds. In other words, the relationship with the doctor tends to be more than a role interaction; doctor and patient know each other in a broader context than that.

Community Services Visited
Visits to doctors' surgeries and filling prescriptions Approximately two-thirds of respondents go to the doctor's surgery in the nearest village. Walking is the most usual method of access (36 per cent), followed by driving (25 per cent) or getting a lift (16 per cent).

While chemists in the rural areas are limited to the small towns, several local adaptations exist for prescriptions. Some doctors do their own dispensing and have developed delivery services such as using the voluntary co-operation of village shop, local bus service, and others who provide a courier service. In other local communities volunteer rotas exist so that prescriptions may be filled without delay and urgent medicines may be delivered by a district nurse on her rounds.

The figures for access are not directly comparable with Hunt's findings, since she was concerned with the main means of transport rather than how people actually obtained the service, and therefore did not include categories which involved other people going or services coming to the home. What is most striking is the very low proportion using public transport for all services. Even in Hunt's low population density regions 24 per cent and 19 per cent respectively get to the chemist and doctor's surgery by bus, compared with only 7 per cent and 8 per cent in this study (see Hunt, 1978, pp. 120–2, Tables 14.6.2 and 14.6.6). Since attendance at the doctor's surgery by someone else is less likely, it is clear that less than half as many use the bus in the more sparsely settled areas. Buses simply are not conveniently available. However, similar proportions walk to their doctor's surgery in both studies.

The most frequent forms of access to both doctors and chemists are walking and driving, although more rely on lifts and public transport than they do for shopping. Over three times as many of those over 75 have their prescriptions brought to them by someone else. Single people are more likely to see the doctor only on house calls, or to travel to the doctor by bus or lift.

Two-thirds of those without a car manage to make their own way to the doctor's surgery, as do nearly half of those where the household car belongs to another member of the household. Most of those with cars of their own drive. Half of those in households without cars walk to the doctor's surgery but substantially higher proportions rely on public transport or lifts than they do for shopping and filling prescriptions, where it is feasible for someone else to go. Among those who are housebound or can only go out with help, a high proportion (37 per cent) claim that 'someone else goes', presumably for new prescriptions or to ask the doctor to call. But for most the doctor always comes to the house.

Only 14 per cent of respondents had visited the doctor within the week of the interview. Interestingly, the under-75s were twice as likely to have seen the doctor in the preceding week as the over-75s, although equal proportions had received attention in the last month. A fifth had not seen a doctor within the last year and of those 5 per cent *never* see a doctor. Those who never see a doctor are more likely to be single. Twelve per cent of those who have never married never see a doctor and one-third of them had not seen a doctor within the last year. Overall, however, the rural elderly are more likely to have seen a doctor within the year than the national average for the elderly, more than a third of whom do not see a doctor in any given year (Age Concern, 1977). It is difficult to know how to interpret this finding. If, as Luft *et al.* (1976) have suggested, need is the essential predictor for medical contacts, then it would appear that the rural elderly suffer more ill health than their urban counterparts. This, however, is in conflict with the data which indicate comparable levels of disability and chronic limiting conditions. However, data on constraints on use of medical services by the elderly come mainly from the United States where the absence of a national health service cannot be ignored. While no data exist to support this suggestion, it may well be that fewer constraints exist on visiting the doctor in rural communities. One doctor commented that many elderly patients are in need of merely 'tea and sympathy'! The greater familiarity between doctor and patient commented on above may reduce social distance and constraints on going to see the doctor.

More had received prescriptions within the last month than had seen the doctor. A quarter had had a prescription filled within the last week, again more of the under-75s. Married people were more likely to have had a prescription filled in the last month (61 per cent) than either the widowed (55 per cent) or single (45 per cent). This may reflect the fact that married people are more able to remain at home when ill than others; however, they had not had more contact with the doctor. Satisfaction with services of both doctors and chemists is high with less than 2 per cent dissatisfied.

Chiropodist In spite of conventional wisdom regarding the scarcity and need for chiropody services, two-thirds of respondents claim they have no need for a chiropodist, less than one-fifth had seen a chiropodist within the last six months and only 2 per cent express dissatisfaction with the chiropody service.

Optician The majority, on the other hand, need the services of an optician and such facilities are less easy to find than those discussed so far. As the tables show, more people have to travel to find an optician. More than twice as many use public transport for access to this service than for any other, and higher proportions drive or seek lifts. However, three-quarters had had no contact with an optician within the preceding year. Only 4 per cent overall are dissatisfied with the services they receive. However, several do not use the nearest optician, but travel to a different town. The reason for this is that they find the local one expensive. This adaptation is demonstrated by the figures which show that more people travel to an optician than for access to other professionals even in those towns where the service is available. In contrast with the use of doctors and chemists, single people are just as likely to use chiropodists and opticians as others.

Dentist Data were not collected on access to dentists' surgeries. However, data from a pilot study and a consumer study show that less than half of the elderly visit a dentist mainly because they have no teeth! The distribution of dentists is similar to that of opticians with lifts, driving and public transport being the most common modes of access.

Home Visits from Community-Based Services
All respondents were asked if they had been visited in the six months preceding the interview by each of a list of people from health and social services, voluntary organisations and others who might be likely to visit their homes at regular intervals providing support and thus likely to become aware of emergencies. For the purpose of comparison a similar list was used to that of Hunt's study, with three additional categories of privately contracted services: chiropodist, private household help and private nurse. In most instances figures for our rural sample are comparable with Hunt's (see Table 4.5). This seems to indicate that population density does not affect service provision on a regional basis but may affect intra-regional distribution, since some differences between communities exist.

Visits from the doctor Twenty-eight per cent overall had received a home visit from the doctor in the half year before the interview. Contrary to the situation of more house calls in rural Wales suggested by Moyes (1976), this is slightly less than the 33 per cent who had received a visit in Hunt's survey. However, it is equivalent to visits received in her retirement areas and 28 per cent of those living alone had received a visit in both studies. Within Hunt's study, however, a wide range of difference was noted between standard regions (OCPS, unpublished tables), ranging from 23 per cent visited in the Greater London area to 44 per cent (almost double) in Yorkshire and Humberside. Retirement areas at 28 per cent are comparable with rural Wales, only slightly higher than London at 23 per cent. Those rural elderly who are visited, however, appear to be more likely to receive regular visits. The majority of those who had received a visit had seen the doctor less than fortnightly, but almost a tenth were visited at least every two weeks (more than twice as many as in Hunt's study.) Those over 75 are twice as likely to be visited but of those visited a similar proportion receive frequent visits.

A similar proportion of both men and women receive house calls, in spite of the greater mean age of women. Widows receive one-and-a-half times as many calls as the married or single; however, they are visited less frequently. Although those who have never married receive fewer visits, more than half of those who *are* visited receive visits at least fortnightly, reflecting the greater age of this category. The fact that more widows receive visits may reflect greater age but it may also reflect greater dependence, as an analysis of support networks to be reported elsewhere will indicate. Those who came to the community after 40 are slightly more likely to receive doctors' visits than local people. On the

Table 4.5 *Home Visits Received from Professionals during the Six Months Preceding Interview (percentages)*

| | Rural Wales | | | Hunt[1] | | | |
N =	All (688)	Living alone (221)	Not living alone (467)	All (3,869)	Retirement areas (458)	Living alone (1,144)	Not living alone (2,725)
Doctor	28	28	28	33	28	28	36
District nurse	18	22	16	8	7	8	8
Health visitor	5	4	5	4	3	6	4
Home help	8	11	6	9	6	19	4
Social worker[2]	6	8	5	5	2	6	3
Social security	7	11	6	6	6	9	5
Meals on wheels[3]	7	13	4[4]	3	1	6	1
Voluntary organisation	3	3	3	3	2	3	3
Minister[5]	50	51	49	16	17	18	16
Insurance men	37	33	40	49	46	37	54
Chiropodist[6]	9	10	9	—	—	—	—
Private nurse[6]	1	1	1	—	—	—	—
Private household help[6]	8	12	6	—	—	—	—

[1] Hunt (1978), Table 11.2.1, p. 87.
[2] Equivalent to Hunt's 'Council Welfare Officer' which may include housing as well as social services.
[3] Highly variable.
[4] Three per cent live with spouse only.
[5] Over 70 per cent in one area.
[6] Not enumerated by Hunt.

basis of the data it is impossible to interpret this. It may reflect a difference in expectation and demand of services but it is more likely to indicate that where local relatives are available they will take care of the sick with less recourse to the doctor.

There are some quite distinct differences between communities. The proportions visited at home range from less than a fifth to half. The reason for this wide range of difference was at first felt to be patterns of attendance at the doctor's surgery, perhaps affected by proximity, since the two communities with the highest proportions visited were those with the longest journey to the doctor's regular surgery, and the community with the least house calls had a doctor's surgery in the village where most population is concentrated. However, this was not borne out by comparison with surgery visits over the same period. The differences are best explained as the end product of a number of factors which affect the communities differently, including doctors' attitudes, state of health, geographical factors and mean age.

In all communities respondents comment positively about the services received from the doctor. However, the elderly generally are known to be undemanding patients so it is difficult to accurately assess the service. The comparable level of house calls in both the rural sample and Hunt's study, however, deserves some comment. Because of the distances involved – a doctor may, for instance, cover a 12-mile radius from his surgery – travel distances and times are more demanding, particularly in bad weather. The region is typically one of narrow lanes and high hedges and in the worst winter weather such lanes quickly become blocked by drifting snow. Doctors told of problems in reaching remote dwellings, sometimes abandoning cars and finishing the journey on tractor or even on foot.

District nurse   District nursing services were at a transitional stage during the conduct of the survey. Previously nurses had been patch-based and tended to be attached to particular practices. This structure survived in some communities whereas in others the change-over to district nurses being attached to health centres covering a wider area had been completed. Under the new system doctors requiring the services of a district nurse for a patient contact the health centre with each specific request.

More than twice as many of our rural elderly receive visits from the district nurse as did respondents in any standard region (OPCS, unpublished tables) in Hunt's study, and for those living alone the proportion is almost three times as many. Those living alone are more likely to receive visits, despite the higher incidence of impaired health of those who live with others. The most common service is regular help with bathing and treatment or monitoring during convalescence of those who have been identified as 'at risk'. Those who are married are least likely to receive visits (12 per cent) underlining the importance of care received from a spouse, and while almost twice as many of the single and widowed receive visits (21 per cent and 24 per cent respectively), those who are single are visited more frequently, as a reflection of household composition – that is, they are more likely to be living alone or with elderly siblings than with younger relatives. The higher incidence of singleness may thus contribute to the higher level of contact.

In those communities where the district nurse was still patch-based within a catchment area, she was known personally to many of the elderly. In one village the nurse was highly visible as she did her rounds on her bicycle and several very elderly respondents said that they did not know how to answer the question because although the nurse 'pops in to see me, to see how I am', they were unable to say whether it was an 'official' visit. Since the monitoring value of such calls is self-evident, they are included in our figures and this informal aspect of the service may also go some way to explaining the higher proportions visited. In another village, in which a district nurse was resident, she said that frequently she was sent for when elderly persons were ill in preference to a doctor being called. She always went (though the formalities require all visits to be initiated through the doctor) and then contacted the doctor herself subsequently. However, this particular nurse has now retired and she doubted whether the 'younger ones' would adopt such a flexible approach. The OPCS has recently conducted a survey of patterns of working of district nurses (Dunnell and Dobbs, 1982).

Here again patients express a high level of satisfaction with the services they receive, though 10 per cent of those visited would like more frequent visits and 6 per cent longer visits (N = 123).

Private nurse In addition to visits from the district nurse, nine households had also received visits from a private nurse. In every case these visits were considered to have been too short and too infrequent. In some households where there was an old person too sick to be interviewed the carer was not over 65, so when we add these instances to the elderly people who were interviewed and who were either providing or receiving home nursing care it is likely that the need for additional home nursing is greater than these figures suggest. Unfortunately, the data do not include details of what duties private nurses undertake.

Health visitor Only 5 per cent had received visits from a health visitor, three-quarters of whom were over 75. This is also comparable with Hunt's findings, although here again there were wide differences between standard regions, ranging from 3 per cent in London and in retirement areas to 10 per cent in the Northern region (OPCS, unpublished tables). A third of those receiving visits (N = 34) are in poor or only fair health; three-quarters suffer from chronic limiting conditions and nearly nine-tenths had not been out of the house in the month preceding interview.

Chiropodist Less than a tenth had received a home visit from a chiropodist within the preceding six months (N = 64). Since two-thirds report that they have no need for chiropody services this would seem to indicate that a quarter of those needing attention receive this in their own home, nearly three-quarters of whom are over 75. Our findings *vis-à-vis* chiropody service suggest that concern felt about its availability may be exaggerated, for while help with cutting toenails is the most frequently needed item of personal care, very few voice dissatisfaction with or a need for additional chiropody services. However, both doctors and district nurses report doing some minor chiropody.

SOCIAL SERVICES AND SOCIAL SECURITY

Social services and social security have been purposely linked together since it seems important to discuss some of the problems which these categories pose both for respondents and consequently for the research. Pilot work for this project had confirmed fears and reinforced the findings of other researchers that it is difficult for most people to distinguish between the two agencies. Indeed it was found that even when a person has been in contact with one or the other agency, they still are either unable to make the distinction or, in some cases, remain unaware that two separate agencies exist.

In addition to being asked whether they had received a visit from a social security officer, a social worker, a home help, or meals on wheels, respondents were also asked whether they had 'ever asked for help from the social services' and an attempt was made to identify this agency by then listing some of the more likely services they might have requested. Those who said they had asked for help were then asked about the outcome of their request. For a variety of reasons the data produced from these questions proved to be unreliable. Not the least of reasons was that the majority of contacts are not initiated by clients themselves. They come preponderantly from the health services or from relatives (Grant, 1981a). In order to analyse the situation accurately, therefore, it was necessary to consult social service records.

Most of the study communities are more than 20 miles from the social services area office. Just over a quarter of elderly households are known to social services, that is, social services have records of contact with that household, and approximately one in seven elderly households is on a social worker's current caseload. This includes those registered as blind or physically handicapped in addition to those monitored as elderly-at-risk or receiving home helps, meals on wheels, or day care. Some of those cases which had been closed between the time of the sample lists being compiled and interviews being attempted had died, gone into hospital, or gone to live with relatives outside the area. Overall, more than a quarter of the elderly households sampled had had some contact with social services and 14 per cent represent current cases.

Some differences between communities merit comment. The proportions known to social services are lowest in the most dispersed and the retirement destination communities. The most dispersed community has the highest proportion of the elderly living in households with younger adults present so it would appear that this reduces demand on social services.

The fact that only 10 per cent of elderly households in one study community are social services open cases is significant since the influx of retirement migrants to this community is frequently commented upon as a source of concern to social workers. Because the area represents one of the population concentrations of the region, it produces more cases numerically than less densely settled areas. However, the stereotype of the retirement migrant who has no local relatives is widely accepted by the local social workers, who claim that as a result the area places a disproportionate demand on their resources (Black, 1981). Another small town, however, with a much higher *proportion* of open cases (17 per cent) and fully one-third of the elderly known to social services (compared with less than a quarter in the first town), is seen as a self-supporting community. The subconscious effect of the stereotype on service provision cannot be calculated but it is worth asking the rhetorical question whether the low proportion of open cases reflects the effect of such stereotype in assessment and allocation of limited resources. Neither the age structure nor the health of these two populations explains the difference in social services input. (More detailed information regarding social services clients is available in Black *et al.*, 1983.)

Home Helps
Home helps visit 8 per cent of respondents, comparable with Hunt's 9 per cent (range between standard regions 6 per cent – 13 per cent), but higher than her retirement areas – 6 per cent (OPCS, unpublished tables). Those who live alone are slightly more likely to receive a home help, although in Hunt's study those living alone are more likely to receive home help than in the rural region. The home help is, of course, in a slightly different category from other professional visitors because she comes at least once a week and therefore has an ongoing, regular relationship with the client. However, the provision of home helps shows a great deal of variability from one community to another with the two most sparsely populated communities apparently receiving no home helps at all, although this is probably explained by the small numbers involved. Differences however exist between other com-

munities, suggesting that the correlation between need and service may
not be uniform throughout the region but affected by local problems of
availability, household composition, expectations, knowledge, and so
on, although sparsity of population does not appear the main cause of
differences (Grant, 1981b).

As with other services, those over 75 are more likely to need and
receive help: more than four times as many of those over 75 receive
home helps (17 per cent against 4 per cent). Sixty per cent of home
helps see 40 per cent of the elderly population, that is, the over 75s. In
spite of their lower mean age, men are as likely to receive home helps as
women and they also receive help at a lower level of dependency. In
other words, less physically dependent men may receive home helps
where they are perceived as unable to keep house adequately for themselves. The same is true for informal help, as Part Four will show. Men
also get more frequent visits than women. It may be that in some
instances independence and self-image could be enhanced by helping
such men to become more self-sufficient in household tasks, particularly
basic cooking, rather than perhaps reinforcing dependency through
home helps. In one instance a man whose general health was fair but
who was very deaf, and depressed over the death of his wife from
cancer, commented that the only hot meals he had were those made by
the home help or when his daughter came 20 miles on the bus to see
him. Otherwise he lived on cold food, largely tinned meat and bread and
butter. Several men commented on their gratitude to home helps who
made a 'hot meal'.

Half of those receiving home help are in poor or only fair health
and a third suffer from low morale (probably related to health). More
than half of those receiving home help are visited more than once
weekly but all receive at least one visit a week. Home helps appear
to have minimal involvement in personal care tasks. Apart from
general housework, home helps concentrate, in order of prevalence,
on making fires, ironing, carrying fuel, doing laundry and doing
shopping.

Satisfaction with the home help service is generally high. Although
specific complaints are made, these concern aspects of the service only.
Several comment that they can still dust but want help with cleaning the
outside of windows, polishing the brass, or spring cleaning, all of which
are excluded from the remit of home helps. While cooking is not central
to the home help's responsibilities it appears that some home helps are
willing to cook if necessary. Other complaints refer to change without
warning of either times or incumbents and several express anxiety over
cut-backs. Most appear to rely heavily on their home helps and structure
their lives around these expected visits.

In addition to the 8 per cent receiving home help, an equal number
are visited at least once a week by a privately paid household help.

Meals on Wheels

In spite of the difficulties encountered in supplying meals on wheels in rural areas, more than twice as many of the elderly respondents receive such meals as in Hunt's study. Hunt's average conceals considerable variations between standard regions, from 1 per cent in the North-west, South and retirement areas to 5 per cent in the North and Yorkshire and Humberside (OPCS, unpublished tables). The figure for rural Wales is higher but the data are, of course, influenced by the almost total absence of day care and luncheon clubs in the region. In most communities meals are organised by social services and delivered by volunteers through the WRVS. Again there is considerable variation between communities, very scattered areas receiving no meals at all. The majority receiving meals get them twice a week. Those who live alone and the over-75s are again twice as likely to receive meals.

In some communities the number of meals available is limited by the education authority who tell the local school how many they can provide. This means that eligibility is related to availability rather than need. In a few communities, old people's homes provide some meals and a few elderly people are able to come and eat at the home as part of day care. It would seem that the potential exists for volunteers to provide hot meals on a neighbourly basis, particularly in the most rural areas. Perhaps some of the same volunteers who now deliver meals would be willing to do this. Informal arrangements of this nature do exist. In one case a woman living alone explained that she had felt rather ungrateful because sometimes the meals were too much for her to eat and on other occasions she did not like what was served, but she had continued to receive meals because she did not want to hurt the feelings of the person who brought them. When she had discussed her dilemma with a neighbour, the neighbour had immediately offered to cook her what she liked. As the neighbour's husband came home for lunch every day, it was very little extra work for her. Under these circumstances, the meals on wheels had been discontinued. In another instance, an old lady reported that she used to always invite an old man who lived nearby in for Sunday dinner, but had had to stop because it was proving too expensive, although she felt she could not tell him that. Innovations and willingness to help already exist and could well be co-opted by social services to extend the service on a less formal basis, where the formal service cannot help or is inappropriate.

Social Workers

Respondents were asked if they had been visited by a 'council welfare officer, social worker, or occupational therapist'. As previously mentioned, the findings here must be treated cautiously, for while the question and resulting data are comparable with Hunt's, it is difficult to gauge the accuracy of respondents' understanding of the question.

Housing officers may also have been included in this category or confusion may exist with social security officers. While figures for contact are comparable with Hunt's overall figure, compared with M. Abrams's urban survey (1978) contact with social workers is considerably lower. Those under 75 have little contact with social workers in either survey. Hunt gives no breakdown by population density but comments on higher proportions visited in Greater London, although still far less than in Abrams's study. However, variation in contact between standard regions ranges from 2 per cent in the North-west and retirement areas to 7 per cent in Greater London and 6 per cent in the West Midlands (OPCS, unpublished tables), the most urbanised regions. It appears, therefore, that elderly urban populations place greater demands on social workers, that is, a higher proportion of the population is visited. However, this does not immediately explain the fact that those who are visited in rural Wales receive less frequent visits. (See also Grant, 1981b.)

More of those living alone (8 per cent) and those over 75 (9 per cent as opposed to 3 per cent) are visited by a social worker. More than twice the overall proportion are visited in one community and this is difficult to interpret since there does not appear to be a higher level of dependency in that community. It is also one of the most distant communities from the district office. It is known to social workers as a 'self-supporting' community, and one worker commented that 'when we get a call from the . . . Valley we know we'd better go that day, it must be urgent'. Whether this image affects the pattern of social work it is hard to say, particularly in view of the small numbers involved and confusion with social security personnel.

Visits from social workers are infrequent, the majority being less often than once a fortnight, and data from the study of clients indicates that they follow no prearranged system and that the majority receive one visit for any particular input, that is, to deliver aids or assess for home help. A quarter of those who have been visited (N = 42) say that they feel the social worker does not come often enough, and 15 per cent feel that the social workers do not stay long enough when they do come.

Social Security Officers

The problem of definition which exists for social security officers is the same as for social workers since these two categories are frequently confused. Respondents were asked if they had been visited by a 'social security or supplementary benefits officer'. While the categories and responses are comparable with Hunt, a significant difference was found between districts, with respondents in one almost twice as likely to have been visited as those in another. Hunt's figures for standard regions also showed a range of difference from 3 per cent in the Northern region to 10 per cent in Greater London. Again those living alone are more likely to be visited (11 per cent as opposed to 6 per cent), as are those over 75 (11 per cent as opposed to 4 per cent). The widowed are twice as likely to have been visited as the married (10 per cent as opposed to 5 per cent). Widowhood often carries with it the double shock of loss of spouse and immediate and sudden reduction in income. This is particularly hard felt by those whose only income comes from the old age pension, causing considerable hardship in some cases at a time when emotional resources are least able to cope with the situation. Two-thirds of those visited had a weekly income of less than £30 a week at the time of the survey.

VOLUNTARY ORGANISATIONS

A very small percentage have any contact with voluntary organisations, although the same is true for Hunt's sample for all regions and Abrams's (1978) retirement towns. Those voluntary organisations that are mentioned tend to be local or youth groups rather than local branches of national organisations. In spite of the fact that meals on wheels are delivered by the WRVS, this is not acknowledged by respondents who see this as part of social services.

All national charities appropriate to the elderly were contacted and, in addition, local district branches of larger organisations (for example, the Red Cross, St John Ambulance, Abbeyfield Homes) were asked about their provisions in the districts studied. At the national level activity is concentrated in the larger cities, many charities acting on the basis of direct requests from those needing assistance or from social workers on their behalf. At the local level, activities are centred on the larger towns. Help in the rural areas is more difficult to come by because there is usually no local branch of the specific charity or a lack of available volunteers. Because of low regional wage levels, rural families rely heavily on the part-time earnings of wives to supplement family incomes (Wenger, 1980). This means that married women, who have traditionally provided the bulk of volunteers, are seeking paid rather than volunteer work. In fact, during the recent downturn in the economy the Red Cross and St John Ambulance branches in the region have experienced a falling away of established volunteer members. At the same time social workers in the area report a very low level of contact or co-operation with voluntary agencies (apart from the WRVS), while admitting that more contact is desirable (Grant, 1981a).

CLERGYMEN

More elderly people receive visits from clergymen than from any other professional. Half the respondents had been visited within the six months preceding the interview. This is three times as many as in Hunt's overall study. While Hunt's figures for standard regions show a wide range, from only 9 per cent in Greater London to 26 per cent in the Northern region (OPCS, unpublished tables), the figure for rural Wales is twice as high as for any other region. However, there are quite significant differences between communities, which appear to be related to the proportion of the elderly who are members of a church or chapel and whether or not there are resident clergymen in the community. Although some of the clergy interviewed claim to visit non-members of their congregation, this is not the rule. They say they have to be careful not to tread on the toes of other clergymen who might have prior claim! In those communities where nine out of ten have been members of a church or chapel for more than twenty years, where the chapels continue to play an important social role and where all the main denominations have resident practitioners, three-quarters had received a visit. Membership is high and more than half report that they talk regularly with other church or chapel members. Membership and attendance are lowest in the community with most retirement incomers but even here a third had been visited by a clergyman in the six months before interview.

The likelihood of visits is not related to household composition, but those over 75 are more likely to receive visits since they are less likely to be able to attend services and widows are slightly more likely to receive visits than either the single or the married. Retirement migrants, however, receive far fewer visits than long-term residents, less than one-third having been visited – more being non-members. This is one area where integration into the community is more difficult, especially for incoming Nonconformists since in some communities all chapel services are in the Welsh language, while others hold English services only in the summer when there are tourists in the area. Others do not choose to affiliate. The net outcome is that migrants are less well integrated into the religious organisations and pastoral networks.

At the time the survey was conducted, only the larger communities had resident clergymen, although in one other case this absence represented only an interregnum. In discussions with these clergymen local patterns are discernible. Due to the overall shrinking rural population, today's clergyman covers a larger area than previously, especially less popular Nonconformist denominations. One minister, for instance, shepherded a flock spread over an area of 68 miles from end to end. All of the religious groups have a high proportion of elderly members, higher in the dispersed areas.

One aspect that all have in common is that they see their pastoral care responsibilities primarily in terms of support for the elderly. There are slight differences between the denominations, but the Nonconformists in particular undertake to visit all member households at least once a year and the elderly more frequently. This is stressed less by the Anglican Church since this tends to form a residual category with a less formal membership. In addition to visiting the elderly at home, all clergymen visit any member who is in hospital, travelling long distances as far as Liverpool. They are also involved in taking relatives to hospital to visit. Hospitals will occasionally call ministers to ask them to come to sit with the dying or to bring and support the relatives of the dying. Most say that their usual role as visitor is to allow elderly people to talk: 'My pastoral work is listening. They tell me their troubles.' Topics of discussion are often mundane problems; common are troubles of communication with adult children (not necessarily lack of instrumental care) and the decision by those living alone to enter an old people's home. However, most discussion is not about problems.

In one small town, the two largest chapels have teams of women members distributed throughout the town on the basis of more than a dozen small districts, who have a special responsibility for the old, the sick, the bereaved and others as need arises. Most of the women involved are non-working housewives in the 40–60 age range. One minister here remarked that he had been told by a social worker, 'You do all the work in B . . .'. All clergymen try to provide help and support where the need is known without recourse to social services except for access to home helps and old people's homes. And all comment on the fact that *they* at least are available around the clock!

INSURANCE MEN

Hunt found that the most common visitor to the elderly in a professional capacity is the insurance man. Nearly half her respondents were visited compared to less than two-fifths of the rural Welsh elderly, less than in any other standard region (OPCS, unpublished tables). The younger elderly are more likely to be visited, and visits from the insurance man are likely to be more regular than visits from other professionals, with 13 per cent being visited at least every fortnight. In the rural Welsh context more had been visited by a clergyman although such visits are less frequent.

SATISFACTION WITH PROFESSIONAL SERVICES

Satisfaction of recipients with professional services is generally high, particularly with the home help service. Although the real numbers are small, satisfaction is lowest among those who claim to have been visited by social workers. Satisfaction with health services, particularly doctors, is high.

OVERALL SATISFACTION WITH COMMUNITY SERVICES

In addition to being asked about their satisfaction with each specific service, respondents were also asked how satisfied they felt with services in the community in general. This is not a measure of community satisfaction, but specifically relates to service provision. Satisfaction with services in the community is high overall, as we might expect with an elderly population. Only 3 per cent say they are generally dissatisfied with the services in their community. Satisfaction is lower in those communities with higher proportions of incomers.

Respondents were also asked whether there was anything that they missed by living in their particular community – something they might appreciate if they lived elsewhere. The difference in the proportions who feel that they miss things is of the same order as satisfaction with community services, with only 14 per cent of long-term residents missing anything compared with 55 per cent of retirement migrants. The most commonly mentioned things that are missed are theatres, symphony concerts and large shops. However, the overall levels of satisfaction with services are generally so high that it can safely be said that the elderly feel well provided for, although those planning retirement migration from the conurbations might well be advised to choose a small town rather than a more rural area.

THE QUESTION OF ACCESS: SUMMARY AND CONCLUSIONS

Chapters 3 and 4 have discussed the mobility of the elderly and their access to formal services. The literature on rural deprivation is persuasive. Rural areas suffer from inadequate transport, depressed income levels, cut-backs in or lack of various services and amenities, exacerbated by uneven distribution within rural areas and centralisation and rationalisation. In terms of service and amenities provision, the rural areas are less well served than urban areas and people within rural areas have unequal access to facilities. This last point, however, can be just as true in urban areas. An old lady on the sixth floor of a tower block in an inner city may be further from a bus stop, a grocer, or a doctor's surgery than an old lady in a small village.

In this rural study half of the elderly never use public transport at all and those who do appear mainly to use it occasionally for trips or to satisfy long-interval needs, such as access to the optician. The use of public transport to gain access to such short-interval needs as food shopping and the chemist is very low. However, among users dissatisfaction with public transport is higher than that for any other service and it is in this area that improvements are most frequently sought. Fare concessions are minimal and fares the most frequently mentioned problem for users. It is, therefore, difficult to assess the potential use of an efficient public transport system since car use may be merely a reflection of its absence. However, in those areas where community car schemes have been introduced, the main uses are to visit hospitals and for evening activities involving long journeys and night driving. It is likely that the automobile is embedded in the adaptive behaviour of rural regions where flexibility is essential.

High car ownership offsets the lack of public transport but 'forced car ownership' (Coles, 1978) is evident in frequent anxieties voiced over the costs involved in running a car. Many women in the present elderly cohort never learned to drive, so it is possible that future cohorts of the elderly may include more drivers, but the possibility of increased car ownership appears to be unlikely in view of increasing costs. Telephone installation is also higher particularly among those whose children live outside the area, but average bills are higher due to the greater distances involved, and the number of SSD telephones supplied to the elderly is lower in Wales than in any region of England. Both cars and telephones in the community can also be seen as a resource for those who do not have their own car or telephone. The giving and receiving of lifts and providing access to telephones appear to be established practice.

In spite of high levels of dissatisfaction with public transport among users, access to necessary goods and services does not appear to present great problems, with a high level of satisfaction with services being expressed and a high level of frequency of service provision for short-interval needs. What is most striking is the adaptability of the individual and community in meeting needs, which is further illustrated by the growth of innovatory forms of public transport such as the community car schemes.

More frustrating problems of access were discovered to be the result of poor planning, such as the local authority bungalows at the top of a very steep hill or the steps and steep drive up to similar bungalows in another village, where pensioners also have difficulty getting into baths where the sides are too high. In three communities occupants of sheltered or local authority pensioners' housing become trapped on the first floor when their mobility is curtailed by advancing arthritis. Such problems are widespread and not limited to rural areas. The implications here are obvious. A more informed approach to such planning decisions not only improves the mobility and independence of the pensioners involved, but by so doing could reduce pressures on domiciliary services and old people's homes. The doctor's advice to sufferers of arthritis/rheumatism (the most common limitation on mobility) is to keep moving. If it is possible to walk to the nearest shop mobility may be longer sustained.

Contrary to findings in the United States (e.g. Youmans, 1977), the health of the rural elderly appears to be no worse than that for the urban elderly and certainly the take-up of social services among the elderly does not reflect any reluctance or sense of stigma. Pilot work for this project had included one or two questions designed to test for feelings of stigma. One asked the elderly if they minded others knowing they received help. Since sense of stigma seemed to be virtually absent, it was decided not to include the questions in the final questionnaire. Where the elderly are concerned, the rural population appears to have no inhibitions about accepting help from social services, and levels of domiciliary support from both health auxiliary and social services personnel are equal to or higher than in Hunt's (1978) survey. Contact with social workers does appear to be higher in urban areas (M. Abrams, 1978) but this is more likely to reflect need than resistance to take-up of services.

One United States finding which the survey appears to validate is the propensity for the rural elderly to report a higher level of functional performance on items of personal care, in spite of minimal differences in reported limitations on physical activities (Schooler, 1975). This seems to support the high value placed on independence and self-reliance which has been attributed to the rural elderly, reinforced in the Welsh context by lower proportions with non-elderly members of the household. This resourcefulness is apparent in the adaptations which are made to accommodate the restrictions of increasing age and infirmity.

One might question whether the greater independence of the rural elderly reflects a survival phenomenon: that is, that those who remain in or migrate to the rural areas may be a self-selecting group of more independent people. This argument has been countered by those who see the drift of rural youth to the cities as selective migration of the more independent and innovative sector of the rural population. So far as the elderly population is concerned the higher proportions living alone, together with higher levels of functional capacity for self-care, raises important questions about taught dependency and the reinforcement of independence.

One aspect of the rural ethos which became apparent from the research is the discontinuity between objective and perceived deprivation, particularly amongst the old elderly. As the high levels of satisfaction indicate, the elderly accept their situation and in the main do not feel deprived. Questions to those few without plumbing facilities, for instance, elicited responses to the effect that since they were used to nothing else it had never been a problem, as did questions about loneliness to those living in extremely remote situations. There was at times a wry amusement on the part of the interviewee at the interviewer's naivety and a modest pride in their own self-sufficiency. Others are more explicit and say that the inconveniences of rural living are acceptable because the advantages far outweigh them. Adapting to the rural milieu is seen as merely a question of proper planning and compromise. For many, of course, the adaptation is to move from the small hamlet or isolated cottage into the village or market town, and such moves on retirement, widowhood or with increasing dependence are common.

The cultural distinction between town and country has become increasingly blurred with the spread of the automobile and the mass media. In terms of material culture they are indistinguishable. The world-view of the rural elderly person, however, is part of a non-tangible sub-culture which still contains elements which are different from the world-view of an elderly person living in the city. As Collier suggests (1977), the situation of rural populations needs to be assessed in its total cultural or phenomenological context rather than through the eyes, values and categories of outsiders. Central to the rural world-view is the element of security which has been referred to above. 'All the neighbours are my friends' was a frequently voiced response to a question asking if the interviewee had friends in this area. The Celtic countries have a cultural tradition of agricultural co-operation (Arensberg, 1937: Jenkins, 1971; Rees, 1950), and while the modernisation of agriculture has reduced the necessity for co-operative labour (Hannan, 1972), the spirit of co-operation still exists and becomes active in emergencies. In bad winters farmers will use tractors to get doctors to outlying homes. In some communities the chapels have their own system of community support. Many of the elderly commented that 'the neighbours are very good' and mentioned examples of help and offers of help. It was suggested in one community that 'when there are not so many people about, everyone counts'. While these observations reflect ideal behaviour they also indicate an ethos where an expectation of good-will, co-operation and support exists. In this context, and given the common problem of access, offering and asking for help becomes institutionalised.

While access does not appear to be a problem and satisfaction with services is high, there are areas of concern. The data show that a high proportion of the elderly rely on the village shop or delivery services for their food shopping. In some instances shops in small villages are excellent, in others they offer a limited range and very little fresh food, but in all instances prices are high and this is true too in the small towns. Given lower rural incomes, higher food prices and lack of choice, particularly of fresh foods, there is room for concern about the nutritional value of the diets of the rural elderly, particularly those in the remoter areas relying on deliveries and mobile services. It is felt that this is an area which warrants further investigation and one to which health education efforts might be beneficially addressed.

The problem of access to hospitals has not been treated in this survey. Reference has been made to the problem of hospital visiting and the centralisation of services. This is definitely one area in which access is difficult and where questions about the quality of service provision should be raised. In addition, no data were collected which would give an indication of the comparative level of specialist services. It would seem likely that the problem of sparsity and distance may be reflected in a lower level of provision of rehabilitative, preventive, diagnostic and emergency services.

It is apparent that the independence of the elderly is reflected in a stoical and tolerant attitude towards their physical limitations. They are undemanding patients. We need more comparative information about access to and use of specialist services and diagnostic tests, as well as more detailed data on problems of access to hospitals for patients and visitors. This would involve data on, for instance, rehabilitative services to stroke victims, tests for anaemia, diabetes and high blood pressure, preventive and educational approaches to arthritis/rheumatism, and so on. The current data only demonstrate that access to and contact with general practitioners is equivalent; data on hospital and specialist services may give a completely different picture of rural health care.

In conclusion, despite the obvious objective problems presented by the rural environment, the elderly demonstrate the capacity to adapt to and cope with their situation. Dependence on others increases with age and remoteness, but access to goods and services does not appear to be a serious problem in the cultural context, although retirement migrants may initially have more difficulty in adapting to the local ethos. However, scope exists for the development of more innovation and flexible and community-based approaches to planning, particularly in the fields of transport and social services.

On the other hand, while service provision presents the rural elderly with particular problems, the urban elderly are also constrained in their access to such services. While public transport may be more available, it is also likely to be more crowded and more impersonal. The walk to the shop may be shorter but the urban old person must face crowded pavements, traffic and the fear of crime. The figures on achieved access appear to be comparable: the rural and the urban elderly make different adaptations to overcome the difficulties posed by their own environments.

SOCIAL ENVIRONMENT

Chapter 5

FAMILY, FRIENDS AND NEIGHBOURS

Part Two has shown that the elderly are for the most part able, competent people who make those adaptations necessary to overcome the problems posed by their environment to achieve access to necessary goods and services. In Part Three we move on to look at the social environment of the elderly. In other words, having looked at how instrumental needs are satisfied, we now look at the social and emotional resources available to the old people before proceeding in Part Four to a consideration of that help which they receive from the informal sector: family, friends, neighbours and other members of the community.

This chapter seeks to explore the availability of relatives to the elderly, the amount of contact they have with family and the levels of satisfaction experienced, and examines the role played by friends and neighbours. It also compares, where possible, the current rural data with findings from urban areas.

CLOSE RELATIVES LIVING

Nearly all (97 per cent) of the elderly people interviewed feel they have close relatives living, comparable with Hunt's (1978) finding of 95 per cent (para. 12.7, p. 94). The interpretation of 'close relative' was left to the respondent since a cousin with whom one is in friendly daily contact would be a close relative, but a cousin never seen would not. This imprecision in definition means that responses should be interpreted as a subjective rather than an objective response, relating more precisely to how people feel. The very few without close relatives represent in real terms 22 people. They tended to live in the small towns rather than in the villages or out in the countryside.

Those without close relatives are spread across the whole age range but three-quarters are women and half of them are single, separated, or divorced. Two-thirds live alone. They are just as likely to be Welsh as non-Welsh. While we are talking about small real numbers, the fact that they are three times as likely to be very lonely and eight times as likely to be very isolated (see subsequent discussion) underscores the vulnerability of this small group and the importance of family support for the majority lucky enough to have close relatives. Most however do form close relationships with non-kin.

CHILDREN

Availability (see Table 5.1)
In addition to the 15 per cent of elderly persons who never married, another 15 per cent are childless (that is, never had children or have no surviving children), so that nearly one-third of the elderly population are without children. (Four per cent of those who have never married had children.) This figure is comparable to that of M. Abrams (1980) for the United Kingdom urban elderly. Forty-four per cent of those who live alone are childless, although this is lower than Power's (1980) figure for Eire (53 per cent). Of those who have children, two-thirds have only one or two children, so families are mainly small. Interestingly enough, the small seaside town with high retirement migration has the smallest proportion of childless, which is in marked contrast with Karn's (1977) findings in English resorts and Clwyd County Council's findings for the North Wales coast that retirement migrants (moved more than 15 miles after age of 60) are more likely to have no children (personal communication, Stuart Hatch, Clwyd Planning Department). But retirement migrants, generally speaking, do have smaller families than other groups, with three-quarters of parents having only one or two children. In the more agricultural communities more than one-third of those with families have four or more children.

Table 5.1 *Number of Children by Age of Arrival in Community and Household Composition (percentages)*

	Number of children					
	0	*1*	*2*	*3*	*4+*	*N*
Total	30	22	24	10	14	(696)
Age at arrival						
Under 40	32	17	24	11	17	(315)
41–60	39	22	19	8	12	(137)
Retirement movers	18	32	20	9	21	(71)
Retirement migrants	25	27	30	12	7	(171)
Household composition						
Living alone	44	18	20	8	9	(228)
With spouse only	18	26	33	13	10	(275)
With younger relative/s	8	23	19	14	36	(135)
With elderly relative/s	78	8	8	0	5	(60)

Proximity (see Table 5.2)

There is a clear relationship between migration and proximity to children. Parents tend to have either a child within 5 miles or no child within 50 miles. This reflects two forms of migration: the outmigration of the local young and the immigration of retirement migrants. However, retirement migrants are more likely to have *all* their children outside the region. Those communities with high proportions of incomers thus have higher proportions of the elderly with no children living nearby. In the seaside towns two-thirds or more have no child within 50 miles, but even in the total sample (including the childless) more than half of the elderly have no child within 50 miles. In the most rural communities approximately one-half have children within 5 miles. Long-term residents are more than twice as likely to have children nearby as retirement migrants. Among the retirement movers (moved less than 15 miles after age 60) the proportions are even higher, indicating that such moves are likely to be towards children.

As a result of the increased geographical mobility of the middle classes (Bell, 1968) at all stages of the life cycle, proximity to the nearest child is also related to social class. Middle-class parents are less likely to have children within 5 miles and, as Hellebrandt (1980) has noted, are likely to stress independence of children.

Proximity to children increases with age and widowhood. More than half of those who have children are living within 5 miles of at least one of them. The shift to living closer to children seems to start after 75 but accelerates after 80. However, a quarter of parents over 80 are more than 50 miles from their nearest child, although often near or with other relatives, as subsequent data will show. The importance of widowhood as the impetus for moving is obvious: more widowed parents live within 5 miles of a child than married parents. Twice as many of those widowed less than a year preceding the interview live more than 50 miles from their nearest child compared with other widows, providing evidence of subsequent moves towards children. Forty-two per cent of parents who moved from one community to another within five years before being interviewed moved to within 5 miles of a child, some into the same household. Nearly half of those living within 5 miles of a child are living in the same household, and the majority of those living more than 50 miles away from their nearest child are married couples under 75. Of those living alone only a quarter have a child within 5 miles.

Compared with M. Abrams's urban study (1978, 1980), the incidence of childlessness among the rural elderly is similar in spite of higher proportions who have never married. Among younger elderly parents (under 75) the proximity of the nearest child is also comparable but more of the rural over-75 parents have children living within 5 miles. Rural women living alone (in both age groups) are also more likely to be

Table 5.3   *Proportion of Parents with Children Living within Five Miles (percentages)*

	Urban[1]		Rural	
	Living alone	*Not living alone*	*Living alone*	*Not living alone*
Men				
75+	36	56	29	66
65–74	27	52	50	50
Women				
75+	42	55	57	71
65–74	37	49	42	48
All				
75+		50		63
65–74		47		48

[1] M. Abrams (1978).

within 5 miles of a child compared with urban women (Abrams, 1978). (See Table 5.3.)

In summary, a third of the elderly are childless and half of those without children live alone. Less than two-fifths overall have a child living within 5 miles, but proximity to children increases after age 75 and frequently widowhood results in a move nearer to children. Overall, however, fewer than half the over-80s are within 15 miles of a child, due in part to high proportions in this age range who never married. Looking to the future, however, we can assume that since more have married, more of the very old in subsequent cohorts could have children near at hand.

Contact (see Table 5.4)
Proximity obviously affects frequency of contact and figures for contact with children follow the same bimodal distribution. Overall two-fifths see a child at least once a week, but well over half of parents do so and three-quarters of parents over 80. At the other end of the scale only 2 per cent of parents never see their children. All these parents were under 75 and many of the children concerned had emigrated and were living abroad. Contact as well as proximity increases with age and widowhood.

In comparison with M. Abrams's (1980) study, availability and frequency of contact with children is roughly equivalent in town and country. However, younger retirement migrants rarely have frequent contact with children. Figures on migration history were not available in the

Table 5.4 *Contact with Children by Community, Age at Arrival, Age, Social Class and Household Composition* (percentages)

	N	More than once a week	Weekly	2–3 times a month	6–12 times a year	Less often	Never	No children
Total	(691)	37	3	7	13	10	1	31
Age at arrival								
Under 40	(310)	47	3	6	8	4	1	33
41–60	(136)	29	2	6	10	13	3	39
Retirement movers	(70)	51	6	11	4	9	0	19
Retirement migrants	(170)	20	2	8	25	19	1	25
Age (all)								
65–69	(181)	39	1	11	14	11	2	22
70–74	(220)	30	2	8	13	15	2	30
75–79	(146)	40	4	6	14	4	0	33
80–84	(82)	43	2	1	11	4	0	39
85+	(62)	42	3	0	5	10	0	40
Age (parents)								
65–69	(141)	50	1	14	18	14	3	
70–74	(154)	43	3	12	19	21	3	
75–79	(98)	59	6	8	20	6	0	
80–84	(50)	70	4	2	18	6	0	
85+	(37)	70	5	0	8	16	0	
Social class								
I	(35)	17	0	3	37	17	0	26
II	(249)	43	3	7	11	4	0	33
III	(241)	35	2	10	13	13	3	24
IV–V	(129)	40	17	17	9	5	1	38
Military	(18)	11	0	0	17	61	0	11
Household composition								
Living alone	(224)	26	3	5	13	6	1	46
With spouse only	(271)	27	2	13	21	17	2	19
With younger relative/s	(131)	90	1	0	0	1	0	8
With elderly relative/s	(60)	7	5	2	0	8	0	78

Abrams study but our figures would seem to indicate that residential stability is more of a discriminator than the rural–urban dichotomy. The significance of retirement migration is a complex one since the increase in contact with age holds for all migratory categories. In some instances, retirement migration is to the home of a child or to be nearer a child. Although frequency of contact is comparable, the fact that more of the rural *old* elderly have children within 5 miles is important in terms of their availability to help in crises and the psychological importance to parents in knowing that they are there.

Compared with long-term residents and retirement movers, retirement migrants and middle-aged movers have less contact with children, with retirement migrants having least contact. Long-term residents are more than twice as likely to see a child at least weekly. Most of those who have children within 5 miles see them more than once a week, as do more than half of those with children more than 5 but within 15 miles. However, even among those whose nearest child is more than 50 miles away, more than half see at least one child at least every two months. For those who have more than one child this can mean more frequent visits. But for two-fifths overall visits are less frequent.

Satisfaction

So far as satisfaction with the frequency of contact is concerned, satisfaction was tabulated for each child, so that it is impossible to say of any one respondent that they want more contact with their children, since they may wish more contact with one out of four, for instance. Overall, a fifth of all children are seen less frequently than desired by their parents, but this does not mean that a fifth of parents are dissatisfied as some parents may wish to see more of more than one child. It is possible to say, therefore, that at *least* 80 per cent of elderly parents are satisfied with the frequency of contact with their children. In another context, 84 per cent state that they see enough of their relatives, which confirms this high level of satisfaction. For Abrams's urban parents, two-fifths of the old elderly and over two-fifths of the young elderly would like to see more of their children. The degree of difference indicates that in spite of similar levels of contact, satisfaction with contact is far higher in the rural communities. It may be that satisfaction is greater because needs for human contact, interaction and validation are being met by a greater diversity of other forms of association or support.

GRANDCHILDREN

The importance of grandchildren to elderly people is often stressed and certainly the photographs of grandchildren in many an old person's living room are evidence enough to support this relationship as a source of pleasure.

Availability

Slightly more of the elderly are without grandchildren than the numbers without children. Contact with grandchildren is understandably less than contact with children and again there are significant differences between communities reflecting migration trends. However, in the whole sample there are only six grandparents who never see any of their grandchildren. These include grandchildren living abroad and grandchildren estranged through divorce.

Contact

Contact with grandchildren does not increase with age, as does contact with children, but remains fairly constant. Approximately one-third see at least one grandchild every week (two-fifths have no grandchildren). Widowed grandparents are visited more frequently and those who live alone receive slightly more frequent visits than those living with their spouse only. Almost half those living with younger relatives see grandchildren more than once a week, many presumably part of the same household.

Migration also affects contact with grandchildren and retirement migrants have less contact than long-term residents. Local people with local kin networks naturally have more contact with grandchildren on a day-to-day basis than those who have retired to the area or mainly middle-class grandparents whose children have moved out of the area. However, grandparents in rural Wales are a common destination for family holidays when grandchildren (and grandparents!) are young.

Satisfaction

Respondents were asked whether they felt they would like to see more or less of their grandchildren or whether they were satisfied with the amount of contact. Three-quarters say that they are satisfied but many qualify their statement by adding 'They come as often as they can', 'They have their own lives to lead', or 'They are grown up and working now, of course, but they always came for their holidays when they were little'. It is apparent that although they can rationalise satisfaction, many grandparents would like to see more of their grandchildren, and nearly every grandparent must have had pictures of grandchildren displayed or produced photographs to show interviewers. This being so, we can estimate that the numbers saying that they would like to see more of their grandchildren may understate the case.

Just over a quarter of those with grandchildren say that they would like to see more of them, but this figure conceals a considerable difference between those communities with high proportions of incomers and those with more local populations. The desire to see more of grandchildren is greatest where the proportions of incomers are also highest.

The rural residents are comparable with Abrams's (1980) urban residents in terms of contact and availability of grandchildren. However, again rural grandparents seem to be more content with the amount of contact with their grandchildren, with only just over a quarter saying they wished they saw more of their grandchildren (including those who wished to see more of some of them) – approximately half the proportion of Abrams's urban grandparents.

In spite of the fact that they see less of their grandchildren, older retirement migrants are slightly more likely to feel satisfied. Among younger migrant grandparents only 59 per cent are satisfied, compared with 80 per cent of older migrants. While this difference between older and younger migrants is difficult to explain, it may reflect a more recent loss on the part of younger retirement migrants who previously lived nearer to grandchildren but are now able to have far less contact than they had before they moved. Their grandchildren too are younger, or still being born and grow and change more quickly. Older grandparents have perhaps adapted their expectations and are less disappointed by the level of contact. Some grandparents commented of absent grandchildren, 'they hardly know us! ' – a fear perhaps more appropriate about young grandchildren than adult ones.

BROTHERS AND SISTERS

The importance of brothers and sisters to the elderly may be underestimated. Most of the literature concerned with informal caring stresses the role of children, and it has been suggested that sibling relationships are relatively unimportant (Lee and Ihinger-Tallman, 1980). However, as the preceding section has shown, one-third of the elderly have no children and even for those who have, brothers and sisters can fill a special place (Kivett and Maxheamver, 1980). With increasing age the desire for reminiscence increases and those who have shared one's childhood and adolescence have a special role. Brothers and sisters are among the few who have clear memories of one's parents, early home and growing up. Frequently, siblings who may never have been particularly close seek a closer relationship in old age as the threat of loneliness increases (Jerrome, 1981).

Availability
While very few (8 per cent) of the elderly were originally only children, more than a quarter (28 per cent) are now without living siblings, 20 per cent have one, 18 per cent two and 34 per cent three or more. Most (62 per cent) have lost at least one sibling through death but slightly more of the elderly have brothers or sisters than have children. While the families the elderly have raised are typically small, the families in which they themselves grew up were considerably larger. Compared with their own children, where only 14 per cent of families have four or more

children, more than half of the elderly themselves came from families of this size. The significance of this for social services in the future will become apparent when we look at the importance of siblings as a source of support to the elderly; the post-pill families of the third generation will be smaller again so that possible sources of support from both children and siblings in coming cohorts of the elderly will be further reduced. This is important in terms of those who do not marry since siblings and their children are the most important relatives.

Proximity (see Table 5.5.)
Migration patterns also affect proximity to siblings, those who have moved being less likely to be within 5 miles of a brother or sister. Communities with large proportions of incomers have larger proportions without a brother or sister nearby. Although the proportions having brothers/sisters are comparable with those for children, brothers and sisters are less likely to be living within 5 miles. Over half have no brother or sister within 50 miles. Long-term residents are more than three times as likely to have a sibling within 5 miles as retirement migrants.

Those who have never married are twice as likely to live within 5 miles of a brother or sister, and three-fifths of those whose households are comprised of elderly relatives have siblings within 5 miles, usually in the same household. But more than half of those who live alone have no sibling within 50 miles. Those who live with their spouse only are least likely to have a sibling nearby, but there is some evidence to suggest that widowhood may in some instances be followed by a move towards a brother or sister. Among those who have brothers and sisters and who have been widowed for less than a year, twice as many are living more than 50 miles from their nearest brother or sister than those who have been widowed for longer.

Contact (see Table 5.6)
Frequency of contact with brothers and sisters is affected by more constraints than contact with children. Both the visited and the visitor are subject to the restrictions of increasing age, and as the years pass the possibility of contact is more frequently removed by death in addition to factors of mobility. Therefore, less contact may be expected with brothers and sisters than with children, and as the years pass and brothers and sisters die the possibility for contact declines. Overall, there is some decline after 75, attributable to the decreased numbers who still have living siblings, but among those who do, contact increases after 75 with as many of those in the over-85 category having at least weekly contact with a brother or sister as those in the youngest age range 65–69. In part this reflects the higher incidence of singleness and sibling households in the older age group, but as Jerrome (1981) has

Table 5.5 Proximity to Brothers and Sisters (percentages)

	N	Within 5 miles	5–15 miles	15–50 miles	50 miles	(+)	No siblings
Total	(694)	28	5	13	27	(55)	28
Age at arrival							
Under 40	(311)	36	7	15	16	(42)	26
41–60	(133)	23	6	11	32	(61)	29
Retirement movers	(71)	41	6	17	13	(37)	24
Retirement migrants	(170)	11	1	9	47	(79)	32
Age (all)							
65–69	(184)	34	3	10	30	(52)	22
70–74	(219)	29	5	17	27	(50)	23
75–79	(144)	22	4	11	29	(64)	35
80–84	(83)	23	15	12	19	(50)	31
85+	(64)	25	2	8	20	(65)	45
Age (those with siblings)							
65–69	(143)	44	3	13	39		
70–74	(169)	37	7	22	34		
75–79	(94)	34	5	17	45		
80–84	(57)	33	21	18	28		
85+	(35)	46	0	3	11		
Marital status							
Single	(106)	49	6	6	14	(40)	26
Married	(332)	24	2	15	34	(59)	25
Widowed	(250)	24	8	12	22	(56)	34
Household composition							
Living alone	(225)	29	8	10	24	(54)	30
With spouse only	(273)	21	3	16	38	(61)	23
With younger relative/s	(133)	27	7	14	17	(53)	36
With elderly relative/s	(58)	59	0	3	7	(38)	31

Table 5.6 *Contact with Brothers and Sisters (percentages)*

	N	More than once a week	Weekly	2–3 times a month	6–12 times a year	Less often	Never	(+)	No siblings
Total	(696)	17	7	6	12	25	6	(34)	28
Age at arrival									
Under 40	(311)	22	7	7	11	24	4	(30)	26
41–60	(134)	14	7	5	16	22	6	(35)	29
Retirement movers	(71)	20	14	10	10	20	3	(27)	24
Retirement migrants	(170)	10	2	3	12	31	10	(42)	32
Age (all)									
65–69	(183)	21	6	7	12	30	2	(24)	22
70–74	(220)	18	7	7	15	22	9	(32)	23
75–79	(147)	13	5	4	12	26	6	(40)	34
80–84	(83)	15	8	6	7	30	2	(33)	31
85+	(63)	14	5	3	10	14	8	(54)	46
Age (those with siblings)									
65–69	(142)	27	8	8	15	39	2		
70–74	(170)	24	9	9	19	28	11		
75–79	(97)	20	8	6	18	39	9		
80–84	(57)	21	12	9	11	44	4		
85+	(34)	26	9	6	18	26	15		
Marital status									
Single	(105)	45	3	1	9	15	2	(28)	26
Married	(333)	10	8	8	13	29	7	(32)	25
Widowed	(252)	16	6	5	11	25	5	(38)	33
Household composition									
Living alone	(225)	21	5	4	12	23	6	(36)	30
With spouse only	(274)	9	8	8	15	30	8	(31)	23
With younger relative/s	(134)	10	9	6	10	26	2	(38)	36
With elderly relative/s	(58)	55	0	3	3	7	0	(31)	31

found, siblings tend to re-establish or reaffirm ties with their brothers and sisters with increasing age, even where previous relationships have been strained.

Fewer retirement migrants have brothers and sisters than other groups, and as a result of the lack of proximity of many of these, contact is far less. Less than half as many retirement migrants see a brother or sister during the week as do long-term residents.

Reflecting greater proximity, nearly half those who have never married are in at least weekly contact with a brother or sister, more than twice as many as those who are married or widowed. Frequency of contact with siblings also increases after widowhood, those who have been widowed for more than five years being almost four times more likely to have weekly contact with siblings than the recently widowed.

There are several households where a widowed sister/brother has moved in with her single sister/brother or vice versa after the death of the husband/wife. The sibling household is the most common form of 'elderly relative household', although in some cases the relationship may be one of marriage with sisters-in-law together or a sister-in-law keeping house for a brother-in-law. This is reflected in the fact that more than half of those living with elderly relatives see a sibling more than once a week.

Household composition, because it is frequently related to marital status, is an important factor in contact with siblings. Fewer of those who live alone with their spouse or with younger relatives in the household have weekly contact with brothers and sisters, while those who live alone are more likely to maintain contact. This is more significant than the proportions here indicate since, because those living alone with their spouses are generally younger, more of them *have* brothers or sisters than those living alone.

Compared with Abrams's (1980) urban study, the availability of and contact with siblings is similar. However, contact with siblings is higher for the old elderly in the rural context, reflecting the high proportions in this age group who never married.

Satisfaction
As for children, respondents were asked of each sibling whether they would like to see more or less of them or whether they were satisfied with the amount of contact. Some wish to see more of one sibling out of two or three, for instance, so it is not possible to say how many are dissatisfied with the amount of contact in any aggregate way. However, most of the elderly are satisfied with the amount of contact they have; only 2 per cent of all living siblings are seen less often than desired. Unfortunately Abrams's (1980) study gave no figures for satisfaction with contact with siblings so it is not possible to say whether satisfaction is higher.

OVERALL CONTACT WITH RELATIVES (*see Table 5.7*)

In spite of the fact that one-third of the elderly are childless and almost one-third have no brothers or sisters, less than one-tenth have neither children nor siblings. Others may live in the same household or community as nephews, nieces, cousins, or even in a few cases, parents. While children, brothers and sisters are the most likely contacts, many elderly people have contacts with other relatives and with a variety of relatives. In order to find out the overall contact respondents have with their families they were asked how often they saw *any* of their relatives to talk to.

Almost half the elderly see a *relative* every day of their lives; and more than 70 per cent in all communities, except the seaside towns, see a relative at least once a week, irrespective of the population density of the community. The childless are slightly less likely to see a relative every day, but over a third do have daily contact compared with half of those with children.

Respondents were asked, 'How often do you see any of your children or other relatives to talk to?' This included relatives in the household as it was felt that the important thing was whether or not there was any *contact* with a relative. Hunt's respondents (1978, pp. 94–5) were asked, 'How often do any of your close relatives manage to visit you?', which implicitly excludes members of the same household, so our figures are not directly comparable. However, both sets of data indicate a high level of contact within families.

With respect to visits from outside the household, Hunt found that age and sex make little difference to the frequency of contact but that mobility, marital status and size of household do (p. 94). She found that the frequency of visits to the married and widowed is identical, but that the single and the divorced/separated are visited approximately half as frequently. Bearing in mind that the figures are not directly comparable, one would still expect to find similar differences in frequency of contact in this survey if singleness is a critical factor with respect to family contact. What one does find is that the widowed have more contact with relatives than the married but so do those who have never married, at least half of whom have daily contact compared with only two-fifths of those who are married. This can be attributed to factors which are associated with the rurality of the region. Since there is a significant proportion of retirement migrants in the total sample, the distance from adult children decreases the frequency of contact. Many married couples in this category reported contact less often than once a month. Widowhood, however, changes the picture, with children visiting more frequently and widowed parents moving nearer to children or going away to visit them, especially during the winter. Single persons, on the other hand, are more likely to be locally born and to have family ties in the region. Their most frequently seen relatives reflect the existence of local extended family networks, as the next section will show.

The numbers of divorced/separated persons in the survey amount to less than 1 per cent, so that it is impossible to make any confident statement about their situation. However, on this scant information it was found that two-thirds see relatives less than once a month, so that Hunt's observation that the divorced/separated form a special group with reduced family contact appears to hold in rural areas. While numbers are very small, the incidence of divorce is increasing with each age cohort and so indicates a growing area of concern for the future.

Of some concern within the rural area is the pattern of retirement migration, which means that in some communities significant proportions of the elderly are incomers, who have arrived there late in life. In looking at frequency of contact with relatives by age of arrival in the community, there is an obvious difference between those who came before they were 40 and those who came after that age. However, there is barely any difference between those arriving between 40 and 60 and those after 60, clearly indicating that it is migration after middle age that decreases contact and not migration after retirement. Like the decreasing size of families and the growing incidence of divorce, increase in geographic mobility means less available family support in the future, and the figures indicate that the greater the distance moved, the less frequent contact becomes.

Although children's contact with parents increases with age, overall contact shows little change, reflecting the loss of older relatives such as brothers, sisters and parents, as well as reduced mobility with waning health. Frequency of contact diminishes from 65 to 80 after which it increases again, with more than half of the very elderly being in daily contact. The sharpest drop is in daily contact between 65 and 70 as aged parents die and adult children leave home. The young elderly are more likely to have children still at home and the older elderly to be living in a child's household. Three-fifths of those aged 90 and older have everyday contact with a relative in the same household. Daily contact therefore declines slightly during the seventies and builds up again in the eighties, as relatives provide more support for growing dependency, but the difference is not as great as one would anticipate. The two-generation nature of the so-called 'elderly' is reflected in the highest figures for daily contact in the youngest and oldest cohorts of the elderly – over the years the carers become the cared for! Approximately one-quarter in all age groups see relatives once a month or less – a cause for some concern with respect to the old elderly. (See Table 5.8)

Nearly three-quarters either live alone or with their spouse only; most others live with relatives and so report a high incidence of daily contact with relatives. Those who live alone and elderly couples show almost identical patterns of contact. (Married respondents consistently inter-

Table 5.8   *Frequency of Contact by Age by Age at Arrival in Community (percentages)*

	N	Every day	At least weekly	Less than once a month
65–69	(180)			
Under 40	(93)	59	78	19
41–60	(42)	52	67	33
Retirement movers	(10)	30	70	10
Retirement migrants	(35)	29	51	37
70–74	(213)			
Under 40	(85)	56	78	19
41–60	(49)	33	57	33
Retirement movers	(24)	50	96	4
Retirement migrants	(55)	29	44	49
75–79	(144)			
Under 40	(76)	49	81	10
41–60	(20)	35	55	30
Retirement movers	(15)	67	80	13
Retirement migrants	(33)	15	40	55
80+	(138)			
Under 40	(53)	60	81	17
41–60	(19)	37	53	37
Retirement movers	(20)	50	85	15
Retirement migrants	(46)	50	63	35

preted 'relatives' to mean other than spouse.) Approximately three-fifths are in contact at least once a week with relatives, as were Hunt's elderly living alone (Table 5.9).

RELATIVES SEEN MOST OFTEN *(see Table 5.10)*

The particular relatives seen most often by the elderly depend, of course, on the family and household composition of the person involved. Where children are available they are the relative with whom there is most contact, but for those who have no nearby child, brothers and sisters are important and with increasing age nephews and nieces.

More than half of all the elderly see one or more of their children more frequently than other relatives. Three-quarters of parents are in more frequent contact with a child than other relatives. (The only other significant category is that of brothers and sisters.) Some respondents mention more than one category of relative, most commonly child and grandchild who visit together, but only one category was enumerated, so it is probable that grandchildren are underrepresented.

Table 5.9 *Frequency of Contact of Those Who Live Alone and Those Who Live with Spouse Only (percentages)*[1]

	Lives alone	With spouse[2] only	Hunt[3] Lives alone
Daily	31 ⎤	27 ⎤	39
	⎬ 50	⎬ 45	
2–3 times a week	19 ⎦	18 ⎦	
Once a week	11	13	19
At least once a week	*61*	*58*	*58*
2–3 times a month	8	7	6
Once a month	5	8	7
Less often	26	27	29
N =	(223)	(265)	

[1] These two categories include 72 per cent of the sample. Other categories report high daily contact because they are mostly living with relatives.
[2] Respondents consistently interpreted question to mean 'other than spouse'.
[3] Hunt (1978), Table 12.8.1, p. 95.

A quarter of respondents are in most frequent contact with siblings, and after 80 the proportion of those whose most frequent contact is nephew or niece is substantially higher, demonstrating the response of the family to increasing age and frailty. The figures for contact with nephews and nieces for those over 80 almost directly reflect the incidence of singleness in those age groups, while below that age they are about half. What seems to happen as time passes is that brothers and sisters are less able to support one another and the younger generation takes on the responsibility. This comes out clearly when relatives seen most frequently are considered by marital status. More than half the single see a brother or sister most frequently, but nephews/nieces and cousins are approximately three times more important to the single than to the married and widowed combined. With increasing age the importance of siblings and cousins declines and for half the single over 80 a nephew or niece is the most frequent contact (Table 5.11). After 80, cousins are important only to those who never married. Among those few who claim to have *no* close living relatives, two-thirds do have infrequent contact with some relative, most frequently a cousin or a niece/nephew. The importance of nieces, nephews and cousins for the single has also been noted by Hunt (1978, Table 12.9.2, p. 96).

For parents, proximity to children appears to be a critical index in terms of frequency of contact with relatives, since even for those whose nearest child lives more than 50 miles away, children are the relative with whom most frequent contact is maintained. Nearly all parents with

Table 5.10 *Relatives Seen Most Often (percentages)*

	N	Child	Brother/ sister	Nephew/ niece	Cousin	Other[1]	No relatives
Total	(681)	54	25	9	6	3	3
Age							
65–69	(179)	56	27	3	10	3	1
70–74	(216)	51	30	7	5	3	4
75–79	(144)	57	18	8	7	7	3
80–84	(80)	53	21	21	1	0	4
85–89	(33)	42	24	21	3	1	9
90+	(29)	66	14	17	3	0	0
Marital status							
Single	(105)	2	53	24	16	4	1
Married	(321)	63	22	4	5	2	4
Widowed	(250)	65	17	9	3	4	2
Household composition							
Living alone	(222)	40	27	14	11	6	2
With spouse only	(265)	59	23	5	6	4	5
With younger relative/s	(132)	86	7	5	0	2	0
With elderly relative/s	(58)	12	66	17	2	0	3
Age at arrival							
Under 40	(306)	54	26	8	7	3	2
41–60	(129)	45	25	12	9	4	5
Retirement movers	(69)	64	25	4	4	3	0
Retirement migrants	(170)	58	24	8	2	4	5

[1] Includes parent, aunt, uncle, grandchild and 'other'

Table 5.11 *Relatives Seen Most Often by Marital Status by Age (percentages)*

		N	Child	Brother/ sister	Nephew/ niece	Cousin	Other[1]	No relatives
Single								
23	65–69	(24)	0	63	8	29	0	0
28	70–74	(30)	0	63	13	20	3	0
17	75–79	(18)	0	56	17	6	22	0
17	80–84	(18)	6	39	50	6	0	0
15	85+	(16)	6	31	44	13	0	6
100								
Married								
33	65–69	(107)	70	20	2	6	3	0
39	70–74	(125)	59	27	5	2	2	5
20	75–79	(63)	68	10	3	10	6	3
5	80–84	(15)	33	40	13	0	0	13
3	85+	(11)	55	27	0	0	0	18
100								
Widowed								
18	65–69	(45)	56	27	2	7	7	2
24	70–74	(59)	58	20	9	3	7	3
25	75–79	(62)	63	16	8	5	5	3
19	80–84	(47)	77	9	13	0	0	2
14	85+	(35)	74	11	14	0	0	0
100								

[1] Includes parent, aunt, uncle, grandchild and 'other'.

children living within 15 miles are visited at least weekly. Of those who have a child within 5 miles more than three-quarters are in daily contact with a relative and in nine out of ten cases that relative is a child. The majority of those with the nearest child living 5–15 miles away receive visits once to three times a week, but of those outside this radius less than half receive weekly visits.

More than half the childless are in at least weekly contact with some relative, mostly daily: half of these are in contact with siblings, a quarter with nieces or nephews and others with cousins; only a tenth have no contact with relatives. Siblings are also important to those with only one child, a quarter of whom report a brother or sister as being their most important contact.

VISITING (*see Table 5.12*)

In addition to receiving visits *from* relatives, visits are also made *to* relatives' and friends' houses either during the day or overnight; obviously, elderly people who do not or cannot make visits have less opportunity for contacts with others. Fifteen per cent overall never visit, directly comparable with Hunt's findings (1978, Table 12.15.1, p. 100). Visits to others are far less frequent than visits received, with only 10 per cent overall visiting more than once a week and two-thirds visiting less than once a month, although this may represent an underestimate since respondents may have under-reported visits which do not involve staying overnight. However, 85 per cent do visit others and there is some interesting variation between communities.

Visiting appears to be more frequent in communities with high proportions of Welsh residents and lowest in the seaside resorts. In fact, those who identify themselves as Welsh or half-Welsh are more likely to make frequent visits and this does not appear to be related to proximity to friends and relatives. The tendency to visit therefore lends some support to the Welsh stereotype of English incomers as 'keeping to themselves'. Among the English this seems to be seen as a virtue, several old people commenting that they had 'never been one for going in and out of other people's houses' or saying, 'I've never bothered people: always kept to myself'. However, comparability with Hunt's findings suggests that residential stability is the key factor. Long-term residents and retirement movers are approximately twice as likely to make weekly visits as middle-aged or retirement migrants but other differences are minimal.

The numbers of those who *never* visit increases with age, with 75 marking a steep decrease in the numbers who make visits; twice as many of those in the age group 75–79 never visit compared with those aged 70–74. Under the age of 80 approximately a quarter visit at least once a week but the frequency of visits drops off after 80.

Table 5.12 *Patterns of Visiting Relatives or Friends (percentages)*

	N	More than one a week	Weekly	At least weekly	2–3 times a month	6–12 times a year	Less often	Never/no relatives
Total	(682)	10	12	22	14	25	24	15
Age								
65–69	(180)	11	13	24	16	25	24	11
70–74	(215)	10	15	25	16	21	28	10
75–79	(145)	9	12	21	14	27	19	20
80–84	(81)	7	7	15	11	31	22	21
85–89	(32)	13	3	16	3	34	19	28
90+	(29)	10	0	10	7	24	28	31
Age of arrival								
Under 40	(306)	13	12	25	13	23	21	16
41–60	(132)	5	7	12	17	31	27	14
Retirement movers	(69)	10	20	30	30	15	16	9
Retirement migrants	(168)	7	12	19	7	28	30	17
Marital status								
Single	(105)	14	10	24	13	23	21	17
Married	(323)	8	12	20	15	25	26	14
Widowed	(248)	10	13	23	13	26	23	15
Household composition								
Living alone	(224)	13	12	25	14	26	21	12
With spouse only	(267)	7	13	20	14	26	27	14
With younger relative/s	(130)	12	9	21	14	25	21	19
With elderly relative/s	(57)	7	8	16	12	19	30	23
Ethnic identity								
English/British/Other	(227)	7	9	16	5	26	35	18
Welsh/Half-Welsh	(456)	11	13	24	19	24	19	14

There is some difference between the visiting patterns of men and women and by marital status. Men are less likely to visit than women. Those living with their spouse only are less likely to make *frequent* visits than those living alone. Those who live with other elderly relatives are even less likely to visit and more likely to visit infrequently. Of those without living relatives, more than a quarter never visit, but members of this category who do visit are more than twice as likely to make visits more than once a week.

Many comment that they visit each of their children living outside the area once or twice a year. Several of the older elderly spend the winter months staying with children. One-third report that they had been away over the preceding Christmas.

SOCIAL CONTACTS ON CHRISTMAS DAY

The media pay a great deal of attention to the plight of the elderly at Christmas and encourage neighbours to be aware of old people living nearby, so respondents were asked how they had spent the previous Christmas. Two-thirds had remained at home, while a third had visited relatives or, in a few cases, friends, but more than half of those who live alone went away for Christmas.

Nine out of ten spend Christmas with family or friends. The majority (51 per cent) spend the day in the company of their children. More than half those who are married and two-thirds of widows are with children. Smaller proportions spend Christmas alone with their spouse (12 per cent), with brothers or sisters (12 per cent), with other relatives (8 per cent), or with friends (8 per cent).

Many of those who have never married spend Christmas with brothers and sisters (40 per cent) and more of them spend Christmas with friends (18 per cent). In some cases 'friends' are neighbours who take an interest in the old person. Sometimes they spend *part* of the day with relatives, or go for Christmas dinner, and several older respondents comment that they go out for dinner but come back afterwards to rest because they find it too tiring to spend a whole day with the younger family members!

However, approximately one-tenth do not spend Christmas in the company of family or friends. Most of these say that they have been alone by choice. Some add that they have invitations but that they decline sometimes because of ill health or special diet. Most stress that they do not mind being alone. Of those who are alone, one in five admits to loneliness. However, some who spend Christmas with their spouse only mention that it is a lonely time. A few have been in hospital over the holiday, all of whom are incomers over 80.

There is little significant difference between communities, the important influences being age, marital status and household composition.

Four times as many of the over-80s spend Christmas alone and lonely as those under that age (4 per cent as against 1 per cent) and more than twice as many spend Christmas alone (14 per cent and 6 per cent). More than a fifth of those who have never married spend Christmas alone, although the majority claim that this is by choice. Because of the relationship with age, almost four times as many women as men are alone over Christmas and women alone are more likely to admit to being lonely. Those who are most likely to spend a lonely Christmas are single or widowed women, probably over 80, living alone. The majority of elderly people, however, spend the day in company.

CONTACTS WITH NEIGHBOURS AND OTHER MEMBERS OF THE COMMUNITY

One of the prevalent stereotypes of country areas is that of intimacy, friendliness and neighbourliness, and mutual trust and co-operation. So it was intended to discover the extent of neighbourhood support available to the elderly and to test the implicit hypothesis of this stereotype. In addition to contact with relatives, neighbours are found to be important to the rural elderly in spite of the somewhat long distances between some households.

Neighbours
The importance of neighbours to elderly people, especially those living alone, goes without saying, and given some of the distances involved in the study area, it is surprising to find that only 2 per cent feel that they are without neighbours and another 2 per cent who have no contact with their neighbours.

Compared with Hunt's (1978) findings, most of the elderly get on with their neighbours; rural residents appear to get on only slightly better, with 96 per cent getting on well with most or all of their neighbours compared with 88 per cent (pp. 108ff.) Differences between long-term residents and retirement migrants are insignificant. Interestingly enough, the proportions saying that they get on well with all their neighbours are highest in the most dispersed communities!

Nine out of ten say they see neighbours to talk to regularly and nearly half are available to provide help *to* their neighbours in a variety of ways: a third are already doing so on a regular basis, mainly by doing shopping. Only 2 per cent say there are no neighbours from whom they can ask favours, compared with five times as many in Hunt's study, although it must be stressed that the majority in both studies have neighbours to whom they can turn.

Age, sex and marital status do not substantially affect relationships with neighbours, although there is some increase in those who have no contact among the over-80s, reflecting the effects of physical mobility.

Eighteen per cent of the bedfast or housebound, and 13 per cent of those who can only get out with help, have no contact with neighbours, compared with only 3 per cent of those who go out without help. While these figures are indicative of isolation, it is perhaps more important for us to note that 82 per cent of the housebound and bedfast and 87 per cent of those who cannot get out without help feel that they get on well with most (at least) of their neighbours. These findings are very comparable with Hunt's figures, given the small numbers and high proportions of proxies (pp. 108 ff.) The problem of immigrants from a different cultural background has received considerable attention in rural Wales, but in general, ethnicity does not appear to affect contacts with neighbours. Age of arrival in the community also has slight effect here.

Three-quarters have neighbours next door. Using these figures as an indication of proximity and population density it appears that distance does not affect the *quality* of relationships. Interestingly enough, hardly any of those whose nearest neighbour is more than a quarter of a mile distant say they have no neighbours. The meaning of 'neighbour' is adapted to suit the rural context and thus the nearest persons become neighbours. However, distance does have some effect on contact with neighbours: 13 per cent of those without a neighbour within 50 yards (18 per cent of the sample) either have no contact or consider themselves without neighbours, compared with 2 per cent of those with neighbours next door or across the road. Whilst physical separation is obviously a contributory factor in social isolation, it is important not to lose sight of the fact that even for the most physically isolated – those without a neighbour within a quarter of a mile – 88 per cent say that they get on well with all or most of their neighbours. Overall, it can confidently be said that the vast majority feel that they have neighbours around them to whom they could turn in an emergency and with whom they have friendly contacts.

Other Members of the Community
While comparable statistics for urban areas are not available, it is also worth mentioning here that in addition to the 91 per cent of the elderly who say that they talk regularly to neighbours, 66 per cent also talk regularly with people in the local shops, 62 per cent with members of the community other than neighbours, 57 per cent with church or chapel members, 55 per cent with the postman and 46 per cent with the milkman. Only 1 per cent say they never talk with anyone in any of these categories.

FRIENDSHIP

In addition to amicable relations with neighbours, most people in all communities feel that they have real friends in the neighbourhood.

Again the imprecision of the term 'real friends' is acknowledged and this response must be seen as a reflection of how people feel rather than an objective assessment. Eighty-five per cent overall feel that they have *real* friends nearby. Differences between communities are minimal. There is no difference between men and women, but increasing age relentlessly takes away friends by death and 42 per cent of those over 90 feel they have no real friends. This unavoidable fact seems to be one of the most prevalent losses associated with longevity. The importance of age homogeneity in friendship patterns has been noted by Rosow (1967).

Those who have never married are most likely to report real friends nearby (89 per cent), perhaps a reflection of their more local origins, but the fact that the married are most likely to be without real friends (17 per cent) suggests that it might also be associated with available time and the need for companionship over the years. Those living in a child's household and couples with a parent or sibling living in the same household are more likely to be without real friends close by (27, 43 and 60 per cent), but since the numbers are small in these categories the figures should be treated cautiously. Often the frail elderly have moved into a child's home when already housebound and have been unable to make new friendships in a strange community.

While the majority feel they have real friends nearby, twice as many retirement migrants are without real friends as long-term residents (20 per cent as against 10 per cent), with middle-aged movers falling between these categories. This also indicates the importance of the investment of time in developing friendships, and twice as many of those who think of themselves as English, British, or some other nationality are without real friends as are those who think of themselves as Welsh or half-Welsh (22 per cent to 11 per cent). This too is presumably related to migration. The data on visiting suggests that there may be a behavioural aspect here in that non-Welsh incomers are less likely to visit and therefore to form new attachments. However, not all friendships need to have been developed since arrival, since retirement migrants sometimes move to be near friends. It is, of course, impossible to attribute this factor to any one feature since recent arrival, outsider ethnic identity and age may all contribute to inhibit the development of new friendships.

Nine out of ten feel that they do not need more friends. Having real friends in the area does not necessarily mean that some people would not like more friends, and by the same token some without friends close by feel that they have enough friends even if they are not nearby. On the whole, the majority both have friends in their area and feel no need for more friends, and while those communities with most immigration show less contact with relatives, there is no difference where friendship is concerned in spite of the fact that the data show retirement immigrants and the non-Welsh to be more likely to be without local friends.

One of the key factors of friendship is feeling important to or needed by another person, so respondents were asked whether there was anyone who depended on their friendship and also if there was anyone who needed them to take care of them. In the latter context, both friends and family would be included, those in the household as well as those outside the household. The responses seem to indicate something else rather than the proportions of persons who are actually providing emotional or other support for others. The elderly seem to take very literally the concept of 'dependent' as meaning that the other person could not survive without them. There is a tendency to undervalue their importance to others. A frequent comment is, 'Well, I don't think they really depend on me, no', or 'Well, I do take care of her/him but whether she/he needs me . . . I suppose she/he could manage on her/his own'. We have only to compare the proportions who are married to see how quick the elderly are to underestimate the value of their own friendship and support. On the other hand, frequently, married people in answering 'no' to the question, 'Is there someone who needs you take care of them?' add that it is indeed they who are taken care of, and others allude to their frailty, disability, or age and suggest that 'I'm not much use' or 'There's not much I can do for anyone'. This last response shows how friendship and providing instrumental help are allied in the minds of people, that is, a friend is someone you help or someone who helps you. Company and emotional support do not appear to be valued as highly by the giver as the performance of tasks, although the receiver may feel quite the other way!

In spite of this tendency towards humility, significant proportions of respondents do feel that they are needed by others, and in the light of the preceding paragraph it can be assumed that the figures reflect considerable commitment. It is difficult to explain large differences between communities. One small village stands out with nearly half who feel someone depends on their friendship and two-fifths who are needed to take care of someone. This community also has the highest proportion of elderly people with dependent members of the household but in addition to that it has the oldest age structure, many of the elderly being retired estate workers who have known each other for a long time although they may have originally come from a distance as youngsters to work in the area and amongst whom a spirit of mutual support has developed. It is tempting to see the higher proportions who feel their friendship is important in the seaside towns as a compensatory adaptation to the lower proportions with local kin networks. The data on the whole, however, support the observation of Windley (1977) in the United States who talks about 'the affection of reciprocity and of assistance among unrelated elderly persons'.

CONFIDANTS

There is a sizeable body of literature which points to the importance (for mental health) of the availability of someone to whom one can talk about the personal and intimate joys, sorrows and uncertainties of life (see Blau, 1973). So respondents were asked whether there is anyone in particular to whom they can talk about themselves and their problems. Ninety-five per cent feel that there is such a person. Not all those without feel this to be a vacuum, however, most commenting to the effect that they have always kept things to themselves. In comparison, M. Abrams (1978) found that almost three times as many of his urban elderly are without confidants.

The nature of the relationship to the confidant is affected by the age, sex and marital status of the respondent. For those who are married the majority confide in their spouse, which of course means that more men than women confide in a spouse because of the greater likelihood of women being widowed. Of those who have never married most confide in a brother or sister, with friends and other relatives being the only other significant categories, and friends are more important for the single than for any other group. More than half of the widowed confide in a child, with brothers/sisters and friends being the next most likely categories. With the passing of the years more of the elderly are widowed, and with increasing age children become more significant as confidants.

The striking aspect of the confidant relationship is its duration. More than two-fifths (43 per cent) have known their confidant for more than fifty years, and three-quarters for thirty years or more. The implications of this for communication in the context of shared knowledge and understanding those things which do not have to be said are obvious. The loss of a confidant through death can, therefore, leave a void which is often hard to fill. It is evident that when a spouse dies, most frequently a child becomes the confidant, but for the single losing a sibling this is usually not possible.

Most confidants for the single are brothers or sisters and predictably in this age group virtually all have known their siblings for more than fifty years, compared with only a quarter of friends or other relatives to whom the single may subsequently turn. Of those who are married or widowed, two-fifths have known their husbands and another two-fifths their children for more than fifty years (although in the latter case the child has not been in the confidant role for as long as that). It may, therefore, be more difficult for the single to find another relationship of the same closeness, and those who are single are far more likely to be without a confidant, although this is also affected by the general independence of those who have not married. Confidant relationships with friends and neighbours are more likely to be of shorter duration and may reflect replacement confidants; more than half are of less than thirty years' duration, but the majority are of more than ten years' standing. The most important feature, however, is that only 5 per cent overall are without someone in whom they can confide. What is reassuring is the apparent ability of the elderly to adjust to the emotional shock of the loss of spouse or other confidant and to establish new confiding relationships.

SUMMARY

The rural findings discussed in this chapter have been compared with the findings of Abrams (1978, 1980) or Hunt (1978) for more urban samples. It appears that overall there is little difference between the rural and urban elderly in terms of the availability of and contact with relatives. However, in rural communities more old elderly parents have children within 5 miles and the single old elderly are more likely to be near to and in contact with brothers and sisters. Retirement migrants, however, are less likely to have close relatives within 50 miles and have less contact. In spite of similar levels of contact, the rural elderly are more satisfied than the urban elderly with family contact.

It is apparent that in most cases those without children or spouses form close relationships with other members of the immediate family. In most cases these are with brothers or sisters and, as time goes by, with nephews or nieces, although cousin relationships can also be important. There is also clear evidence that with increasing age family adaptations take place in order to maintain the security of the old elderly. Moves are made towards both children and/or siblings, and widowhood appears to be one of the prime stimuli for such a decision. There is also evidence to suggest that in spite of distance, adult children maintain close contact with and continue to make regular visits to their parents, so that even for those parents whose nearest child is more than 50 miles away contact with a child is likely to be more frequent than with other relatives. The higher incidence of telephones among retirement migrant parents and comments made also demonstrate that parents and adult children maintain frequent contact even when distance separates. For the single, earlier close relationships with siblings appear to be replaced by siblings' children with increasing age.

While retirement migrants have less contact with family, contacts with friends and neighbours are less affected and the majority of the elderly get on well with their neighbours and have good friends in the community. Proximity *and* contact increase with age, and the elderly show that when a confidant is lost they are able to re-establish a close and confiding relationship with another. Visiting patterns show little difference between the rural and urban studies. The case histories in Chapter 9 illustrate many of these relationships and give concrete examples of the networks within which the elderly live. Overall, social involvement and contact seems to be low for a small minority of the elderly.

Although slightly higher proportions of the rural elderly state that they get on well with all or most of their neighbours, can ask them favours, or have confidants, it is important to stress that in both the rural and urban studies it is a small proportion who respond negatively to these questions. Differences between rural and urban response may reflect differences in the definition of 'neighbour', since we have seen rural neighbours may be quite a distance away. Given the high levels of contact involved it should not be inferred that there is a wide difference between the urban and rural elderly, but rather that despite the different constraints which exist, high levels of social interaction with family, friends and neighbours are prevalent in both environments. It is, of course, very difficult to make any comment about the quality or meaningfulness of these contacts and it may be that differences exist in this dimension. However, that question would require a different type of research.

Chapter 6

VOLUNTARY ASSOCIATION AND SPARE-TIME ACTIVITIES

Participation in voluntary organisations can be looked at as one measure of community integration. It may provide role continuity after retirement and can be an important source of social contacts. For migrants involvement in local groups can provide a channel of entry and ultimate acceptance into a new community. While the social contacts of the elderly show only small variations between rural and urban contexts, participation in voluntary groups is far more common in the rural communities.

MEMBERSHIP (see Table 6.1)

Almost half of respondents (49 per cent) belong to at least one voluntary organisation, other than chapel or church, compared with just over a third (36 per cent) in Hunt's (1978) more urban sample (pp. 125 ff.). Membership in such associations declines with age among rural and urban residents, and in the rural communities is highest among long-term residents and retirement migrants. Community differences in the organisations to which people belong reflect in part the availability and viability of groups. Overall pensioners' groups and women's organisations are the most popular but each community has its own pattern. Membership is unrelated to marital status or ethnicity, but women and those who live alone are slightly more likely to belong to voluntary organisations than men and those who live with others. Hunt (1978), on the other hand, found more male members than female (p. 126).

Higher rural participation in voluntary organisations was contrary to expectation since for many the travelling necessary to sustain membership is difficult, and the smaller communities may not have a wide choice of associations: some, for instance, have no OAP groups. In spite of these drawbacks, twice as many belong to pensioners' groups, twice as many to the British Legion and comparable proportions to trade unions, political and professional organisations, the Red Cross and the WRVS. More than three times as many belong to the Women's Institute – and

Table 6.1   *Voluntary Associations Compared with Hunt[1] (percentages)*

| | Total | | Males | | Females | |
	Rural Wales	Hunt	Rural Wales	Hunt	Rural Wales	Hunt
Church and religious organisations	*	13	*	8	*	16
OAP organisations	16	8	9	6	22	9
British Legion	7	4	7	6	6	2
Women's Institute	10	3	—	—	17	5
Merched y Wawr	7	*	—	*	12	*
Townswomen's Guild	*	1	—	—	*	2
Trade union	2	3	4	6	—	—
Political organisations	5	4	7	5	3	4
Professional organisations	3	2	5	2	1	2
Red Cross	2	1	1	1	1	2
WRVS	2	2	—	—	3	3

[1]   Hunt (1978), Table 15.3.1, p. 126.
*   Not listed separately.

this is one group where membership declines less steeply with age. The Townswomen's Guild was absent from the list since the organisation is rarely found in the small rural towns, but *Merched y Wawr*, which is the Welsh language equivalent of the Women's Institute, was included. In Hunt's (1978) survey 7 per cent of women belong to the Women's Institute or the Townswomen's Guild. In our rural survey, combining the percentages for the Women's Institute and *Merched y Wawr*, 29 per cent belong to a women's group. Even allowing for the very few women who claim membership in both groups, this is approximately four times the proportion of urban women who seek such association.

Women are more than twice as likely as men to join pensioners' groups, and widows are twice as likely to join as married people. Such groups are also more popular with long-term residents than incomers. While twice as many rural respondents belong to clubs for the elderly compared with Hunt (1978), this difference is mainly due to the high proportion of women (22 per cent) who belong. Comparing the rural findings with M. Abrams's (1978) wholly urban sample, again rural membership is higher. Membership is higher for all sub-groups in the rural sample except for men over 75 living alone.

While long-term residents are more likely to belong to OAP groups than others, more of those who have moved since retirement, whether local or incomers, belong to a women's organisation, and retirement migrants are more likely to join hobby, historical and sports societies. More than half of those who belong to hobby groups or historical and conservation societies are retirement migrants and more than a third of those who belong to sports groups (mainly golf and sailing), in spite of the fact that they comprise only 25 per cent of the elderly population. It is evident that the retirement migrant actively seeks community integration through voluntary association, although different associations may be favoured by local people. They are also more regular attenders at meetings than other groups, and Jerrome (1981) has shown how retirement migrants are recruited into voluntary associations by other retirement migrants and in this way enlarge their circle of friends.

The overall evidence is, therefore, that voluntary association is greater in the rural communities than in urban settings. While the level of voluntary association can only be seen as indicative of greater community integration, this suggests that the rural elderly may receive more social support, which may go some way to explaining the higher levels of satisfaction with similar frequencies of contact with relatives.

ATTENDANCE AT MEETINGS

Some of the voluntary organisations to which respondents belong, such as professional organisations and charities, have no local meetings. It is, therefore, significant that over a third of our total sample regularly attend meetings of voluntary organisations. Regular attendance at meetings is highest during the seventies but drops off sharply after 80, paralleling the drop in membership. Widowed members attend more regularly but married members also attend more frequently than single members.

CHURCH OR CHAPEL MEMBERSHIP

Religious observation has long been one of the obvious aspects of community integration and participation. The high proportions of the rural elderly who are visited by clergymen (Chapter 4) are indicative of the importance of the church/chapel in the study communities. More than 80 per cent claim membership of church, Nonconformist chapel, or other religious group, and more than 75 per cent attend at least sometimes. Almost half the elderly attend at least once a month and nearly two-fifths every week. Attendance declines slightly with age but only after 85, and there is little difference between the sexes. Unfortunately, no comparable figures are available for urban populations.

Wales is well known for its strong Nonconformist tradition, so it is difficult to say whether the importance of religious activity is a cultural or rural phenomenon. Recent arrivals are less likely to be members and more likely to be English. Five times as many retirement migrants as long-term residents belong to no religious group. However, church membership is highest in those communities with the largest proportions of Welsh-speakers. Five times as many non-Welsh are non-members, so it is perhaps important to acknowledge that this may be an ethnic phenomenon rather than a rural one. On the other hand, the valid distinction may be between indigenous country people and incomers and it would be interesting to look at comparable data from other rural areas. The findings may also reflect the predominant use of the Welsh language by the Nonconformist groups. In parts of rural Wales, the chapel (Nonconformist) still plays an important, though waning, social role as a focus of the community. Although no comparable figures on membership are available, it seems apparent that the salience of religious membership is higher in the rural community.

HOBBIES, INTERESTS AND SPARE-TIME ACTIVITIES (*see Table 6.2*)

Meaningful activity is important for self-image and life satisfaction. So it is also worth considering differences in participation in hobbies and other interests. Interviewers on the rural survey were instructed not to prompt respondents, but comments from the interviewers to the research team indicate that respondents sometimes asked for examples which were then given. It seems reasonable, therefore, to compare Hunt's total figures, including prompted replies for the commonest activities, television, radio, reading and knitting.

Television and radio head the list for both urban and rural residents and there seems to be little difference between the regions in the importance of this activity. (More of the rural elderly listen regularly to the radio than regularly watch television.) Comparable proportions with Hunt's study (1978) also engage in knitting, indoor games (cards, bingo, and so on), music and sport. But eight times as many rural residents report walking as a hobby and almost twice as many gardening and these proportions hold for men and women. Almost three times as many rural women report various arts and crafts, although for men the figure is comparable. On the other hand, urban residents appear to spend more time reading, particularly men. Differences between long-term residents and retirement migrants are not extreme, but it appears that the migrants are less inclined to watch television and more inclined to engage in craftwork and indoor games such as cards. There are no very significant differences between communities, apart from the fact that sports are only important in a sailing centre.

Involvement in all hobbies and activities, apart from television, radio and reading, declines with age. With gardening, walking and indoor games, participation drops sharply after age 80. In fact four times as many of the over-80s have no hobbies or interests as those under 80 (8 per cent and 2 per cent respectively). Men are more involved in gardening, walking, music and sports than are women, while, as one would expect, more women are concerned with knitting and sewing, but a considerably higher proportion of women mention reading. Those who

Table 6.2 *Comparison of Hobbies and Interests with Hunt*[1] *(percentages)*

	Total		Males		Females	
	Rural Wales	Hunt	Rural Wales	Hunt	Rural Wales	Hunt
TV/radio	85	91/76[2,3]	85	91/72[2,3]	85	91/76[2,3]
Reading	64	82[3]	55	83[3]	70	82
Knitting[4] (needlework)	36	33	2	1	60	54
Gardening	48	26	62	39	39	18
Walking	33	4	45	5	24	3
Arts and crafts (including woodwork)	17	10	17	16	17	6
Indoor games (cards, bingo, etc.)	12	10	14	12	11	9
Music	6	8	9	8	4	7
Sport (of any kind)	4	6	10	12	0	2
Other activities[5]	10	18	15	20	0	2
None[6]	4	22	3	22	4	22

[1] Hunt (1978), Table 15.4.1, p. 127.
[2] TV/radio separately.
[3] After prompt.
[4] Rural study including sewing.
[5] Not included in our list but listed separately by Hunt – repairs and redecorating, cooking, preserving, wine-making, church activities, spectator sports.
[6] Hunt's figures based on non-prompted responses.

live alone do more knitting and sewing and watch more television than those who live with others.

The overall effect is that the rural elderly are more involved in those hobbies and activities that are likely to involve them in outdoor physical activity and manual dexterity. Walking and gardening, of course, in addition to providing exercise and fresh air and thus aiding health and morale, also increase the potential for outside contacts.

The large proportion who mention gardening as a hobby in the rural areas reflects the availability of gardens and deserves separate comment. Only 14 per cent have no garden. Although it might be logical to expect the proportions of those with gardens to be higher in the most rural communities, the availability of gardens follows no pattern and in fact the most dispersed (and highest) community had the fewest gardens. The problem of gardens becoming overgrown and a burden to elderly residents is frequently discussed, so respondents with gardens were asked what their feelings were about them. Only 16 per cent say that they would rather be without their gardens, indicating that upkeep becomes burdensome for a few. However, for more than four-fifths the garden is seen as a positive asset and two-fifths say they would not be without it. Surprisingly, those with small gardens are twice as likely to wish to be rid of them as those with large gardens, more than half of whom say they wouldn't be without them. Gardens become more of a burden with increasing age, particularly after 75, and twice as many of those who live alone would rather be without a garden. However, there is little significant difference between men and women. The majority remain happy to have a garden, but help in this area is sometimes a problem and some gardens are overgrown.

SUMMARY

In summary, it appears that in spite of reduced opportunities, as a result of distance and lack of public transport, compared with the urban elderly the rural elderly are more likely to belong to voluntary organisations, to be in contact with a religious institution, to attend meetings and to engage in those spare-time activities which provide potential for contact with others. Overall, their integration with the community at large seems to be higher than that of the urban elderly.

This difference between the activities of the rural and the urban elderly demands some discussion. There are some contrasting features of the environment which deserve comment. Voluntary groups and religious institutions are not only more visible in rural communities but are frequently the only source of diversion and entertainment available. In some communities, there is considerable overlap between church or chapel and voluntary organisations.

Many informal groups are connected with the chapel, or autonomous groups may use church or chapel premises as a meeting place. Their visibility is assured because not only do many groups use the same meeting place since premises are limited, but meetings are advertised on local notice-boards, in the post office, the local shop, or the pub, and because there are fewer of these a high proportion of people are likely to know of the existence of a group. Added to this, the viability of such groups where the total population is small depends on a higher proportion belonging, and so canvassing for members becomes more important. This activity in its turn is also more easily accomplished since a very high proportion of potential members are known to organisers and so many will receive a personal invitation, and the social milieu is such that reminders are almost inevitable! Because groups are small efforts are made to ensure that everyone who wishes to attend has some way of getting to meetings.

The environment also has an effect on the informal spare-time activities of the elderly. The popularity of walking and gardening reflect the availability of attractive country or seaside and of gardens, but more than that they reflect the fact that being outside is more pleasant when one is assured of peace and safety. The high level of security which the elderly feel in an environment where the crime rate is low and where they know and are known to a high proportion of their neighbours is further enhanced by lower levels of traffic, noise, air pollution and vandalism.

The net effect is that the rural elderly are more visible and more integrated into the community. It seems likely that these factors make an important contribution to the high levels of satisfaction expressed with family relationships and the acceptance of many of the inconveniences of rural life (Lawton, 1980).

Part Four

SUPPORT

Chapter 7

HELP AND HELPERS

INTRODUCTION

Chapters 5 and 6 have shown that the rural elderly are roughly comparable with their United Kingdom urban counterparts in terms of the availability of, proximity to and contact with children, grandchildren and siblings, but that they are substantially more satisfied with the amount of contact. It was suggested that this difference in the level of satisfaction may be related to the higher level of voluntary association and religious membership found in the rural communities, and participation in spare-time activities which are more likely to bring the elderly into contact with others. The most significant finding is that for most of the elderly in both environments, family and/or friends are available as potential sources of support.

This chapter seeks to look in more detail at the types and sources of help available to the rural elderly, the proportions receiving help and the proportions of paid help. It is important to stress that the majority of the elderly are active participants in their social networks, which include those to whom the elderly give support as well as those from whom support is received. In all categories of frequent needs, a minority of the elderly receive help, and in other cases, such as household decoration and repairs, the elderly are not unique in their search for outside assistance. Following a short section describing briefly some of the kinds of help given by the elderly to others, consideration is given to different types of help received by different categories of elderly people; help received by the most dependent in terms of personal care; help with frequently and less frequently needed routine housekeeping chores (for example shopping, cooking and gardening); and sources of help in crises (sickness, anxiety, bereavement, and so on), that is, unpredictable needs.

One of the most evident findings is the heavy reliance on family help. Awareness of the family as the chief source of help underpins recent policy statements on the need for greater support of the elderly within the community (DHSS, 1981), and is further evidenced by the data which show movement to be with or nearer to children and/or siblings with increasing age. In spite of widespread concern about the attenuation of family support the data indicate continuing commitment. Even retirement migrants appear to be well supported. A cross-cultural study by the World Health Organisation in 1959 denied the contention that families were becoming less willing to care for one another but hinted that distance may make this impossible: 'Wherever careful studies have been carried out in the industrialised countries the lasting devotion of children for their parents has been amply demonstrated. The great majority of old people are in regular contact with their children, relatives or friends ... *Where distance permits* [italics added] the generations continue to shoulder their traditional obligations, of elders towards their children and children to the aged' (WHO, 1959). But even where distance separates, the family often remains the primary source of help for the elderly and the level of contacts through visits, telephone calls and letters remains high (Bell, 1968).

The reciprocal nature of the relationship between parents and children, mentioned in the above quotation, has also been commented upon by Sussman (1965) who describes norms in the United States of financial assistance from parents to newly married children, baby-sitting for young parents and the expectations of care for the aged. He makes an interesting point, that daughters are far more likely to receive and subsequently give services while sons are more likely to receive and give financial support.

The anthropological literature on reciprocity indicates that behaviour and performance are more complex than the one-to-one relationship of the interactants, involving also questions of relative power, community solidarity, reputation and status, individual self-image and the presentation of self to the larger group (see Bailey, 1971; Goffman, 1959; Mauss, 1954). In other words, where the cultural expectation of care exists, social pressures reinforce performance, a point noted by Firth *et al.* (1969) who found that moral obligations were recognised even in the wider kin field and despite the interventions of the state and the greater financial security of the middle-class families he studied.

However, as already noted, the parent–child relationship may not be conflict-free. At the same time, adult children are subject to the role conflicts of being parent, child, employee; sometimes aunt or cousin to other elderly persons; and increasingly grandparent simultaneously (Shanas, 1981). While Blenkner (1965) has commented on the failure of social workers to adequately help such adult children, Goldfarb (1965) identified two types of socialisation styles which he suggests have implications for adaptations of both parent and child in old age. In the first, the child is provided with the necessary skills and information to act independently and given the freedom to do so, and in the second, the child is coerced into accepted behaviour to please the adult, with two resultant basic personality types. These he characterised as independent and dependent and suggested they were self-perpetuating within the family. Independent persons cope better with ageing – their own and their parents!

The word 'dependency' is used frequently in the context of the elderly. It has acquired a connotation of stigma and may indeed have something to do with the vehemence with which many elderly people stress their independence. Yet everyone is dependent to some degree or another; we all need help and support throughout life, albeit most support is needed in the first and last few years. Since the age range within the so-called 'elderly' cohort may include two generations, it is a minority who at any one time have a high level of dependency. The elderly, like every other group in society, give and receive help as and where necessary or appropriate and, like every other group, those who live with others naturally expect and receive more help than those who live alone. At the risk of belabouring this point, it is important to accept at the outset that the majority of the elderly are competent, capable adults who give as well as receive and that receiving help is not necessarily a measure of need or dependency. By the same token, the fact that increasing age brings ultimately increasing frailty and the curtailment of physical capacities to perform mundane tasks of everyday life and personal care cannot be denied. The sick and the frail need more help than the able-bodied. This chapter seeks to look at the situation of the elderly with respect to help given and received, but because the primary focus of the research was to discover the availability of help for the elderly within the community setting, the emphasis has been placed on help received rather than help given, although that is where the chapter begins.

HELP GIVEN BY THE ELDERLY

As noted in Chapter 6, 96 per cent get on well with most of their neighbours and 72 per cent with *all* their neighbours. One-third of elderly respondents help their neighbours out in various ways and a further 12 per cent say they would if asked. The likelihood is that more than this 12 per cent are realistically *potential* helpers as this was a volunteered response and may not always have been elicited. Helping neighbours is more common in those communities where settlement is less dispersed. The most common form of aid is help with shopping (56 per cent of helpers do this) followed by gardening (20 per cent), giving lifts (17 per cent), bringing in fuel (9 per cent) and small numbers doing cleaning, cooking, baby-sitting, looking after pets, or keeping a key to the house, and a large category of other tasks (35 per cent) reflecting the idiosyncratic pattern of flexible co-operation. Neighbourhood support is obviously a highly flexible area. The likelihood is, of course, that some respondents do not even think of what they do in these terms and so these figures perhaps understate the amount of mutual help that exists.

Those elderly who are regularly involved in helping out their neighbours are more likely to be single (35 per cent) or married (38 per cent) than widowed (24 per cent), and more likely to be men (39 per cent) than women (27 per cent), irrespective of marital status. This does not appear to be merely a reflection of age since a high proportion of the single and married continue helping after 75, while help from widows drops off more steeply. Overall, helping is, as expected, most usual in the 65–69 age range and drops steeply after 80. Those who live with their spouse only are more likely to be helping out neighbours (40 per cent) than those in other types of households. Giving help to neighbours is also class-related, with the middle class more likely to help neighbours. Helpers are more likely among those with large networks and those without close relatives.

In addition to the practical types of help mentioned by respondents, the elderly provide emotional support to friends and relatives, although as already discussed, this type of help tends to be undervalued by the giver. Almost a quarter were prepared to say that there was someone who depended on their friendship and a fifth had someone who needed them to care for them. In half of these cases, that person was a dependent member of the household. The majority of dependants were of the same generation as the interviewee, usually a spouse. In a very small number of cases the dependant was a parent but a fifth of dependants were adult children and in two instances the interviewee was caring for more than one dependent relative.

In most instances the dependency relationship is such that one spouse is ambulatory but housebound or able to go out only with considerable difficulty. In only two cases was the dependant permanently bedfast. Some instances involve mental handicap or mental illness. Since care for dependants has important implications for social services, it seems worthwhile to describe actual situations as examples of the type of care informally provided by the elderly in the community and the type of strain carers are often under.

In one instance, a widow of over 80 (referred to here as Mrs Hughes; see Chapter 9) lives alone with her mentally handicapped niece aged 73. The house is some distance from the nearest village and not within walking distance of a shop. Mrs Hughes is childless and has cared for her niece with some short interruptions since she (the niece) was 16. At first contact she was at great pains to stress how well they manage and how happy her niece is. From her report they are well looked after by neighbours and are known to the social services.

While Mrs Hughes's situation appears to be a mutually gratifying relationship, the position in another household is far from satisfactory. Mr and Mrs B. live on a small council estate in a village with their mentally handicapped son in his late forties. The son has always been difficult and with the parents' increasing age is becoming very demanding and aggressive. At the time of the interview Mrs B. was tearful, anxious and worried about the future. She has managed so far but suddenly is realising that the strain is proving too much. Although the family is in contact with social services, the parents remain under considerable stress and have little day-to-day support.

In a very rural area, two elderly bachelor brothers live together on a remote farm. One has suffered a stroke and has been completely immobilised in bed for over a year. The older brother, who acted as proxy, continues to work the farm and to care for his brother with the daily help of nieces, who live on adjacent farms, and who come daily to cook and to bath and tend their uncle. The able-bodied brother comments that his brother looks forward to his coming in at night for a cup of tea and a chat about what he's been doing and what he's heard during the day.

On another farm, an elderly couple have the husband's brother living with them. He has been a member of the household for many years but has been in and out of the psychiatric hospital. The wife finds his behaviour very difficult to cope with and impossible to understand. The patient's reaction when angry with his sister-in-law is to refuse to speak for weeks and to soil his bedding.

In a small village with one shop, Mrs C., a widow in her late seventies, lives with her daughter, who is chair-bound, suffering from rheumatoid arthritis. The daughter's condition is acute and her diction affected. There is no way the mother can take her daughter out since the old person's bungalow in which they live has a steep slope to the road and in any case Mrs C. is not strong enough to wheel her. She also worries about the future of her daughter.

These are all extreme cases. For the most part elderly carers are looking after others of the same generation who are able to perform some personal care tasks for themselves but are chronically ill, unable to get out, or have difficulty moving around the house. Frequently, carers are up in the night to tend to their dependants. Most of those who find themselves in the caring role do not question their responsibility but in many cases the strain is evident. One common factor of such caring relationships is that they develop gradually as a result of deterioration in the condition of the dependant. At the outset, the responsibility is assumed willingly and inevitably. To shift the responsibility elsewhere would not occur to most carers and in some cases the recognition of a need for help comes later, experienced as anxiety about fulfilling commitments.

The range of help given by the elderly covers the full gamut from taking full responsibility for the care of a dependent adult to the triviality of keeping an extra key to a neighbour's house. What seems evident is that a general willingness to help exists amongst the majority of those capable of helping and a high proportion are committed in one way or another.

HELP RECEIVED BY THE ELDERLY AND SOURCES OF HELP

Help received by the elderly covers a broad range, including, at one end of the scale, essential personal care which cannot be done by the person themselves, and at the other, occasional expressive help such as doing errands or washing up. For those who are physically limited and/or frail only regular care makes it possible for them to remain at home; others like many in most age groups need occasional help with specialised tasks such as house repairs; some need regular help with more routine chores such as shopping, cooking, and so on, and everyone needs help in times of crisis. Some tasks have to be done at least daily (such as feeding and cooking), some at frequent intervals (such as shopping); others infrequently (for example, painting the house) or at unpredictable intervals (for example, in cases of illness, need for advice or comfort). Different types of need call for different types of help, differing degrees of commitment and hence, in some cases, different sources of help.

At the same time, not all help is received as a direct result of need. Much helping is expressive, particularly within the household or between close friends. Mutual help is also part of the rural ethos, such as offering lifts to pedestrians, sharing garden produce, picking up a neighbour's bread or papers if one happens to visit the shop before he does, or passing on crucial information about local events. There is bound to be a difference between the amount and sources of help of those who live alone and those who live with others. We all expect others in the household to help with household chores irrespective of the necessity for such help.

This section looks at types of help in terms of first, regular, predictable needs, for personal care, routine chores and emotional support; and secondly, unpredictable needs for practical help, advice and emotional support, in what may be seen as crises. It also looks at the sources of help: family, friends and neighbours and others. Where family are concerned, a distinction is made between spouse, another member of the same household and relatives outside the household. However, the important distinction is between help from within the household and help from outside.

Personal Care

As discussed in Chapter 3, the majority of the elderly are well able to care for themselves, but for a small minority help is needed for various tasks of personal care. With increasing age more help with personal care is needed. Since the numbers receiving such care are small, detailed analysis would be misleading. Most receive help from other members of the household, with small proportions receiving care from outside relatives. Professional help is significantly limited to longer-interval care such as that provided by district nurses and chiropodists. Help from friends and neighbours is negligible.

Although the real numbers of those needing help are small, sources of help where needed are clearly related to household composition. Those living alone are least dependent and need help with a narrower range of tasks. Their help with bathing comes mainly from the district nurse although a quarter of those needing help are helped by relatives living in another household. Help with dressing is provided, in the one case where needed, by a home help. Four-fifths of those needing help with toenails receive help from the chiropodist, with small numbers getting help from an outside relative or the district nurse and only one from a friend. Help with mobility is provided mainly by outside relatives. Apart from help in moving around, those who live alone are more likely to rely on professional help than those who live with others.

Those living with their spouses only present an entirely different picture, their husband or wife being the main helper for every task with back-up being provided in a small number of cases by the district nurse (bathing), chiropodist and outside relatives. More than half of those living with younger relatives receive help with bathing from the district nurse. For all other tasks helpers are mainly members of the household including cutting toenails, where only a fifth receive chiropody help.

The real number of dependent people living with other elderly relatives is too small for convincing analysis but the data indicate a more complex network of support. Surprisingly, reliance on other members of the household is far smaller than would be expected. Help with bathing comes most fequently from the district nurse or an outside relative. The district nurse is also mentioned as the main source of help with dressing and shaving, while outside relatives provide help with other short-interval help: toileting, feeding, putting to bed and getting up, and helping to move around the house. Other members of the household are mentioned only as the main source of cutting toenails and going out (however, some in this category do not go out).

Households where dependent elderly persons are being cared for by elderly relatives other than a spouse appear to receive a higher professional input than similar households where the dependant is the husband or wife, or where the principal carer is a younger relative. However, data from a parallel study of elderly social services customers indicate that domiciliary services are provided to those living alone at a much lower level of physical dependency than that of those living with others. Informal carers, particularly elderly spouses, apparently provide the bulk of support for the frail elderly at home. However, the breakdown of carers is a frequent reason for Part III and hospital admissions (Townsend, 1965; Pope, 1978). Given the small numbers of households involved it is difficult to draw any conclusions from our data, but the situation raises important questions about the support of carers, and further commitment in this area of social provision is indicated.

Routine Chores

Routine chores can be roughly divided into housekeeping tasks which are fairly critical and needed at frequent intervals, ranging from more than once a day, such as cooking, to once a week, such as laundry or ironing; and property maintenance jobs which are necessary at longer intervals and could possibly be ignored, such as gardening and structural repairs.

Help received may be daily or on some other regular basis or it may be occasional, depending both on need or inclination. In some cases help may be paid for, in other cases it may be given freely and in many cases payment would be totally inappropriate. On the other hand, for some people paying for help may be the only way to get help, although for those few who can easily afford payment it may be a preference.

The following section looks at sources of help with routine chores by task for both frequent (short-interval) and infrequent (long-interval) needs (see Table 7.1).

Proportions receiving help and sources of help   Where frequently needed chores are concerned, most help is received with shopping which necessitates leaving the house and carrying provisions home. Almost two-fifths receive at least occasional help here and a quarter receive regular help. Most of this help comes from the family (three-fifths) and much (two-fifths) from within the household. However, help from neighbours (12 per cent) is more frequent with shopping than other routine chores. More than half the help with shopping comes from outside the household and one person in ten receiving such help pays (including local authority and private household helps).

Help with laundry and ironing is received at least occasionally by a third of the elderly and here too regular help is received by a quarter. Similar proportions of such help come from within the household and from the family. However, approximately a quarter who receive help with laundry or ironing pay for such help (including household helps and commercial laundry services).

Help with cooking is slightly less frequent. A quarter receive at least occasional help and one-fifth regular help, more than half of which comes from within the household. A tenth of such help is paid for.

Almost three-fifths of the rural elderly rely on open fires for their main source of heat and thus the critical tasks involved in maintaining the fire can become burdensome. However, 84 per cent of those relying on fires receive no help with them, although approximately a quarter get at least occasional help with cutting wood or carrying fuel. Smaller proportions, however, get regular help with this demanding chore than receive help with cooking, laundry, or shopping, and while approximately two-fifths of such help comes from within the household, only just over half such help comes from the family and less than one-fifth is

Table 7.1 *Help with Routine Chores (%)*

		Help received								Sources of help						
	N	Never	Occasionally	Regularly/ daily	N	Spouse	Household member	Within household	Outside relative	Family	Friend/ neighbour	Home help	Other/ unclear	Outside help[1]	Proportion of help paid
Short interval															
Shopping	(665)	61	13	26	(291)	29	15	44	18	62	12	2	23	55	10
Laundry	(665)	68	6	27	(254)	29	17	46	16	62	5	4	30	55	23
Ironing	(658)	70	4	26	(242)	30	18	48	13	61	4	5	29	51	21
Cooking	(666)	74	6	20	(210)	38	20	58	11	69	4	3	24	42	11
Making fires[2]	(550)	84	3	13	(137)	25	22	47	4	51	2	8	39	53	16
Cutting wood[2]	(533)	74	8	18	(118)	20	19	39	15	54	5	1	40	61	12
Carrying fuel[2]	(529)	79	5	15	(163)	21	22	43	10	53	4	3	41	57	13
Long interval															
Gardening	(620)	65	14	21	(265)	19	14	33	14	47	7	—	46	66	29
Decorating	(642)	43	35	22	(419)	8	11	17	17	36	2	—	61	81	54
Household repairs	(633)	35	42	24	(468)	5	9	14	8	22	3	—	74	85	57

[1] It is assumed that other/unclear is outside help, that is, from the household.
[2] Where appropriate.

paid for. Helpers include local children as well as household helps and contributions of fuel (particularly around Christmas) from local charitable groups such as the Scouts.

Help with less frequently needed chores – gardening, decorating and household maintenance – is less likely to come from informal or family sources and more of this help is paid for. A third receive at least occasional help with gardening, two-thirds of which comes from outside the household, less than half from other members of the family and nearly a third of this help is paid. More than half the elderly receive help with decorating, only a fifth of which is from within the household and a third from the family. More than half of such help is paid for. Two-thirds receive help with household repairs (that is, property maintenance), only one-fifth of which comes from the family. Again, more than half is paid for. Council tenants, of course, receive free help with decorating and repairs.

Age   With increasing age the elderly become more dependent on help from others and more likely to live with others. Up to the age of 80 approximately one-fifth receive regular help with shopping, laundry and ironing after which the proportion helped doubles in the early eighties, and approximately two-thirds of those aged 85 or older receive help with shopping and laundry and more than half with ironing. Fewer overall receive regular help with cooking, and here again those under 80 are half as likely (16 per cent) to receive help as those in the early eighties (28 per cent) and almost half those over 85 receive regular help. A very similar pattern exists for help with fires. In fact it is possible to say that under 80 a fifth or less receive regular help with frequently needed routine chores, twice as many in the 80–84 age range and half as many again after age 85. It seems important to draw attention here to the fact that increased dependency seems to occur after 80, rather than 75, as much of the literature, particularly statistical analyses (e.g. M. Abrams, 1978, 1980), implies.

Sources of help reflect the changing household composition of the elderly in the face of widowhood and increasing frailty and provide a reminder of the danger of seeing them as a homogeneous group. Under the age of 75, approximately half of help with shopping, laundry, ironing and cooking comes from within the household, mostly from a husband or wife. After this age, approximately three-fifths of such help comes from outside the household. During the seventies help with shopping is more common from neighbours than outside relatives, although neighbour help generally is less likely to be regular. However, after 80 reliance on the family become greater. Home helps are only significant shoppers for those over 85. Help with laundry, ironing and cooking follows a similar pattern except that help from neighbours is minimal. The proportion paying for laundry service increases slightly with age.

The real numbers of those receiving help with maintaining fires are too small when broken down by age to be meaningful. However, they appear to demonstrate a similar pattern, with a fall-off of help from the household during the seventies (as the incidence of widowhood increases) and a build-up during the eighties (as the frail elderly move in with others). The proportion receiving help from neighbours is small and nearly all such help is for the over-80s. Help from home helps is only significant for *making* fires and concentrated in the over 75 age group.

Where less frequently needed chores are concerned help is sought at earlier ages. Up to age 80 approximately seven out of ten manage without help in the garden but after that age three-fifths receive help. (Some presumably receive no help but do no gardening!) Again, with the younger elderly help comes mostly from a spouse and subsequently from other household members. The youngest age group of the elderly (65–69) are more likely than other age groups to receive help from relatives outside the household and from friends or neighbours, although those over 80 receive a similar amount of help from neighbours. Those in the 75–85 bracket are more than twice as likely to pay for gardeners than those in other age groups! Reliance on family declines with age but appears to increase after 85.

At least two-thirds of those over 70 and more than half of all the elderly receive help with decorating and household maintenance, and more than three-quarters of those over 80. Most help here is paid for, although slightly less than half the under-75s pay for decorating help. Other than paid help, help with decorating comes mainly from relatives living outside the household. Reliance on family help increases after age 80.

Those who previously did their own less frequently needed chores appear to give up household repairs by 70, decorating by 75 and gardening by 80. After these ages, less than half get by without help.

Gender The patterns of help received by men and women reflect the gender stereotypes of appropriate tasks held in society at large and this holds even when age and marital status are controlled for. Similar proportions of men and women receive help with shopping. More than twice as many men as women receive such help from their spouse (more are married), while twice as many women receive help from relatives outside the household and from friends or neighbours (more live alone). However, twice as many men receive help with laundry and ironing and three times as many with cooking. Women are also twice as likely to be paying for help with these 'housewifely' chores.

A comparable proportion of men and women receive help making fires but eight times as many women pay for this help, even though a similar proportion comes from the family. On the other hand, three times as many women as men receive help cutting wood and twice as many carrying fuel. Here again, women are at least three times more likely to pay for help even though women are twice as likely to get help from the family.

Where less frequently needed chores are concerned the picture is slightly different. Although women get more help than men, it is the men here who are more likely to pay for help. Twice as many women as men receive help with their gardens. More than a third of this help is paid for and a third comes from younger relatives. Women pay for a quarter of the help received with gardening, and while a similar proportion comes from the family, four times as many women receive help from neighbours.

More than two-thirds (68 per cent) of women receive help with decorating compared with two-fifths (43 per cent) of men, and women receive more help from the family. Men are more likely to pay for decorating but they are also more likely to get help from neighbours. A similar pattern holds for household maintenance. Here again, women receive more help from the family – more than twice as much in this case – while men pay for more of their help. However, here women are more likely to get help from friends and neighbours.

It is difficult to know why women are more likely to receive help with gardening and household maintenance from friends or neighbours but less likely to receive help with decorating. The numbers receiving help from friends or neighbours are small. It seems significant, however, that with these less frequently needed chores, which are customarily in the male domain, women are more likely to receive neighbour help with those chores which are mostly outside the house. It may be that a privacy constraint exists which inhibits neighbours from offering help with a job which would require them to spend a substantial length of time in the woman's house. By the same token, there may be a constraint on offering help to men with chores seen as within man's domain for fear of causing offence. In other words, to offer help where there is no one of 'appropriate' sex to do the job is acceptable, but offers to help in the same sex domain imply a recognition of loss of competence or ability which may be hurtful. This type of response on the part of potential helpers is worth while exploring.

Overall, it is apparent that women and men are more likely to receive and less likely to pay for help with those chores which fall within the traditional domain of the opposite sex. The same pattern has been observed when help comes from the statutory social services, with men receiving help with housekeeping chores at a very much lower level of dependency.

Family versus non-family   It is evident from what has already been said that the family provide the bulk of informal help to the elderly. However, there are sub-groups within the elderly category for whom family are less available. Much has been written about neighbourhood support, and while it is evident that for most, support in the near vicinity comes from the family, in most cases the younger generation and frequently from within the household, those who have never married, those who live alone, those who have retired to the area leaving family and friends behind, those who have no living close relatives and those whose health is impaired, may have special problems in finding needed help. It is, of course, difficult to estimate unmet needs since much help is expressive. Those who have never married, for instance, may have developed greater independence as a result of their life experience; those who live with others inevitably receive more help than those who live alone and those in poor health receive more help because they need more help.

While most sub-groups receive more than half the help they receive from the family, some groups rely to a larger degree than others on friends or neighbours. For frequently needed help these groups include the single, those who live alone or with other elderly relatives and those with no close living relatives. Retirement migrants rely more than others on friends and neighbours for help with shopping.

The very old, women, the widowed, those who live alone or with elderly relatives, the locally born, those in poor health and those with no close relatives are also more likely to receive help from social services in the form of home helps. Overall, however, more help with household chores comes from friends and neighbours than from home helps, except for help with lighting fires. Those who live alone, those whose health is impaired, those with no close relatives and the middle class are more likely to pay for help.

Very little help with property maintenance comes from friends and neighbours and family help is also much less here. Informal help is more likely with gardening than with decorating or repairs but a large proportion of all such help is paid for. Help in the garden from friends and neighbours represents only 7 per cent of all such help but is more common for the very old, the single or widowed, those who live alone or with elderly relatives, retirement migrants and the working class. The over-75s, males, the single, those who live alone or with elderly relatives, the middle class and those in good health are more likely to pay for gardening help. The majority pay for decorating and household maintenance, and significantly more of those who are single, living with elderly relatives, the middle class, and those in good health.

In summary, the evidence shows that most informal help with household chores and property maintenance comes from the family, either from within or from outside the household. Where family are not available nearby and where the ability to pay for such help is not evident, friends and neighbours step in to help, supplemented in a minority of cases by social services home helps. However, whether help comes from family or non-family, more than half of all help (except with cooking) comes from outside the household.

Help from friends and neighbours, however, is less likely to be regular and the evidence suggests that where day-to-day commitment is needed the family usually takes on this responsibility. However, it should be stressed that more than half of help received from friends or neighbours *is* regular. This seems to suggest that although in most cases the family provides help, when they are not available to help friends and neighbours fill the gap. It seems likely, then, that support from home helps becomes necessary only in those cases where family and neighbourhood informal care is unavailable or has broken down under strain, emphasising once again the importance of informal care-givers.

Help in Crises

Ninety-eight per cent of respondents feel that there are people around from whom they can ask favours. In the most scattered community where 73 per cent live more than a hundred yards from their nearest neighbour, the proportion is lowest, but still 92 per cent, compared with 90 per cent of Hunt's sample, feel they can ask neighbours for help (Hunt, 1978). In real terms, of the 676 weighted responses to this question, only sixteen feel they have no one nearby to ask favours. However, a further 14 per cent overall state that they would never *ask* favours. This may have something to do with the interpretation of the word 'favours' since a higher proportion are able to say where they would go for help in case of several hypothetical situations.

The question was worded as follows: 'One of the things that we are interested in is the kinds of local help available to people. Can you tell me who you would have turned to:

    if you were ill and could not leave the house,
    if you wanted advice about money problems,
    if you were worried about a personal problem,
    if you were feeling 'down' and just wanted someone to
        talk to,
    if you needed a lift somewhere,
    if you needed to borrow something (e.g. food, tools, etc.).'

Here, too, the primacy of the family as a source of support is clear. Table 7.2 shows where the elderly would turn for help in the event of various necessities.

The more intimate the problem the more likely it is that the family will be asked for help, with personal problems, sickness, bereavement and money problems falling clearly in the family domain. Friends and neighbours, however, are turned to by almost half as a source of borrowing things and are also important as a source of transport, both it can be

Table 7.2 *Sources of Help in Crisis/Emergency (percentages)*

Crisis	N	No one don't know	Spouse	Other in household	Within household	Outside relatives	Family	Friend/ neighbour	Professional help	Other
Actual										
Death of spouse	(243)	4	—	26	26	54	80	15	2	0
Hypothetical										
Personal problem	(664)	7	36	12	48	30	78	9	3	3
Taken ill	(675)	2	40	14	54	20	74	18	6	2
Financial advice	(663)	9	20	12	32	30	62	4	13	13[1]
Feeling 'down'	(649)	12	23	9	32	16	48	33	2	4
Lift	(695)	10	7	12	19	26	45	40	1	6
Borrowing	(651)	26	1	5	6	17	23	48	0	5

[1] May also include professional people (not necessarily financial advisers), often retired, who are consulted as members of local community.

assumed because of their proximity. Friends and neighbours also appear to play an important mental health role. One-third of respondents would go to talk to a friend or neighbour if they felt 'down'. This is more than would talk to their spouses (almost half are married) and, significantly, more than half would seek someone outside the household, whether friend, neighbour, or relative, in this context. What is most significant again is the high reliance on informal sources of help. Even money problems would only be taken to professionals by 13 per cent. Note also that in cases of sickness only 2 per cent either have no one or do not know whom to ask for help.

Widowhood Perhaps the most traumatic crisis for the elderly is the loss of a spouse. Over a third of respondents had been widowed and they were asked to whom they had turned for help. Four-fifths named a member of the family. In most cases this was someone living in another household. Fifteen per cent, however, turned to a friend or neighbour and the remaining 6 per cent either coped alone or sought help from the clergy. This pattern of reliance on the family is consistent for most sub-categories of widows (male and female), with the exception that retirement migrants, having no family close by, rely more heavily on friends and neighbours or the clergy than other groups, although even among migrants two-thirds turn to the family for help. (Reliance on family is lowest in the community with the highest proportion of retirement migrants. Incomers are also more likely than others to cope alone, although the real numbers are small.) However, the soft data suggest that while it is the family who provide the bulk of support through bereavement, friends and neighbours and the clergy may play an important immediate intermediary role in contacting family and providing short-term emotional support until the arrival of close kin. For those who have no close family living nearby, the support of friends and neighbours is again critical after the funeral, when supportive relatives have returned home and they are faced with the long-term adjustment to the loss.

Personal problems The definition of 'personal problems' was left to the respondent but was generally interpreted as relating to intimate health and/or confidential family matters. It is not surprising, therefore, to find that apart from bereavement, reliance on family is greatest when the elderly are worried about a personal problem. Almost four-fifths would turn to the family and nearly half to a member of the household. Less than one in ten would turn to a friend or neighbour, and professional or other sources are negligible. However, 7 per cent would not turn to anyone or do not know to whom they would turn.

The family is the most important source of help with personal problems for all sub-groups, with the exception of those with no close relatives (3 per cent) who rely more heavily than all other categories on friends or neighbours (29 per cent), although nearly two-fifths have no one or would turn to no one. Friends or neighbours are also more important to the single (21 per cent), and those who live alone (18 per cent), than to other groups. Single men are the most dependent on friends and neighbours (24 per cent), but men rely more heavily on family advice than do women irrespective of marital status. Single women and to a lesser degree widowed women seem less likely to seek informal help with personal problems. Those over 75, the single, those who live alone, those who live with other elderly relatives and those who have small support networks are more likely than others to be without someone to talk over personal problems or to choose not to discuss them, and those over 80 are more likely than other groups to confide in a clergyman (although very few overall choose this last source of help). As with other needs, reliance on family increases with age for the married and widowed. For the single the opposite is true and with increasing age more and more have no one to talk to about personal problems.

Illness

While three-quarters of the elderly would receive help from their families if they were ill and could not go out, more than half of whom receive help from within the household, there are some significant differences between various sub-groups. Family help declines with increasing age up to age 85 after which it increases. Reliance on professional sources of help increases with age, particularly home helps. More of the over 85s receive help in illness from home helps than in any other age category, although this is attributable in part to the high incidence of singleness in this age bracket. Only 2 per cent overall would not know whom to ask or would not ask anyone. Those who would not know whom to ask had lived alone for less than five years but made up only 3 per cent of those living alone.

In spite of the high reliance on family, certain sub-groups are more reliant on friends and neighbours than others. Less than half the single or those who live alone can count on family help in illness. Single women appear to be least likely to turn to informal sources of help in illness. However, single persons rely more on friends, neighbours and home helps with increasing age until 80. While the married and widowed rely increasingly on family, this increase among the single is much less and occurs only after 85. Reliance on friends, neighbours and professionals is therefore higher for these categories, as it is also generally for women, the widowed, those living with other elderly relatives, immigrants to the region, professional people (due to mobility) and those with no close relatives. Of those in poor health, 62 per cent are cared for by a spouse, 23 per cent by another household member and 8 per cent each by outside relatives or neighbours. Men rely more heavily on family than women irrespective of marital status.

Predictably, demands on professional help (home helps, district nurse and doctor) are greatest from the over-80s, the single, those who live alone and those with no close relatives. Reliance on the doctor appears to be directly related to social class, the working-class elderly appearing to be less likely to call the doctor.

Those who live alone were, in addition, asked how they would summon help if they were taken ill or had a bad fall. The responses to this question support the high proportions in this category who rely on friends and neighbours, since the majority who have worked out a plan would rely on shouting, banging, or waiting for help. Those who have a telephone would use it (37 per cent) but very few have any prearranged way of communicating an emergency (9 per cent) and some do not know what they would do (6 per cent). Telephones are most commonly suggested (and available) among the younger elderly and the middle class. Very few (N = 59) have in fact experienced such an emergency, but it seems significant that more than twice as many in the event had just waited for someone to come, than anticipate that that is what they would do.

Financial advice   Money problems appear to be the most private area. Seven per cent would not discuss these with anyone and 11 per cent only with banks, accountants, or solicitors. While the majority would still turn to a relative, this is much more likely to be someone outside the household. Money problems are clearly not something to be discussed with friends and neighbours or home helps.

While the family remains the main source of help when financial advice is needed, a smaller proportion rely on this source and more turn to help outside the household. Three-fifths would seek advice from the family, half of which would be from a relative in another household. More would seek professional (bank manager, accountant, solicitor) or other help on financial matters than in other types of crisis and very few would turn to friends or neighbours. However, the 'other' category includes informal advice from other professionals in their role as helpful community members. But nearly one in ten would either ask no one or not know who to ask. (Only 1 per cent would turn to a social worker or social security.)

Reliance on family remains fairly stable up to 85, after which it increases significantly. Those living in households with younger members of the family or with other elderly relatives are also more likely to turn to family members for financial advice. In contrast with sickness, women, irrespective of marital status, turn more readily to the family than do men, while men consistently rely more heavily on professional help. Reliance on family increases with age among the married and widowed but decreases after 80 among the single where reliance on 'other' sources increases. Reliance on family is also clearly related to social class, with the middle classes tending to rely less on the family than working-class persons and more heavily on professional or other sources of advice. Those few with no close relatives rely heavily on friends or neighbours and professional sources of advice, but a third would not turn to anyone or would not know where to turn.

From the point of view of policy-making, those who either do not know where to turn or who would not ask for help are perhaps most significant. The proportion in this category increases with age, they are twice as likely to be female, are most likely to be single and more likely to be widowed, to live alone, have a small support network and (as already stated) most likely to have no close relatives. Almost one-third of those who have never married and are over 85 are in this category, as are nearly one-fifth of those widowed for less than one year.

Needing someone to talk to   The crises discussed so far have been fairly specific in their focus and have all concerned fairly intimate or private aspects of life. Those discussed subsequently refer to more generalised or less personal crises. Respondents were asked to whom they would turn if they were feeling 'down' and just wanted someone to talk to. In this instance, less than half would turn to a member of the family, one-third overall would seek out a friend or neighbour but 13 per cent either do not know or would not talk to anyone but would distract themselves in some other way, such as going for a walk or talking to a pet. A few claimed that they never felt the need to talk to someone.

Reliance on family remains fairly constant with increasing age but more of those over 75 were unable to give a name of someone to whom they would turn, and after 80 fewer turn to friends and neighbours and more to home helps, ministers and others, although again the real numbers here are very small. Friends and neighbours are more important to women, the widowed, those who live alone, professional people and, predictably, those with no close relatives. Women rely more on friends and neighbours than men do irrespective of marital status, but married women rely *most* heavily (45 per cent) on friends and neighbours. This finding is supported by Lipman and Longino's (1981) finding that while married women receive most instrumental help from their husbands, expressive support is more likely to come from a daughter or female friend. Single men appear to be fairly isolated in terms of someone to talk to: only half would turn to family, friend, or neighbour and almost a third would turn to no one. In addition to those over 75, the single, those living alone (particularly if for less than a year) or with elderly relatives, professional people, those who have moved *less* than 15 miles since retirement, those with small support networks and those with no close relatives are more likely than others to be unable to name someone they would talk to or to describe other distractions.

Lifts If the elderly need a lift somewhere, they are just as likely to ask someone outside the family as they are to rely on a family member. Again, approximately one in ten would not ask or did not know anyone to ask. Two-fifths would rely on a friend or neighbour and the majority on someone outside the household. Reliance on friends and neighbours is slightly higher in communities with a higher proportion of incomers. Only 5 per cent would use a taxi or any other source of transport.

Those under 75 appear to be less inclined to ask for lifts – twice as many in this age range were unable to name a potential driver – and after the age of 85 reliance on family is substantially increased. Those who cannot get out alone rely mainly on members of the family and very few on neighbours. Men are more independent of family than women, more relying on friends and neighbours or choosing not to ask anyone, although widowed men are more dependent on their families than married or single men. However, single women and married men are less likely to approach informal sources for transport than others. Reliance on family increases with age irrespective of marital status. Certain other sub-groups are also more likely to rely on the family than on others, including the widowed, those living with younger relatives and long-term residents. Reliance on friends or neighbours is highest amongst retirement migrants, professional people, those who have lived alone for less than a year and, of course, those with no close relatives.

Borrowing The need to borrow something from another – a cup of sugar or a hammer, for instance – is perhaps more common in rural areas because of reduced proximity and range of shops, but it is, of course, an accepted part of the give and take of community life in many neighbourhoods. It is not surprising, therefore, to find that friends or neighbours are the most common source of borrowing (48 per cent), mainly on grounds of proximity. A quarter of respondents state that they never borrow from others – more than the proportion who borrow from family – so that approximately two-thirds of borrowers borrow from friends and neighbours.

Reliance on family, however, is greater among more vulnerable inter-related sub-groups: those over 85, the widowed, those living in households with young family members, those in only fair or poor health and those with large support networks. Reliance on friends and neighbours is pronounced among the under-70s and professional persons. Reliance on friends and neighbours declines for all categories of marital status with increasing age, with a shift to greater reliance on family. However, among the single this trend reverses after age 80 and reliance on neighbours increases again. The least likely to borrow are those in their early eighties, those who have moved *less* than 15 miles after retirement and those with small support networks.

Discussion What becomes clear from these figures is the high level of interdependence which exists. Not only do the elderly rely significantly on their families for help, support and reassurance but, for significant subgroups and minorities, needs are met by and demands made upon friends and neighbours. The informal web of supportive reciprocity provides the majority of help and care received by elderly people in the community. The indications are that statutory or formal services are only called upon when for some reason informal carers are not available or cannot cope with the burdens of their responsibilities (Bytheway, 1979).

Most instrumental help comes, of course, from the family, a large proportion from within the household, usually from a spouse, daughter, or daughter-in-law. However, relatives living in other nearby households also provide substantial amounts of help. In some instances, children visited weekly even when this meant a journey of over 50 miles. In a few instances, where amenities are not available at home, baths are taken at a relative's house and frequently those living alone, especially men, take some meals at the nearby home of a married child. However, much expressive help in the way of emotional support comes from friends and neighbours.

What the figures do not illustrate is the variety of commitment which exists. This ranges from the relative, friend, or neighbour who drops in to chat two or three times a week with the frequent reminder, 'You know where I am if you need anything', to the woman or man carrying the full responsibility of a bedridden and ailing relative. In some communities, obvious natural helpers were identified, whose names recurred as sources of help or friendship on several questionnaires. In one village, the interviewer had to finally accept that she could not talk to one of the sample because he was just too busy. Every time she called at the house he was absent cutting wood for Mrs Jones or fixing Mrs Williams's window latch or just leaving to take Miss Roberts to the clinic. Although this helper was himself elderly all those whom he helped – and it seemed he chopped wood for all the old elderly widows in the small community! – referred to him as 'Uncle Jack'. (All names have been changed.)

All the relatives, friends and neighbours involved in caring relationships with the elderly are in some sense volunteers. Any moral or ethical pressures which exist are internal; there is no compulsion on anyone to perform these services or to offer the affection, friendship and commitment which is self-evident in many of these interactions. It is obvious that caring people exist who are prepared to make commitments to others. Because the commitment of 'volunteers' is so often questioned by professional carers it is perhaps worthwhile to consider some instances of commitment and concern which were witnessed.

During the first phase of the research, a couple in their eighties were interviewed. They are a bright and talkative pair and engaged their visitor in a discussion about the problems of elderly people in their community. When asked about other elderly households in their street, they advised that there was no point visiting one particular house because although the occupant was elderly she would not answer the door. Then unfolded the following story:

Twenty years previously, when they were already in their sixties, the woman in question had been companion to a neighbour of theirs. During her final illness this neighbour had expressed concern about her companion, who had moved to the area only to support her friend. Turning to the couple, she had asked them to 'Take care of Dolly for me. She won't linger long when I have gone.' Twenty years later, at the age of 95, Dolly is still there. Now frail and almost blind, she spends most of her time in bed. Having made the commitment to 'take care of Dolly', her neighbours, in spite of their own advancing years, go daily to help her. They go early to take her to the toilet, make her breakfast and light the fire; they go later to make sure she has some lunch and to see to the fire and they go in the evening for a chat and to settle her down for the night. Now they are concerned that they might not be able to carry on. 'We promised', they say, 'but we never dreamed that we'd still be doing it after twenty years!'

In another instance, a woman who kept a guest house also expressed interest in the research and said she had a lodger who was elderly and giving her problems. She tearfully explained that she had taken the old man in because his only other relatives, a brother and sister-in-law, could not get on with him. She had felt sorry for him and offered him a permanent room. As the years passed, he became increasingly dependent and now, although ambulant, is incontinent and subject to 'funny turns'. She is spending more and more time worrying about him and cleaning up after him and finds the arrangement is now costing her money; she refuses to turn him out but is feeling the strain.

Most caring relationships, however, are not as demanding on the helpers as the two referred to above. An old elderly widower reports that his neighbours are wonderful and 'just take care of me'. In his case, this is mainly emotional or expressive support. A couple in another community, who are both in poor health, say they manage because all the neighbours help out and even do the garden for them – an example of instrumental neighbour help.

While the data in this chapter refer to help in specific ways, each person experiences support, friendship and help as an aggregate which has a direct bearing on their outlook on life. The interweaving of various types of support is amply illustrated in the case studies presented in Chapter 9, where networks can be appreciated as whole social environments.

The following 'true story' in which names are fictitious illustrates the embeddedness of helping behaviours:

A woman enters a small village shop. Two related women keep the store and both are behind the counter. The woman, Mary, waits as two other customers are already at the counter. As she serves, one of the proprietresses notices an elderly woman approaching the shop. She stops serving and goes to Mary to tell her quietly that the brother of the woman approaching – Gladys – has died the previous day. Shared knowledge provided the information that Gladys was a childless widow, not in the best of health, and that her brother was her only relative.

Gladys enters the shop and Mary, a younger woman, expresses her condolences and asks if she can be of any help. Gladys thanks her and says she has come to find out the results of two telephone calls which one of the women in the shop has made for her. One call must now be repeated because the line was previously engaged. As Gladys waits, other customers are served and Gladys tells Mary that her brother in another village had suffered a heart-attack. She explains that her sister-in-law had known he was very ill because their next-door neighbour had been a sister at the hospital and 'knew the signs'. Mary asks how her sister-in-law is managing. Gladys explains that she is staying next door with the nurse, but that she, Gladys, is concerned because the nurse had a problem with leaking pipes and has had to have the floor of her house taken up! Water could be heard running only at night when the street was quiet. While the two women had rested another neighbour, a retired plumber, had sat up to try to locate the leak.

At this point, the shopkeeper returns from the telephone to speak to Gladys and almost immediately Mary's father enters the shop. In a whisper he is told of Gladys's bereavement. He waits quietly until Gladys leaves the shop and follows her to express his condolences and asks her if she needs a lift anywhere. She thanks him, tells him the same story about her brother's heart and that she is all right because someone else has already offered her transport the previous day when they had taken her to visit her sister-in-law, also now a childless widow. Those left in the shop express concern about Gladys and agree that she will have to be 'kept an eye on' and visited frequently over the next few weeks.

This actual event demonstrates not only the concern of neighbours one for the other but underscores the lack of symmetry in reciprocity. People help and helpers are helped in their turn, not necessarily by a person they have already helped. Both instrumental and expressive support are interwoven through the community as well as round the individual in crisis. While support through crises is more evident, the data already discussed show that routine help also goes on in a day-to-day way. Being accepted as a member of the community can hinge on the degree to which one is known to engage in such co-operative behaviour. Helping out, therefore, becomes important for self-image and a form of assurance of mutual aid when help is needed.

CONCLUSIONS

This chapter demonstrates that for routine types of help, most of the elderly are self-sufficient.

What is clear is that there are more elderly providing help of one sort or another than there are receiving help, and where help is given it comes preponderantly from spouse, family, or friends and neighbours, while help from formal services is minimal! It is also evident that apart from cooking, more than half the routine help received comes from outside the household. While overall friends and neighbours provide a low proportion of total help received, help in this category is much more important for those who live alone, those who have no family nearby, the single and the middle class (reflecting geographic mobility).

The need for help with routine chores increases with age, steeply after 80. As dependency increases so too does reliance on the family as a source of help. However, it is difficult to know whether this reflects the greater likelihood that those supported by family can *remain* in the community or the rallying of family to compensate for dependency. More over-80s without family may be in residential care. The single, however, rely increasingly on extra-familial sources of support with age and are more likely to be without someone to confide in. Gender appears to play a significant part in the availability of help, with each sex being more likely to receive help and less likely to pay for it if the task falls in the opposite gender domain. So men are more likely to receive help with cooking and laundry and women with cutting wood, gardening and household maintenance. A similar pattern holds true for help in crises, with women turning more to the family for instrumental help and men for expressive help. The middle class are less likely to depend on family help and more likely to rely on friends and neighbours or professional help, whereas the working class rely more heavily on the family. While Chapter 5 has shown that family availability and contact is comparable in rural and urban areas, Chapter 6 suggests that community integration is greater in the rural environment. At the same time, it has been shown that rural social networks include more friends and neighbours (Walker, 1975). The position of the elderly person in the rural community is, therefore, not only more integrated but, because of the smaller population, more visible. The vignette reported above might be less likely in a large urban context because its basis is shared community knowledge. Warren (1981) has demonstrated that help seeking behaviour is related to community type. It may well be that those who in the rural community are more reliant on help from friends and neighbours may be less able to find such help in an urban context. Some of these sub-sets may, therefore, be those more likely to seek formal help in other types of neighbourhood.

What the data do not indicate is the extent of unmet need. There is no measure of how many need help and do not get it, neither is there any measure of how adequate the help supplied actually is. Unfortunately, the methodology used in this study was not really appropriate for measures of this type, which would require repeat visits to the same households over a period of time. Those who were receiving routine help were asked if the help they received was adequate and the majority felt that it was. However, given the facts that in some cases helpers were present and the known tendency of the elderly to refrain from complaint, it is impossible to confidently state that all those who need help receive it. All that can be said is that substantial amounts of help are provided for the elderly, coming preponderantly from informal sources. However, the next chapter will show that the majority of the elderly do have support networks with five or more members.

Chapter 8

SUPPORT NETWORKS, ISOLATION LONELINESS AND MORALE

So far consideration has been given to the type and incidence of various categories of social interaction and the sources and incidence of various types of help and support. This chapter now considers some of the outcomes of the social environment of individuals by presenting data which represent aggregate measures of the effects of the social milieu upon the individual. It considers the size and nature of support networks (for definition see below) and isolation which are essentially objective measures, and loneliness and morale, which represent the subjective responses of the elderly to their social environments.

SUPPORT NETWORKS (*see Table 8.1*)

The discussion has dealt with separate categories of relationships, but for the individual, the web of social contacts is experienced as a whole, a network of social resources from within which company, moral support, help and affection can be sought, given and received. It was felt to be important that some measure of the extent of such networks was made before a realistic picture of the social situation of the elderly could be arrived at. The method used was based on the work of McAllister and Fischer (1978) in the United States. Since the focus of the research was its relevance for social services, it was important to emphasise only those relationships which were meaningful in terms of supportive potential. In other words, role relationship and casual acquaintanceships, however important to self-image and personal validation, would not be significant in the event of personal crisis. It was decided, therefore to limit this measure to what will be referred to as the 'support network'. This includes all those with whom the respondent has close ties or from whom he/she receives regular help.

Respondents were asked to give the first names of all those who stood in particular roles and relationships to them as listed below. Having the first names made it possible to check for overlaps since most members of the network, by its very nature, fill more than one role. Those counted as in the support network include:

Table 8.1 *Support Networks (percentages)*

	N	Small	Average	Large
Total	(684)	24	43	32
Age				
65–69	(179)	18	48	35
70–74	(215)	27	44	28
75–79	(147)	22	43	35
80–84	(80)	33	39	29
85–89	(33)	12	33	55
90+	(30)	37	40	23
Age at arrival				
Under 40	(308)	19	49	32
40–60	(134)	34	39	27
Retirement movers	(69)	25	33	42
Retirement migrants	(164)	27	40	33
Household composition				
Living alone	(226)	27	49	25
With spouse only	(265)	21	42	36
With younger relative/s	(133)	25	38	38
With elderly relative/s	(58)	29	38	33
Marital status				
Single	(106)	30	40	25
Married	(322)	21	42	37
Widowed	(250)	26	44	30
Health				
Good or excellent	(296)	24	41	34
All right for age	(242)	24	44	32
Fair or poor	(144)	26	48	26

(1) All members of respondent's household
(2) Home helps
(3) Relative(s) seen most frequently (more than one tabulated only if seen equally often)
(4) Confidant
(5) People who can be asked for favours
(6) Real friends in the area
(7) Anyone who needs respondent to care for them
(8) Anyone who depends on respondent's friendship
(9) All those who provide informal help with tasks of personal care (excluding district nurse, chiropodist, and so on)

(10) Person respondent would turn to in case of illness
(11) Person respondent would ask informally for financial advice (excluding bank managers, and so on)
(12) Person respondent would talk to about a personal problem
(13) Person respondent would talk to if feeling 'down'
(14) Person respondent would ask for a lift (excluding taxi)
(15) Person respondent would ask to borrow things from
(16) Persons who give unpaid help with shopping, cooking, ironing, laundry, making fires, cutting/gathering firewood, bringing in fuel, gardening, decorating or household repairs.

In items (5) and (6) an arbitrary limit of five names was imposed and respondents cued to list the five most likely helpers or closest friends. In this way we sought to avoid exhaustive listings of acquaintances but recognise that this restriction may place an artificial limit on some networks. However, it is not felt that this affects the overall categories of small, average, or large network size.

Obviously, such information could not be collected by proxy; short form questionnaires had to be omitted, and in a few instances respondents refused to give first names; however, complete network data were collected for more than nine out of ten respondents. The size of networks ranges from one to eighteen, with the modal range being five to seven. Networks of less than five and more than seven were, therefore, considered to be small and large respectively.

Comparable with the findings of Stephens et al. in the United States (1978), three-quarters of the elderly have support networks of five or more persons and a third have what have been defined above as large networks. A quarter have only small support networks but this should not be seen as an evaluative statement. Small networks may be just as meaningful and supportive as large ones. However, in times of crisis the strain placed on members of small networks may be more severe, thus the proportions who do have small networks have obvious implications for social services. However, in some instances large networks may be more indicative of respondents' reluctance to rely on one or two close supporters and may be less effective than those in the middle range. Craven and Wellman (1973) found that small networks were more likely to have strong linkages and to provide better access to emotional resources, whereas large networks were more loosely knit and provided better access to tangible resources. Similarly, Warren (1981) found that small close-knit networks, while providing more psychological support, could be dysfunctional by excluding outside professional sources of help, for example in cases of mental illness. More diffuse networks, on the other hand, are typically more heterogeneous and thus afford a broader range of referral and advice offering greater flexibility. This suggests that in crises small networks may be more likely to provide the necessary supportive environment, whereas large networks may be more inclined to rally professional help.

Network size does not appear to be clearly associated with any obvious demographic factors. Walker's (1975) findings that network size is proportional to length of residence are not convincingly supported by the findings in this study. Warren (1981) suggests that helping networks can no longer be based exclusively on local ties but include telephone links and rapid travel. Some members of the network may not live near to the respondent even though they are an important source of support; for instance, a family member seen most frequently or the source of financial advice. Long-distance support is more common among the middle class. Bell (1968) has commented on the importance of telephone and letters in this context, and Laslett has characterised this as 'psychic' support (1981).

Slightly more of the single have small networks while the married are the most likely to have large networks (and to be younger). Small networks are most common among single men, followed by widowed men, while married men are the least likely to have small networks (Table 8.2). Among women, however, network size is unrelated to marital status. While approximately a fifth of both married men and married women have small networks, men's networks appear to shrink at widowhood with almost twice as many widowed as married men having small networks. There is some indication that support networks become smaller with increasing age, but not as much as one might expect owing to natural attrition; and after age 85, support networks increase in size for both men and women as a reflection of increasing dependency and the likelihood of living in a relative's home.

While those whose health is only fair or poor are less likely to have large networks, there is no evidence to indicate that networks shrink substantially in the face of ill health. Given the overall uniformity of distribution it appears likely that network size may be more affected by the personality and temperament of the persons involved. There appear

Table 8.2 *Support Networks[1] by Sex by Marital Status (percentages)*

		Males				Females		
	N	Small	Average	Large	N	Small	Average	Large
Single	(36)	42	36	22	(70)	24	50	26
Married	(186)	20	38	42	(136)	22	48	30
Widowed	(59)	37	32	31	(191)	22	48	30
All[2]	(284)	26	36	37	(402)	23	48	29

[1] Small networks 1–4; medium networks 5–7; large networks more than 7.
[2] Includes a small number of divorced/separated.

to be significant gender differences which may reflect the emphasis on communication skills which has characterised the socialisation of girls.

There does, however, appear to be some relationship between network size and reported loneliness. No one with a large network claims to be often lonely, and more than twice as many with small networks as those with average networks say they feel lonely often. It should be stressed, however, that those who claim to experience loneliness are in the minority whatever the size of their network.

The networks of the married and widowed are more likely to concentrate demands on one significant other, the spouse or one child respectively, while those of the single tend to assume a less dependent nature with demands spread throughout the network. If government policy, which is shifting towards recognition of the central role of informal support networks, is to be well founded, variations in structure of this type and the resilience of different types of network configuration and composition in the face of crises and long-term need require further study.

As examples of networks, Mr A. is a very frail man of 74 living alone in poor health (very anaemic with stomach trouble). His wife has recently died and he is very lonely. His small network of only two consists of a daughter who lives 50 miles away but who visits every week, and a cousin of his wife who lives very close by and who does his shopping, is very attentive and helps in other ways but with whom he does not really get on very well. He gives the impression of being very dependent on his daughter. All his brothers and sisters (seven) and his son live in another part of the country and he rarely sees them, although they keep in touch by letter. He receives meals on wheels twice a week but no home help.

Miss B. is a spinster of 78 who also lives alone; she claims she is never lonely, but admits to having no friends in the area and no one in whom she can confide. She is entirely self-sufficient and her small network consists of a cousin who lives nearby and a neighbour on whom she can call for favours. Her only sister is very elderly and lives more than 5 miles away so she sees her infrequently but more than six times a year. She has lived in the community all her life.

Mrs C., a married woman of 70, has an average-sized network of five which includes her husband, her son who lives more than 50 miles away, and three friends on the same bungalow estate. She has lived in the community only seven years and is mainly dependent on her husband. Mr D. also has an average network of six. He is a 71-year-old widower, living alone on an isolated farm. His support network of six consists of his sister, three friends living nearby, his nearest daughter and his nearest son who live within 5 miles. He has lived in the area all his life but moved to his present farm only three years ago as semi-retirement!

Mrs E. has a large network of nine. She is a married woman of 71 living in a small village. Her network consists of her husband, two daughters, three grandchildren, a niece nearby and two friends next door. She has lived in the same house all her life. Mr F. also has a large network of nine. He is a married man of 67 with two daughters and two grandchildren living at home. His network consists of his wife, three daughters, a son, two grandchildren and two friends. He has lived in the community more than thirty years.

ISOLATION AND LONELINESS

Isolation and loneliness are both aspects of the deprivation of social contact. The fact that there is no direct relationship between isolation and loneliness has been well established. However, in much of the literature neither isolation nor loneliness is well defined. Assessments of isolation are based on empirical factors such as living alone, having no close relatives, few visits, or a small social network, whereas loneliness is a subjective measure of how people feel about their situation. In many instances, isolation is poorly defined, undefined, or even limited to living alone, and in most studies loneliness is measured by a self-assessment of the degree of loneliness experienced (e.g. Karn, 1977; Kivett, 1979; Shanas, 1968; Weiss, 1973). M. Abrams's (1978) study of the urban elderly used aggregate measures for isolation and loneliness. While the importance of replication is not ignored, it is felt that the questions used to measure isolation and loneliness in his study were not appropriate. He based his isolation measure on answers to eighteen questions. Unfortunately, some of these questions are not independent of others. For example, respondents were asked both if they *belonged* to a religious group and if they *attended*. Some questions are not appropriate to all the elderly, for example, whether they were visited by social workers. Other questions seemed marginal to the problems of isolation, for example, whether they have great-grandchildren! Loneliness was measured by seven statements with which respondents were to agree or disagree. These appeared to be based on the LSIA test (devised in the United States), which has proved unreliable with rural populations (Wood *et al.*, 1969). It was felt, however, that aggregate measures would best reflect the extent and complexity of the problem and questions were devised which it is felt have a more general application.

Where loneliness is concerned it was felt that self-perceptions may be unreliable since there is a stigma attached to loneliness (Weiss, 1973), and since this can be a painful subject, the potential for rationalisation or denial is high. In instances where other members of the family are present during interviews respondents may be unwilling to admit loneliness because it might seem ungrateful or critical of other household members. A series of eight questions relating to the feelings of respondents about their level of social contact were therefore included, only two of which referred directly to loneliness, in addition to but independent of the standard question about the self-perception of loneliness. A similar range of questions was devised as an aggregate measure of isolation.

Isolation (see Table 8.3)
Many of the elderly in this study live in what might be termed isolated households but the study was more concerned with social isolation. Although it might be thought that having small support networks might be indicative of isolation, this in fact is not the case and nearly half of those with small networks are not considered isolated at all. Some iso-

Table 8.3   *Isolation (percentages)*

	N	Low	Moderate	High
Total	(664)	60	34	6
Age				
65–69	(175)	70	26	3
70–74	(217)	67	29	4
75–79	(139)	52	36	12
80–84	(77)	36	55	9
85+	(56)	50	43	7
Age at arrival				
Under 40	(302)	56	35	9
41–60	(130)	55	42	3
Retirement movers	(61)	69	26	5
Retirement migrants	(164)	67	29	4
Household composition				
Living alone	(219)	12	71	16
With spouse only	(261)	89	10	1
With younger relative/s	(123)	76	22	2
With elderly relative/s	(57)	70	26	4
Marital status				
Single	(104)	38	42	20
Married	(317)	88	11	1
Widowed	(237)	33	60	7
Health				
Good	(294)	63	32	5 (N = 14)
All right for age	(239)	58	35	7 (N = 17)
Fair	(117)	58	34	8 (N = 9)
Poor	(13)	46	39	15 (N = 2)

lates may be perfectly happy with their situation but isolation even in these cases does have important implications in terms of risk and help in crises. This is a factor which appears to be well recognised by social services since in the study area those known to social services who are living alone and thus more likely to be isolated are more likely to be in receipt of domiciliary support despite their generally lower levels of dependency, and isolation is cited as a common presenting problem (Grant, 1981b). If isolation reflects the degree to which a person is separated from contact with others, then it also measures the degree to which others are aware of the subject and thus the likelihood that they will become aware of that person's needs. The questions used in the isolation scale, therefore, were devised to measure the likelihood of others becoming quickly aware of such needs. The scale was applied as a crude measure, one point being given to each question with no weighting. Those responses which were felt to indicate isolation were as follows:

(1) Lives alone
(2) Has no close relatives
(3) Never visits anyone
(4) Has no contact with neighbours
(5) Has no telephone
(6) Is alone for more than nine hours a day
(7) Nearest neighbour is more than 50 yards away (out of earshot)
(8) Never goes out of the house
(9) Does not know how to get help in an emergency
(10) Does not talk to any community personnel (milkman, postman, shops, and so on).

On the basis of this, respondents were arbitrarily classified as not isolated if they scored 0 or 1, as moderately isolated if they scored 2–3 and as very isolated if they scored 4 or more isolation points. The highest score was 6 and the mode 1. Six per cent are identified as being very isolated, 34 per cent as moderately isolated and 60 per cent as not isolated.

The most usual factors for both the moderately and very isolated turn out to be living alone, spending more than nine hours a day alone, having no telephone and never visiting anyone. The factors which distinguish between the moderately and the very isolated are, in addition, not knowing how to get help, having no contact with neighbours and no living relatives. Moderate isolation, therefore, could amount to living alone with no telephone. In fact, only 12 per cent of those who live alone are considered not to be isolated in any way.

High isolation is most common in the most dispersed community and in a seaside resort with the highest proportion of retirement migrants;

and, on the basis of mean scores, isolation demonstrates a high correlation with sparsity, with the exception of the seaside town where a higher than expected proportion are highly isolated. However, it is important to stress that only 6 per cent overall are highly isolated and 60 per cent are not isolated at all.

Isolation increases up to age 80 but then appears to decrease as family adaptations bring kin closer together in order to provide care, or as those at risk enter Part III or other institutional accommodation. Isolation also increases with failing health. Those who live alone are the most isolated group, 16 per cent being very isolated. Contrary to the stereotype, retirement migrants are less likely to become isolated than long-term residents. Few who are married are isolated and isolation among widows is less extreme than among those who have never married, a fifth of whom are very isolated. Half of those who are very isolated have support networks of four or fewer but a quarter also have large networks, probably loosely knit.

More women are isolated than men in all age groups but they are likely to be moderately isolated. Men and women are equally likely to become highly isolated. While overall men are less likely to be isolated than women, there are significant differences by marital status (Table 8.4). For those who are married there is little difference between the sexes, but while widowed women are more likely to become isolated than widowed men, single men are more isolated than single women. Overall the most isolated are single men, followed by widowed women, then widowed men, single women, married women and married men.

Compared with the total population, the very isolated are more likely to have been born in the same county, within 15 miles of where they now live, and less likely to have moved within the last ten years. They are more likely to be over 75 and more than three times as likely never to have married. They are also three times as likely to live alone, seven times as likely to have no living relatives and more likely to have lived alone for more than twenty years. They are twice as likely to be childless and less likely to have high morale. While there is no direct link between

Table 8.4 *Isolation by Sex by Marital Status (percentages)*

		Males				Females		
	N	Low	Moderate	High	N	Low	Moderate	High
Single	(35)	29	43	29	(69)	42	42	16
Married	(187)	88	12	0	(130)	88	11	2
Widowed	(57)	39	53	9	(180)	31	63	7
All[1]	(280)	70	24	6	(384)	52	41	7

[1] Includes a small number of divorced/separated (N = 6), one male, five females.

Table 8.5 *Proportions Who Feel Lonely Much of the Time by Isolation Measures (percentages)*

	Single men	Married men	Widowed men	Single women	Married women	Widowed women
Isolation						
Low	0	0	14	3	12	9
Moderate	20	5	43	10	50	23
High	20	-	60	27	-	|50

isolation and loneliness, more than a third of the very isolated say they are lonely much of the time – more than twice as many as in the total sample.

Those who are very isolated are like Miss G., and 81-year-old spinster who lives alone, never visits anyone, has no telephone and is alone for more than nine hours a day; or Mrs H., a 90-year-old widow who lives with her bachelor son but who never visits anyone, talks to no one outside the immediate family, has no contact with any neighbours and lives more than a hundred yards from the nearest household. Among those who are moderately isolated are Mrs J. who lives alone more than 50 yards from her nearest neighbour and Mrs K. who lives alone, never visits and is alone more than nine hours a day. There appears to be a high level of toleration of isolation among the single and married men. Among the widowed, however, at least half those who are very isolated say they feel lonely much of the time. Among widowed men and married women even moderate isolation is associated with loneliness (Table 8.5).

Loneliness (see Table 8.6)
Loneliness among the elderly has received a great deal of attention and has become one of the features of the negative stereotype of ageing. Perhaps for this reason loneliness is one of the aspects of ageing most feared (Hunt, 1978). Like ill health, therefore, it was suspected that some denial of loneliness might be anticipated. One respondent went so far as to state that anyone who said they were never lonely was lying! In order to try to assess the level of un-admitted loneliness, but also to replicate other findings (e.g. Karn, 1977; Shanas, 1968), respondents were asked about loneliness in what might be perceived as a more acceptable form. In the same manner as for the isolation measure, responses which were felt to indicate loneliness are as follows:

(1) Feels lonely much of the time
(2) Does not see enough of friends and relatives

Table 8.6 *Loneliness (percentages)*

| | | Self-perceived loneliness | | | Loneliness measure | | |
	N	Never or rarely	Sometimes	Often/most of time	Low	Moderate	High
Total	(683)	76	19	5	63	29	9
Shanas[1]		72	21	7	—	—	—
Age							
65–69	(176)	78	19	3	69	24	7
70–74	(221)	80	16	5	61	32	8
75–79	(148)	71	20	10	66	27	8
80–84	(79)	75	22	4	65	25	10
85–89	(34)	59	29	12	47	37	17
90+	(25)	84	16	0	39	50	12
Age at arrival							
Under 40	(306)	78	17	5	70	27	4
40–60	(133)	79	12	9	62	28	11
Retirement movers	(45)	58	35	6	59	26	15
Retirement migrants	(170)	77	19	4	54	33	13
Household composition							
Living alone	(226)	58	33	9	53	37	10
With spouse only	(266)	87	8	5	65	25	10
With younger relative/s	(130)	78	20	2	70	23	7
With elderly relative/s	(56)	91	9	0	74	26	0
Marital status							
Single	(106)	85	10	5	59	36	6
Married	(326)	87	9	5	68	23	9
Widowed	(246)	58	35	7	57	33	9
Health							
Good/excellent	(297)	88	10	1	73	24	4
All right for age	(243)	73	21	5	61	31	9
Fair/poor	(137)	55	32	13	45	36	18

[1] E. Shanas *et al.*, *Old People in Three Industrial Societies* (London: Routledge & Kegan Paul, 1968), p. 271, Table II.

(3) Does not meet enough people
(4) Has no one to confide in
(5) Wishes for more friends
(6) Has no one to ask favours of
(7) Has no real friends living nearby
(8) Spent the previous Christmas alone and lonely.

On the basis of these responses, respondents were classified as not lonely if they scored 0, moderately lonely if they scored 1 or 2 and very lonely if they scored 3 or more. The highest score was 6 and the mode 0. The four most important factors in order of importance for high loneliness are not meeting enough people (79 per cent), not having enough friends (71 per cent), not seeing enough of friends and relatives (67 per cent) and feeling lonely much of the time (66 per cent). For the moderately lonely, the most important factors, again in order of importance, are having no real friends in the area (33 per cent), feeling lonely much of the time (28 per cent), not seeing enough of friends and relatives (26 per cent) and not meeting enough people (22 per cent). However, overall lack of real friends in the area is the most commonly admitted problem. Impressionistically the main difference between the very lonely and the moderately lonely appears to be that the former experience a lack of friends, while the latter feel separated or cut off from friends.

On the basis of self-perceived loneliness more than three-quarters report that they are never or rarely lonely, a fifth admit to being lonely sometimes but only 5 per cent say they are lonely often or most of the time, comparable with Shanas's findings for Britain as a whole (1968) and with Karn's (1977) findings for retirement migrants. The fact that these figures also correspond very nearly with Sheldon's study of old people in Wolverhampton conducted in 1945 (Sheldon, 1948), demonstrates that the incidence of loneliness amongst the elderly has remained stable and not deteriorated, as is often suggested. However, in an independent question which formed part of the morale scale, 14 per cent claim to feel lonely 'much of the time'.

Loneliness is higher among the older elderly, those living alone, the widowed and those in poor health. However, the aggregate loneliness measure does appear to have discovered feelings of loneliness which were not admitted in answer to the self-perception question. Using this measure only 63 per cent are not lonely, while 29 per cent are moderately lonely and 9 per cent very lonely. The increase in loneliness with advancing age is more pronounced and there are obvious differences among certain sub-sets of respondents.

As Table 8.6 shows, it is, for instance, surprising to find that loneliness among retirement migrants based on self-assessment is comparable with that of those who have lived in the region all their lives. The aggregate measure, however, shows that for both middle-aged and retirement migrants loneliness is higher than admitted, while figures for long-term residents and short-distance retirement movers are comparable. And while the aggregate and self-perceived figures for those who live alone are comparable, the levels of loneliness among those living with a spouse only and those living with elderly relatives are higher using the aggregate measure. By the same token, while the aggregate and self-perceived levels for widows are equivalent, the single and married show higher levels of loneliness using the aggregate measure. This would seem to indicate that where loneliness might be seen as acceptable – those who live alone and the widowed – it will be admitted; but where a need exists to rationalise or conceal loneliness – migrants, the single, the married and those living with others – it will not be admitted or perhaps recognised.

Using the aggregate measure, men overall appear to experience less loneliness than women (Table 8.7). Loneliness increases with age but more women than men are lonely in all age groups. After age 85 more than half are lonely to some extent. However, more single men are lonely than single women and more widowed men are lonely than widowed women. What is surprising is that loneliness among married women exhibits a higher level than among other groups. More married women are lonely than widowed or single women and more than twice as many are lonely as married men. As the findings in the preceding chapter show, visits from other relatives are less frequent to married couples than to those living alone, and couples who spend Christmas without other company also experience loneliness. There is some indication here that relatives underestimate the social needs of elderly couples. In rank order, the loneliest group are widowed men, closely followed by single men, then married women, widowed women, single women and married men. However, married women are the group most likely to be *very* lonely.

Compared with the total sample the very lonely are less likely to have been born in the county in which they now live and more likely to have come to the county within the last ten years. As a result, they are twice

Table 8.7 *Loneliness by Sex and Marital Status (percentages)*

		Males				Females		
	N	Low	Moderate	High	N	Low	Moderate	High
Single	(35)	49	46	6	(69)	64	30	6
Married	(185)	79	19	2	(128)	52	30	18
Widowed	(57)	49	37	14	(180)	60	32	8
All[1]	(278)	69	26	5	(382)	58	31	11

[1] Includes a small number of divorced/separated.

as likely to have moved after age 60. They are almost twice as likely to be women and more than twice as likely to be living in a child's household. They are less likely to have been living alone for more than twenty years and less likely to be childless. They are more than five times as likely to have low morale and twice as likely to have small support networks.

Amongst the very lonely is Mr L., a recent widower aged 74 living alone. He feels lonely much of the time, feels he does not see enough of his friends and relatives, does not meet enough people and feels he has no real friends in the area. His situation is exacerbated by poor health and grief over his wife's death. Although he has lived in the community since 1949 he still feels an outsider. Mrs M. is also very lonely. She is an 84-year-old widow crippled with arthritis living with her daughter's family. She also feels lonely much of the time, does not see enough of friends and relatives, does not meet enough people, wishes she had more friends and feels she has no real friends in the area. Her situation is made more difficult because she lives in a very isolated house and sees no one but the immediate family. The family moved when she was already housebound. High levels of loneliness are less common among the single but Miss N. was amongst the very lonely. An 81-year-old spinster living alone in a small hamlet within 5 miles of where she was born, she also feels lonely much of the time, does not see enough of her friends and relatives, does not meet enough people and wishes she had more friends. In her case, her loneliness is enhanced by her lack of close relatives, worsening arthritis and an independent streak which resists asking for help from anyone.

The important finding is that the majority are not lonely: only 5 per cent claim to be lonely often, although almost twice as many are very lonely based on the aggregate measure. It does seem that loneliness is an area where rationalisation and denial occur but in spite of that, less than a tenth are very lonely using the aggregate measure. However, loneliness may also be associated with personality and temperament together with life experience. Recent longitudinal research on the elderly at Bonn has identified typologies of adaptation to life which can predispose to or avoid loneliness (Fooken, 1981; Lehr, 1981). These indicate that an extra-familial social life is a protection against loneliness in old age; but this adaptation becomes more difficult to maintain with increasing dependency.

Comparing the very isolated with the very lonely, there are some striking differences. The very isolated are more likely to be local people; they are older, more likely to have never married or to be living alone. They are more likely to be known to social services and to have no living relatives. They are also more likely to have lived alone for more than twenty years and to be Welsh-speakers. They are more likely to have high morale and almost four times *less* likely to have low morale. They are nearly three times as likely to have large, loosely knit support networks!

MORALE (see Table 8.8)

The overall situation of the individual, both physical and psycho-social, is reflected in morale. Morale was measured using the Philadelphia Geriatric Center Morale Scale, which has been found to have high validity *vis-à-vis* clinical tests and has been tested for reliability with rural populations (Lawton, 1975). The scale consists of seventeen items (all of which must be answered) from which an aggregate morale score was

Table 8.8 *Morale (PGC Scale) (percentages)*

	N	High	Moderate	Low
Total	(624)	60	31	9
Age				
65–69	(173)	64	25	11
70–74	(209)	56	37	8
75–79	(137)	65	23	12
80–84	(68)	62	29	9
85–89	(29)	41	52	7
90+	(24)	63	33	4
Age at arrival				
Under 40	(290)	62	32	6
40–60	(120)	61	26	13
Retirement movers	(61)	62	25	13
Retirement migrants	(162)	55	33	12
Household composition				
Living alone	(208)	51	40	8
With spouse only	(245)	62	26	13
With younger relative/s	(115)	67	29	4
With elderly relative/s	(52)	81	19	0
Marital status				
Single	(94)	65	32	3
Married	(230)	63	26	11
Widowed	(225)	55	37	8
Health				
Good/excellent	(285)	78	22	1
All right for age	(225)	56	36	8
Fair/Poor	(113)	25	43	30

calculated (Appendix 2). Scores were available for 90 per cent of respondents allowing for proxies, short forms and incomplete responses.

Three-fifths of the rural elderly are assessed as having high morale, for almost a third morale may be termed moderate but only a tenth suffer from low morale. Low morale has a very high correlation with poor health and loneliness. The evidence does not indicate that morale decreases with age; indeed, after 80 the proportion whose morale is low appears to shrink, although with the small numbers involved this should be treated cautiously. However, low morale is twice as common among those who moved after the age of 40 and reduced morale is most common among retirement migrants. Given the association of morale measures with loneliness, this supports the contention that the aggregate loneliness measure used here does reveal loneliness which is not admitted as such.

Those who live alone are more likely to suffer from reduced morale while those whose general morale is highest are those living with elderly relatives. However, where household composition is concerned *low* morale is more common among those living with their spouse only.

There is some relationship between morale and marital status. The widowed are more likely to suffer from reduced morale than either the single or the married but *low* morale is most frequent among the married. However, again there are significant differences between men and women (see Table 8.9). Women are more subject to low morale than men independent of marital status. Overall, high morale is most common among single men, followed by married men, single women, widowed women, married women and widowed men. While it may not be surprising to find that reduced morale is commonest amongst widowed men, the fact that among women, married women are more likely to suffer reduced morale warrants further consideration and analysis, and may be related to anxieties and/or responsibilities as a result of a husband's poor health and anticipated death. It has been suggested that fear of death (one's own or that of a significant other) is one contributory factor to depression in old age (Levin, 1964) and a

Table 8.9 *Morale by Sex and Marital Status (percentages)*

	N	Low	Males Medium	High	N	Low	Females Medium	High
Single	(30)	0	30	70	(69)	6	32	62
Married	(182)	7	24	69	(127)	18	29	53
Widowed	(55)	7	49	44	(171)	8	33	59
All[1]	(267)	6	30	64	(367)	11	32	57

[1] Includes a small number of divorced/separated.

higher level of loneliness (also correlated with depression) is also found among the low morale group.

It has been established that low morale is associated with loss. The death of a spouse has been identified as the most stressful loss or life change. This explains reduced morale among the widowed and may go some way to explaining generally higher morale among those who have never married since not only do they not experience this most serious of losses but they do not have to anticipate it either. In the general scheme of experience, women are more likely to be widowed than men. Not only do they live longer but they tend to be slightly younger than their husbands. Anxiety over widowhood may go some way to explaining the reduced morale of higher proportions who are married, particularly those living with their spouse only. It is also in this latter category that higher proportions in poor health have been identified which both heightens fear of widowhood and depresses morale. However, Lipman's work in the United States (Lipman and Langino, 1981) indicates that while elderly husbands receive both instrumental and expressive support from their wives, elderly wives, while receiving instrumental support from their husbands, more frequently rely on other sources for expressive support. This may be a contributory factor to the finding that low morale is commonest among married women.

While low morale shows a very high correlation with both ill health and loneliness, there is also some correlation with isolation and small support networks. However, the high morale of single men is negatively

Table 8.10 *Morale (PGC) Scale (percentages)*

| | MORALE | | |
	High	Moderate	Low
By degree of loneliness			
LM low	72	25	3
LM moderate	49	40	11
LM high	9	42	49
Isolation			
IM low	65	27	8
IM moderate	56	34	11
IM high	39	50	13
Network			
Large	69	28	3
Average	60	31	9
Small	51	34	16

correlated with isolation, loneliness and small networks and would appear to indicate an atypical adaptation, although the small numbers involved suggest caution (Table 8.10).

SUMMARY

The overall picture presented by these four measures is one of a generally well-integrated and well-supported elderly population. Less than one-tenth are either very lonely, very isolated, or suffer from low morale and three-quarters have support networks of five or more people. There are, however, sub-sets who are more prone to be very isolated (single men, the older elderly, those living alone, the locally born, those in poor health); very lonely (widowed men, married women, the very old, incomers and those in poor health); and to have low morale (married women, those living with their spouse only, incomers and those in poor health). In many instances, these categories overlap. The case studies presented in the next chapter give more substance to these statistics and it will be seen that even where loneliness and isolation exist, there are people in the immediate neighbourhood to whom the individual can turn for assistance.

Chapter 9

ELDERLY PEOPLE COPING

The aim of this chapter is to provide a more holistic view of the social milieux in which elderly people live. Its chief object is to demonstrate the existence and variety of the supportive networks within which the subjects find ways of overcoming their problems. For this reason, an attempt has been made to cover a wide range of dependency. However, the majority of the elderly manage well with little additional help. As a result, the studies presented here overrepresent the older and more dependent elderly in the community in order to demonstrate the types of care and commitment which come into play when needed. At the same time, the studies also cover overall measures of isolation, loneliness and morale and try to present a composite four-dimensional picture. All the cases are real but names have been changed. The cases have been selected only to reflect the continuum of need which exists and are random examples in as much as the first representative cases which came to hand have been used.

Basically three categories have been included: those who do nearly everything for themselves; those who receive some help; and those who are reliant on help. The first two studies are of self-sufficient and independent elderly households and the following ones trace a scale of increasing dependency.

MR ANNWYL

Mr Annwyl, a 70-year-old married man, was born in mid-Wales and moved over fifty miles to his present community more than fifty years ago, where he worked as a warehouseman. Later he married a local girl and they have lived in the same community all their married lives. He speaks Welsh most of the time. They moved into a new council house twenty-five years ago because their previous residence had no modern conveniences. Their present living room is heated by an open fire but they do not heat the bedroom because 'we couldn't afford heat upstairs as well'. Their only source of income is the old age and supplementary pension, and Mr Annwyl says, 'I worry when it is time for the electricity meter reading'.

Mr Annwyl's health is 'all right for his age' and he suffers from no limiting condition, although he gave up work a year early due to ill health and within the last six years has had four operations! He is not on the telephone and has no car. When he needs to use the telephone he walks 400 yards into the village. He feels that there should be a kiosk on the estate as there are several old people's bungalows there. He uses the bus but finds the fares high and has had difficulty in obtaining concessionary tickets.

Mr and Mrs Annwyl have six children, four sons and two daughters aged from 26 to 40. One unmarried son still lives at home and works full time and their younger daughter lives within 5 miles. The other four children have left the area and live more than 50 miles away. They see their nearby children frequently but see those who live away less than six times a year each. Although they are satisfied with the amount of contact they have with their children, they feel that their relationship with those who live away is based mainly on duty or responsibility. They have eleven grandchildren but while they see the children of the nearest daughter every week, they rarely see the others and wish they could see them more often.

Mr Annwyl himself is the eldest of a family of six and has two sisters and four brothers, aged from 59 to 68. All live more than 15 miles away and he sees little of them, having no contact with one at all, and feels his relationship with the others is superficial. Mr Annwyl sees his nearby daughter more frequently than other relatives and goes to visit her weekly. He says he has plenty of friends and good neighbours. He confides in his wife or his daughter and says he is never lonely.

Mr Annwyl has been a chapel member all his life and attends services every week. The minister visits him once a fortnight and the deacons call quite often. He is the singing leader for the chapel. He also belongs to the local pensioners' club and attends their meetings regularly. His main other interest is gardening. He has a large garden and says he 'wouldn't be without it', and in addition he does the gardens for two of his neighbours. He also spends some time listening to music and singing and attends every singing festival within a 15-mile radius, as well as watching television. He feels there should be more societies for elderly people to attend in the afternoons.

The Annwyls go by bus to the nearby town for all their shopping, to go to the post office, the doctor's surgery and the optician. They never use the library or a chiropodist. At present they are quite self-sufficient without any help from anyone. If Mr Annwyl were ill or worried about money or a personal problem he would turn to his wife. If he needed someone to talk to he has a friend nearby and if he wanted a lift or needed to borrow something he would ask a neighbour.

The interviewer comments: 'They are a happy couple, enjoying themselves by keeping busy' and 'they have plenty of friends'. Mr Annwyl was identified as being neither isolated nor lonely, with an average support network and very high morale. His support network consists of his wife (aged 64), his son living at home, his daughter living in the same community, three friends and a neighbour.

MISS PROBERT

Miss Probert is a 76-year-old spinster who lives in an old and isolated cottage with no modern conveniences except electricity. She heats water in an electric kettle – 'It's quite sufficient for me on my own' – and goes to her nephew's house for a bath when she 'feels like it, but otherwise an all-over wash is all right with me'. She has a chemical toilet outside. She has lived in her two-storey cottage which she owns for more than thirty years. She speaks Welsh most of the time. She says there is nothing about her home which makes any difficulty, although in addition to the lack of conveniences, the interviewer described the outside access as very difficult up a rough and muddy path. Her living room is heated by a coal or wood fire, which she finds very expensive, and she has an electric fire in the bedroom but commented that costs 'have increased a great deal'. She lives on a single old age pension and says that she manages but with nothing to spare, although she has some small savings.

Previously Miss Probert worked on her parents' farm until they retired and 'afterwards it was a full-time job looking after them'. Her surviving parent died fifteen years ago, when she herself was 60, and since then she has lived alone. She claims that her health is all right for her age and suffers from no limiting health condition, although she admits that it is getting difficult to cut her own toenails! She has neither telephone nor car. She walks to her neighbour at the local shop about a hundred yards away if she needs to use the telephone and says, 'I've no idea how to use a telephone. The lady at the shop does everything for me.' She uses the bus and comments, 'It's quite handy. It was stopped a few years ago and we missed it a lot then but we are now able to use the school bus.'

Miss Probert has one younger brother who lives 6 miles away whom she sees about once a month and with whom she says she is close and friendly. She also has cousins in the neighbourhood and a nephew whom she sees occasionally. She sees her brother more than other relatives and says she does not visit much because transport is difficult but she usually goes at Christmas-time. However, she sees her neighbours often and chats with the local shopkeeper and the postman. She seems to be an independent woman for although she says she gets on well with all her neighbours, she says, 'I don't know what they think about me' and 'I seem to be very happy on my own although it is nice to see someone from time to time'. She says she is never lonely; 'I quite like being on my own'. She does have real friends nearby, although she does not confide in any one of them, and says, 'I feel very happy now, everyone seems to be more friendly as we get older'.

Miss Probert has been a member of the same chapel all her life and although she does not attend every week she goes at least once a month. The minister visits her now and again and all her neighbours belong to the same chapel. She also belongs to *Merched y Wawr* (a Welsh women's group) and attends their meetings regularly. She does not have television but listens to the radio and does some knitting and needlework.

Miss Probert walks into the village for her food shopping and to visit the post office and mobile library, and takes the bus into the nearest town to visit the doctor or the optician and to get prescriptions filled. She does not eat meat and does not need the services of a chiropodist. She does all her own housework and cooking but sends the heavy laundry out. Her brother comes to cut wood and to do the garden for her and occasionally brings in her coal while he is there. Overall she says she manages well and needs no additional help. She says that if she were ill and could not leave the house she would ask for help from social services; she would seek financial advice from her brother and borrow from her friend and neighbour. But if she needed a lift she would use a taxi and she would not seek out others for help with personal problems or if she felt 'down' and needed someone to talk to.

Miss Probert seems to have a very high tolerance for isolation and feels she misses nothing living where she does. She had spent the previous Christmas alone and said, 'I didn't mind being on my own. As you get older you don't see Christmas as different from any other day and after Christmas I went to stay with my nephew.' She has great trust in her neighbours despite the fact that no one lives within a hundred yards. When she was asked how she would summon help if she was taken ill or had a fall she said calmly, 'I don't know, but I hope someone would notice I wasn't around and come to investigate', which was exactly what had happened when she had been ill. As soon as she did not go to the shop to get her milk the shopkeeper came over and called the doctor.

In spite of being identified as very isolated, she is not lonely, has an average-sized support network and high morale. Her support network consists of her brother, her nephew, three friends living close by and a neighbour.

MRS CHARRINGTON

Mrs Charrington is a married woman of 66. She was born in London and her husband in Birmingham. She and her husband retired to a modern centrally heated (electric) bungalow in a small seaside resort five years ago from the border counties. 'We decided to sell up and move', she says, 'so we had a winter let at first then we got fed up with that, found this bungalow and bought it.' Mrs Charrington claims her health is all right for her age but she is somewhat limited by arthritis. They are on the telephone and use this to keep in touch with relatives in the Midlands, especially their youngest son. Mr Charrington has a car and they also use the bus and train. However, Mrs Charrington has difficulty getting on to the train and they find that timetables for public transport are inconvenient for hospital visiting. Mrs Charrington refused to divulge their income but they do receive a rate rebate and with electric central heating are concerned about electricity bills.

Mr and Mrs Charrington have two sons, whom they see infrequently and wish they saw more of. One son and their only grandchild live in Australia, the other over 200 miles away. Mrs Charrington was one of five children and has a brother and two sisters still living, but they all live more than 50 miles away and she rarely sees them either and wishes she saw more of them. They also maintain contact with nephews and nieces of her husband who live in the Midlands. They have most contact with their younger son who is unmarried and telephone him every other week, but no longer go to visit relatives or friends. However, they get on well with all their neighbours and help them out as necessary. Mrs Charrington also chats with people in the local shops, the milkman, the postman and other members of the community. She does not meet as many people as she would like to, and wishes she had more friends, but she says she is never lonely and does have real friends in the neighbourhood, including one in whom she confides.

Mrs Charrington belongs to the church but only goes occasionally and does not receive any church visitors. When they first arrived they joined 'everything and became very involved' but when her husband was ill they had to drop everything and doubt if they will start again. The interviewer comments: 'She seemed a little depressed at how the people she thought she had made friends with in the various organisations seemed to lose interest and stopped calling once she was unable to make teas and assist generally because of her husband's illness.' She does not now belong to any local organisations but spends some time walking or gardening and, inside, reading, doing crossword puzzles, or watching television. She misses the big shops and has not really settled down. She says her husband is quite happy and cannot understand her. She is bothered by the constant wind from the sea.

If she were taken ill Mrs Charrington would rely on her husband to take care of her. Her husband had recently been very ill and when he was in hospital their elder son flew home from Australia. For financial advice Mrs Charrington would rely on her younger son and for help with personal problems or when 'down' she would talk with a friend. She makes it a point never to borrow anything. So far the Charringtons are self-sufficient and manage without help for most things, although they hire professional help with decorating and household maintenance.

They walk into the town for all necessary services, except the optician when they go to a neighbouring town because 'the local one is not satisfactory'.

In spite of Mrs Charrington's contacts in the community she refused to name who her friends were and referred repeatedly to her loneliness and distance from relatives in the Midlands. Although on the aggregate scale she is identified as very lonely, she is not seen as socially isolated. However, it was not possible to measure her social network and her morale was low. She also seemed to the interviewer to be very anxious about her husband's health.

MR ELLIS

Mr Ellis is a widower of 71 living alone and working an isolated sheep farm. He moved there when he was 68 as a form of semi-retirement and now only works part time. His son at that time took over the larger family farm. He and his wife bought the present farm twenty-five years previously ready for their retirement but sadly she died within a year of moving and he now finds it rather isolated and is grateful for his car. He has lived in the area all his life and speaks mostly Welsh. Although his home is over 300 years old, it has all modern conveniences and is heated by storage heaters, although he has no heat upstairs – 'never been used to it'. Mr Ellis was unable to say what his income is since it fluctuates, but he said it is adequate and he never worries about bills, although electricity is sometimes hard to meet. He is on the telephone and has a car.

Mr Ellis has four children, a son and three daughters, and all but one daughter live within 5 miles. He sees the three nearest children at least weekly and his other daughter two or three times a month. He also has eleven grandchildren whom he sees every week. He was one of six children and has two sisters still living. One he sees several times a week and the other two or three times a month. He also has seven or eight cousins whom he sees every week. He has most contact with his younger sister but visits other friends and relatives every week. He is also in frequent contact with neighbours and other members of the community, the local shopkeepers and members of his chapel. He gets on well with all his neighbours, although the nearest is over a hundred yards away, and says he would be willing to help them out any time because 'they are very good to me'. In spite of all these contacts, however, he says he does not meet as many people as he would like to and misses many members of the family 'who have passed away'.

His wife had died of cancer and suffered a great deal in a short period during which time the whole family knew that death was inevitable. Of that difficult time, he says, 'The family were very good to me, especially the daughters, of course'. He is alone more than nine hours a day and admits to feeling lonely sometimes. He says, 'It just comes and goes. One feels that it's something that has to be conquered.' However, he is very close to his younger sister and can confide in her and sees most of the neighbours as his friends.

Mr Ellis goes to chapel every week as he has done all his life and sings in a local choir. In addition, he is a keen *penillion* singer, writes poetry and competes in local *eisteddfodau* and sheepdog trials. He also walks a lot, works in his garden, plays cards, reads and watches television. As well as all these interests, he is very interested in local history and his own ancestry. The interviewer comments: 'I could have spent the whole evening in his company!'

He enjoys good health but if he were ill his nearest daughter would come and take care of him. He would take his financial problems to the bank and his personal problems to his sister, but if he felt 'down' and needed someone to talk to he would seek out his only son. If he needed to borrow something he would turn to a friend and neighbour. He does his own shopping, cooking and housework and one daughter does his laundry, while another irons and his son does the decorating for him.

Mr Ellis was identified as being moderately isolated, moderately lonely and having an average support network consisting of his sister, three friends, two daughters and a son. However, his active social network is obviously larger! His morale was medium at the time of interview, although it might be anticipated that as he recovers from the loss of his wife it may improve.

MRS FENWICK

Mrs Fenwick is a 90-year-old widow, keeping house for her unmarried son on a smallholding near a small hamlet, where she was born and where she has lived all her life. She has lived in her present home for over fifty years. Her late husband was also born in the community and she speaks Welsh *all* the time. The house is a two-storey cottage over 200 years old and lacks some modern conveniences. Water is heated by a back boiler, but there is no bath or shower and only an outside privy. But she says, 'We've always managed very well'. Her only complaint is that the house is too small and they have only two bedrooms. The living room is heated by open fire but they use no heat upstairs. She says 'We burn a lot of wood, but there's nothing like a coal fire, especially in winter'. She is happy with her house and 'wouldn't want to go anywhere else'. Her only income is the old age pension but her son works part time and farms part time. She says they manage but 'it's hard sometimes' and 'coal is awfully dear'.

In spite of her age, Mrs Fenwick claims her health is excellent, although she has problems with her eyesight. She can see before her but not downwards and has to be careful not to fall. She says, '*Cyn iached a chneuen: ond am fu llygaid'* (As sound as a nut excepting my eyes). She admits to difficulty cutting her toenails, getting up and down steps and getting out of doors alone. She can get out around the farm but goes no further. They are on the telephone and her son has a car. Of public transport she says, 'The buses are few and far between and a long way from here. I couldn't get down to the buses so I stay home, unless I *have* to go somewhere, then they take me.'

Mrs Fenwick has been a widow for twenty years. She bore five children, two of whom died in infancy. Her son and two daughters all live within 5 miles. She sees them all at least once a week and gets on well with all of them. Their ages range from 52 to 65, and only her eldest daughter is married. She has only two grandchildren, but says she never sees them. She says of them, 'Poorest children I ever saw; they never call to see me'. She was one of seven children, and has one sister and one brother surviving, both younger than she. Her sister lives within 5 miles but she never sees her and does not want to! Her brother lives more than 15 miles away and she has contact with him by letter only.

She has most contact with her children and son-in-law, whom she sees at least once a week, but no longer goes to visit anyone and claims to never see anyone else and to have no contact with the neighbours, which is quite possible since she never leaves the farm and is more than a hundred yards from any other house. Still, she does not regret not meeting people; she says, 'I've got plenty to do to keep me busy. I wash and bake and cook and watch the animals, so I get tired, then I sit down and then I get up and go on again, all day!' She never feels lonely, feels needed by the son for whom she keeps house and while saying she has no friends adds, 'my family is all I need'.

She has been a member of the chapel all her life but she says, 'I've gone too old now to go to chapel, but I like to listen to the services on the wireless'. The minister visits her occasionally. She has no television, although she says she would like one and wondered if the interviewer could arrange it! Due to her advanced age she belongs to no voluntary organisations and says she is too busy for hobbies. When asked if she had a job now she exploded with, 'Of course, I do. I'm like every woman working full time every day' and it certainly seemed that way. As the interviewer left she was starting to make damson jam in a brass pan on the open fire, having gathered the fruit earlier in the day!

All Mrs Fenwick's shopping and other errands are done for her by her daughters and when she needs to see the doctor, chiropodist, or optician they drive her to the nearby town. One daughter occasionally helps her with cooking and the other sometimes with the washing and ironing and her son cuts the firewood and brings in the fuel. No one does any gardening or decorating and although Mrs Fenwick claims she can bathe without difficulty, the interviewer comments, 'Mrs Fenwick obviously does not consider washing herself daily of any great importance!' If she were ill one of her daughters would help and it is to them she would take personal problems or seek to borrow things. For financial advice or a lift she would rely on the son who lives with her. When asked to whom she would turn if she felt 'down' and needed someone to talk to she was indignant, commenting 'I don't feel like that!' The interviewer notes that her philosophy for long life was that she had never harmed anyone so had nothing to feel sorry about! She added that the house and Mrs Fenwick could have been a bit cleaner and tidier but says, 'I suppose you could say she needs a home help and some modern conveniences, but she's well, happy, healthy and content and at 90 years of age what more could you ask for'. Mrs Fenwick, on the topic of home helps, says, 'I've never asked and I wouldn't want one while I can manage; they'd only tidy up so I couldn't find anything'.

However, Mrs Fenwick was identified as very isolated and moderately lonely (on the basis on having no real friends and claiming no one to ask favours of nearby), with a small support network of three children and her son-in-law. But her morale was very high and she claims she is as happy today as when she was 20.

MISS GWYNNE

Miss Gwynne is a 76-year-old spinster living alone in a pensioner's ground-floor council flat in a small town. She speaks mostly Welsh. She was born in the country within 5 miles of where she now lives but moved into town thirty years ago to be nearer her teaching job after her mother died. She moved into her present accommodation seven years ago when her previous garden became too much for her. Although her flat is on an estate not too far from the centre of town she feels rather isolated. The flat has gas central heating . Her only source of income is the state pension but she says she usually manages well because she 'has learnt to economise'. But she sometimes finds her expenses hard to meet, particularly gas and electricity.

Miss Gwynne says her health is only fair. She suffers from rheumatoid arthritis and deafness and claims she has a brain tumour. She has difficulty putting on her shoes and stockings, doing up buttons and doing her hair and can no longer cut her own toenails. She has no car and no telephone because her hearing is too poor. She does use the bus occasionally but finds the fares high.

Miss Gwynne has lived alone for thirty years since her mother died and has no close relatives. The children of a cousin live in the town but she only sees them about once a year. She goes to visit friends occasionally and says, 'I get on very well with the three other ladies in the flats but we don't walk in and out of each other's flats – we keep our independence but everyone helps each other'. She says she helps by doing shopping and cleaning for her neighbours. In addition to her neighbours she talks regularly with others in the community and the postman. She says she meets enough people but does not have any real friends in the vicinity and does not confide in anyone. But she does feel she can ask favours of a neighbour and says she never feels lonely, although she spends most of the time on her own. She says, 'I've learnt to live alone'.

She belongs to a chapel, attends every week and is visited occasionally by the minister. She also belongs to a pensioners' group, the Women's Institute and the local historical society and attends meetings regularly. She had tried to join the handicapped club run by the local social services but although she has arthritis in both hands she was refused as not being sufficiently handicapped. She feels very frustrated by this as there are 'some other people who are not so handicapped that go' and all her friends belong! She spends her spare time watching television, doing crochet work, in spite of her arthritis, reading, playing bingo and cards and walking.

She walks into town for all her needs except the optician, when she gets a lift to Chester. She does all her own housework, cooking and laundry. If she were ill she feels she could call on her neighbour and a friend would give her a lift if necessary. But if she needed financial advice she would see her bank manager; she does not know where she would turn for advice with a personal problem or for someone to talk to, and she never borrows.

Miss Gywnne was identified as being very isolated (in addition to living alone with no telephone, she has no close relatives and is alone more than nine hours on an average day) and moderately lonely. She has a small support network of only three, consisting of two neighbours and a friend. Her morale is moderate.

MRS HUGHES

Mrs Hughes is an 83-year-old widow living with her niece, who is 70 and mentally handicapped. They live in a large house with no near neighbours outside the village in which Mrs Hughes was born. She married at the age of 30 and moved to her husband's home town where she lived for twenty-five years before returning with her husband to her own village when she was bequeathed the house. The house is sixty years old and although it has all conveniences, has not been modernised at all. Since last winter she has been sleeping downstairs. She has a chemical toilet in her bedroom but also has an outdoor flush toilet. She finds the house too large and has difficulty now with the stairs and the outside access. Heating is from an open fire in an old-fashioned range and she has an electric fire in the bedroom, but finds coal and electricity 'very dear' and tries to burn logs when she can. Their only income is from the state pension and she finds rates and electricity bills hard to meet.

Mrs Hughes says her health is all right for her age and claims her activities are not limited by her state of health, but she finds difficulty with all items of personal care except washing, feeding herself and doing her hair and she says she can only go out with help. She goes to a neighbour to use the telephone 'two fields away' but presumably needs help to do so. She does not use public transport but says her niece goes to the doctor by ambulance or 'in a car with a disabled badge and she doesn't like it; she doesn't want everyone to know'! She says she does not use the bus because she cannot get on or off.

Mrs Hughes has been a widow for six years and has no children. Her five brothers and sisters are all dead. She says she has nieces living in East Anglia but she never sees them and does not really want to. But she has a neighbour who calls in to see them every day and sometimes the 'little children' from down the road come. She has a chat with the breadman every week when he calls for his money and says he is very kind and helpful. She also talks to the postman and the coalman, when he comes every fortnight. She gets on well with most of her neighbours and one does all her business and handles her finances. She says she meets enough people but seems to have some paranoid tendencies as she says there are some people she does not want in the house in case they steal things, and she has refused a home help for this reason. She also made accusations about other members of the community which seem improbable. Both doctor and vicar have been rejected.

She said at first that she had no one to confide in but then admitted grudgingly, 'Well, Mr D. if I *had* to'. This referred to the neighbour who seems to look after them and it is obvious that she trusts him. He and the breadman also do favours for her as does the coalman, and it was these three whom she listed as friends. Mrs Hughes says she is never lonely and is never alone as her niece is always with her.

She still belongs to the church but has not attended since her husband's funeral and 'only Mr D., Mary and I went then'. The vicar appears to have offended her in some way about the time of her husband's death. She said of him, '*Haul o'i flaen o a gwynt ai i ôl o*' (May the sun go before him and the wind behind him), which seemed to mean good riddance! However, the vicar *had* visited Mrs Hughes within six months of the interview. She continues to pay her subscription to the local pensioners' club but never goes to meetings. They have no television but Mrs Hughes listens to the radio and reads a little.

Mrs Hughes gets her shopping from a mobile van and sees the doctor and has prescriptions made up on house calls only. But the doctor has only been once when she slipped and hurt her leg! She does her own cooking, laundry and fires and it was apparent that little or no household maintenance is attempted. Her neighbour and his son cut wood for her, bring in the coal (several buckets of which were lined up in a scullery) and until recently did the garden. It was this same neighbour who had helped her at the time of her husband's death and seems to have taken care of her ever since. He appears to be her sole source of help apart from the breadman and coalman. She says she has no one to turn to for help with personal or financial problems or to talk to if she felt 'down', and she never borrows from anyone. However, she does receive meals on wheels twice a week and had recently been visited by a supplementary benefits officer.

Mrs Hughes feels very grateful for the help she gets. She recalled how when her husband was sick in hospital (approximately 10 miles away) before he died, neighbours took her to visit him every night for six weeks. She said she took chocolates and cake for the other patients every night because *he* could not eat them! She also comments that the coalman always comes to see her even when he has no coal for her! The interviews took place after a bad winter and Mrs Hughes's house is in an area always badly hit by snow. She told the interviewer that no one had let her down all winter and she felt very grateful.

Mrs Hughes was identified as moderately isolated and moderately lonely with a small support network consisting of her handicapped niece (?), her good neighbour, the breadman and the coalman. Mrs Hughes's niece was not seen during the interviews in Phase I or II and does not figure as a source of support in Mrs Hughes's account. However, frequent allusions to her are made by Mrs Hughes in terms of what her niece enjoys and how happy she is. She also speaks mainly of 'we' and 'us' when she describes her life, and it is apparent that the care of her niece and the affection she feels for her is an important and central facet of her life. In spite of her situation she has high morale.

MRS IVOR

Mrs Ivor is an 87-year-old widow living alone in a first-floor council flat in a small village. She was born within 15 miles and has lived in the community since she was a child but has only recently moved to her present accommodation and she has difficulty with the steps up to her first-floor flat. The flat is heated by electric fires in the living room and bedroom. Mrs Ivor has only a single old age pension with small interest on savings but manages well, although she finds electricity bills hard to meet. She says her health is now poor since she suffered a fall in the winter, broke her hip and was in hospital for six months. She can now get up and down stairs or out of doors on her own only with difficulty. She does not use public transport and is not on the telephone. The nearest telephone is at the bottom of the steps in the flats, but she says it would not be any use if she was taken ill in the night.

She has been a widow for five years, still misses her husband and has no children. She has an only sister who is 82 and who lives within 5 miles but they only see each other about once every month or so, and she sees their relationship as based on duty or responsibility. However, she has two cousins and two nieces nearby and sees a relative every day. She has most contact with her nieces but does not make visits since her fall. She does talk to the neighbours, church members, the milkman and other members of the community but she feels rather disappointed that she has not made many friends among the neighbours since her move.

Mrs Ivor says she is often lonely, mainly in the evenings, but she is also alone for more than nine hours a day. She says she does not meet enough people and wishes she had more friends. However, she has a cousin nearby in whom she can confide and one real friend. She has belonged to the church all her life but can no longer get there and does not belong to any voluntary organisations. She spends her time reading, watching television, or listening to the radio.

Mrs Ivor is visited by the health visitor once a fortnight and has a home help three times a week. She is also visited at home by the chiropodist who comes to cut her toenails. One niece does her shopping for her regularly and all her other errands while her other niece does her laundry and ironing, but she cooks for herself. If she were ill she feels she could call on a neighbour to whom she would also turn if she needed someone to talk to. She would turn to one of her nieces for financial advice and the other if she was worried about a personal problem. But she never borrows and never goes anywhere that would require a lift.

The interviewer comments that Mrs Ivor seemed rather lonely and depressed. She had moved into the flat five months previously on leaving hospital and was unable to go out much or walk far so has been unable to meet people close by. The steps up to her flat are of concrete with only one handrail and she is very anxious about falling. Mrs Ivor was identified as moderately isolated, moderately lonely, with an average support network, consisting of two nieces, a cousin, a friend and a neighbour. Her morale was only moderate.

MRS JONES

Mrs Jones is a recent widow in her mid-eighties. She now lives with her daughter, son-in-law and three adult grandsons on a large farm. The farm is in her husband's natal village and she herself was born about 15 miles away. She speaks mainly Welsh. She and her husband lived in the north of England for many years, returning when she was in her late fifties. She has been living with her daughter for about a year, moving there after leaving hospital where she had been treated for a broken arm and leg. She now walks with a zimmer and gets rather confused. She has her own bed-sitting room on the ground floor with her own furniture, heated by an electric fire. She has no financial responsibilities.

Mrs Jones has five children, three daughters and two sons. In addition to the daughter with whom she lives, another daughter lives within 15 miles, but her other children live more than 50 miles away. She rarely sees her eldest son but sees her nearby daughter two or three times a month and her other children at least every other month, although she would like to see more of them. They are all married and apart from the daughter with whom she lives, all are working at least part time. She has thirteen grandchildren, now adults, but claims to see the grandsons with whom she lives only about once a month and the others rarely. She would like to see more of them but rationalises that most of them live too far away. Mrs Jones was one of five children but only one sister is still living, also very elderly, so that although she lives within 15 miles they rarely see one another. She also has a close friend in the nearby village but the farm is too far out for her to come to visit often. Occasionally she goes to mid-Wales to visit a son and she is visited by members of the chapel including the minister and occasionally another friend from the village, but she does not meet as many people as she would like to and is very lonely. She said she wished she could go to the local old people's home in the town where she recently lived.

Mr Jones had died, according to Mrs Jones, just six months prior to the interview, although this seems inaccurate, and she admitted that she felt lonely most of the time and wished she could die. She said, 'I miss him very much at night, alone in my bed'. Although she can confide in her daughter and feels she does have real friends, she is conscious of the loss of friends over the years. She spends her time watching television and reading. She can no longer attend chapel.

Mrs Jones is permanently housebound and the interviewer commented that she seemed to be left to herself a great deal. She seemed to be cut off from the rest of the household although until recently she had been taking her meals with the family. However, since she refused to eat when with them she now takes all her meals in her own room. Mrs Jones complained bitterly about her daughter and her daughter finds her very difficult. A community nurse comes to bath her twice a week, the chiropodist to tend to her feet, and she relies on her daughter to take her to and from the toilet, around the house, or to go out (rarely) in the car. She had not been out in the past six months. She relies entirely on her daughter for all housekeeping and care. Her daughter receives an attendance allowance for her mother. However, the interviewer comments: 'It was obvious that the old lady was being awkward and the daughter did not really want her there. She felt the rest of the family were not helping', and also 'she was very lonely as her daughter does not have enough time (or inclination) to spend with her'. From the daughter's point of view, as a busy farmer's wife on a large farm with four men to cook for, the additional responsibility of caring for an infirm and slightly confused parent who is admittedly awkward is a major undertaking.

Mrs Jones is identified as very lonely, moderately isolated with a large support network, consisting of her daughter, son-in-law and three grandsons in the household, a daughter living nearby and two friends. Due to her confusion it was not possible to measure her morale.

MRS KING

Mrs King is a 78-year-old widow, living alone in a small village with no real shop. She and her husband were both born in Liverpool where they ran a family business. Their dream had been to retire to a cottage in Wales. Just after they had found their cottage her husband died suddenly after fifty years of marriage, but one of their sons bought the cottage and she moved in ten years ago. The cottage is over 150 years old, has been well modernised but seemed rather cold. It is heated by electric fires which Mrs King finds very expensive 'but clean and convenient'. Mrs King's only income comes from the state pension and a supplementary pension. She says she manages but finds heating bills hard to meet.

Mrs King says her health is only fair. She suffered a stroke two years ago which left partial paralysis of her left side and her arm is badly affected. She describes how she makes her way cautiously to the post office (50 yards away down a short slope) which also sells bread, papers and a few groceries, saying she says a little prayer before she leaves asking 'Him' to take care of her and see her safely back again. She has difficulty cutting up her food, doing up buttons, and moving about generally, particularly negotiating steps, and she can no longer cut her toenails. Obviously she does not drive, but she is on the telephone and sometimes uses the bus. This appears to be quite difficult and she says, 'my stick causes trouble on the buses'. She finds the fares high. With only £6 in concessionary tickets (at the date of interview), the return fare to the nearest town is nearly £1. The timetables are also difficult for her, she says she sometimes sits in the shelter in town for over an hour waiting to come home. But the bus driver is very kind and carries her shopping to her door for her.

Mrs King has been a widow for ten years. She has four sons, ranging in age from 50 to 60, all living more than 15 miles away. They are all married and she sees them about every three months but they all telephone often and she gets on well with them. She also has ten grandchildren and eight great grandchildren and although she rarely sees them, 'They all speak to me on the 'phone and I'm very glad to hear from them. I thank God for them.' She says she is satisfied with the amount of contact she has with all of them. She had no brothers or sisters.

She had been seeing her eldest son more frequently than any other relative but was upset at the time of interview as he had suffered a stroke the week before. She never goes herself to visit any of her relatives or friends. Although she says she talks regularly with neighbours, church members, the milkman and the postman, she says, 'I am very reserved and I don't go knocking on people's doors but I do go to church each Sunday and everyone is very friendly. I talk to everyone on the bus and on the streets, especially little children.' She says she does meet enough people and has real friends close by, one of whom she can confide in and who she thinks probably depends on her friendship. She sees friendship very much in terms of reciprocity and feels sorry that 'I can't help because of my arm, so there's nothing I can do to help others'. Most of her friends belong to the church and they come to visit her when she is ill. But, perhaps due to her reserved nature, she feels lonely most of the time. Sadly, she had spent the previous Christmas alone and 'rather lonely', although saying 'I had everything I needed', to which one might add, except company.

Her church membership and religious faith are very central to her life. She attends services every week and is visited by the rector, other church members and a voluntary organisation attached to the church. She says, 'The members are very, very kind and I could send for them if I needed them'. In fact, two church members arrived at her cottage as the interviewer was leaving. They had seen her 'looking poorly' in church on Sunday and wanted to make sure she was all right. Due to her poor health Mrs King does not belong to any voluntary groups. She spends her spare time watching television and reading.

Mrs King takes the bus to a nearby town to do her shopping and to visit the doctor or the optician, although since her stroke the doctor calls every three weeks and the district nurse every fortnight, bringing her tablets, so she does not need to go to the chemist. She praised both the doctor and nurse for their support and kindness to her. She walks to the village post office and to the mobile library van. She says she has no need of the chiropodist – a friend cuts her toenails for her – and eats no meat. She pays the same friend to do her laundry for her, but she does her own ironing and most of her own cooking, although she does have meals on wheels. She is also visited occasionally by the community officer from the social services office. If she were ill and unable to leave the house, she feels she could rely on her close friend, to whom she also turns when feeling the need to talk to someone. However, she would turn to another friend for advice on personal problems. If she needed financial advice she would ask one of her sons and if she needed a lift she would ask one of the church members. She makes it a point, however, never to ask favours and never to borrow from anyone. She has had two falls when alone. The first time she 'waited until I felt better, then crawled to the sofa and waited for help' and when she had the stroke she says, 'I dragged myself downstairs and telephoned the doctor. He came within half an hour.'

Mrs King finds transport is a big problem but says of her environment, 'this is a small isolated community, still enjoying the old fashioned ideals of caring for the weaker folks'. The interviewer comments that 'Mrs King is a very lonely woman, living in the past with her memories', but in spite of her poor health and loneliness she has a caring family, most living in the north-west of England, who although unable to support her in a day-to-day way keep in constant touch by telephone. She has a strong faith in God and believes He will take care of her and says she fears nothing, not even death.

Mrs King was identified as being moderately isolated but very lonely, with low morale. She has an average-sized support network consisting of her four sons and three friends living close by. However, in spite of her poor health and low morale she feels that things are better for her than they were ten years ago when her husband died.

MRS LOWELL

Mrs Lowell, aged 65, lives with her husband on a council estate in the small town in which she was born. Her husband came from the north of England, where they were living when war broke out in 1939. When her husband left for the army, she returned to be near her parents and they have lived in the town ever since. Mrs Lowell speaks Welsh most of the time but her husband is English. Their two-storey council house is centrally heated by solid fuel and because Mrs Lowell is not well they find the heating very expensive. Their only income is the state pension. They receive a rent rebate but find it difficult to manage on their current income. 'We don't like debts, so it's natural that we worry about how we're going to pay these bills', she says. The cost of coal and food bothers them most.

Mrs Lowell says her health is only fair. She has had two major abdominal operations recently and 'cannot travel very far from the toilet'. Her husband is also in poor health, suffering from angina, and needs occasional oxygen. Although her physical mobility is not impaired her condition restricts her mainly to the house. The doctor visits her regularly every two weeks but she has sometimes to telphone for help during the night. It has been suggested to Mrs Lowell by the consultant that she should drink three pints of milk a day and eat plenty of eggs but she says they cannot afford so much milk. They have a car and use no public transport. Mrs Lowell sees both the telephone and car as essential because of her state of health.

The Lowells have five sons, ranging in age from 24 to 39. The eldest lives within 5 miles but the others have all left the district and live more than 50 miles away. They are all married and working full time but she sees her eldest son more than once a week, and three of the others two or three times a month. They have thirteen grandchildren and see all but one of them two or three times a month when their parents visit. Mrs Lowell was one of nine children and has four living brothers and two sisters. Her two sisters and one brother live within 5 miles. She sees her sisters more than once a week but rarely sees any of her brothers.

She sees her eldest son and his daughter most frequently of her relatives – they visit at least once a week, but she no longer goes to visit relatives or friends. She does not go out much but does talk with neighbours and the postman and very occasionally the local shopkeepers. She says she gets on well with all her neighbours, 'they are very good neighbours indeed'. She has good friends living nearby and can confide in her husband or a close friend and feels she can ask favours of her neighbours. She says she is never lonely.

She has belonged to the local chapel nearly all her life but now only attends occasionally, although the minister visits her regularly and 'has been very good' to her, especially when she was in hospital. She still belongs to the British Legion but her health prevents her from attending meetings. She spends her spare time watching television and knitting.

All necessary services are available in the local town, except for the optician for which she travels to another town. A friend and neighbour does all her shopping for her, her prescriptions are delivered and her husband drives her to the doctor. She uses neither library nor chiropodist. She does all her own cooking, ironing and makes the fire but receives help from her husband with the laundry, cutting wood and bringing in the coal. While she was in hospital neighbours did their garden and planted potatoes for them. When she is ill her husband takes care of her. She takes personal problems to her sister and when needing to talk to someone or to borrow something, turns to a friend and neighbour.

The interviewer comments: 'This last operation seems to have knocked her around a bit . . . she manages fairly well but has to take her time. Although it is she who has received the operation, he seemed in a worse state of health . . . he had to keep going to stand in the doorway to get his breath.' Mr Lowell is younger than his wife but has been forced to retire owing to ill health. However, in spite of their health problems, the Lowells 'seemed very happy and talked a lot about their children and grandchildren'.

Mrs Lowell was identified as being neither isolated nor lonely and to have moderate morale. She has an average support network of seven, consisting of her husband, eldest son, granddaughter, sister and three friends who are also neighbours.

MR MORGAN

Mr Morgan is 80 and lives with his wife and a son from a former marriage in a council bungalow in a small village. Mr Morgan remarried twenty-three years ago after the death of his first wife and his second wife is twenty years his junior. He was born in South Wales but came to his present community as a small child. They moved to their present home eleven years ago after the doctor advised them to find single-storey accommodation owing to the ill health of both Mr and Mrs Morgan. The bungalow had gas central heating when they moved in but they found this too expensive and asked the council to disconnect them. They now have an open fire in the living room and an electric fire in the bedroom.

Mr Morgan is in poor health; he has suffered both a stroke and a heart-attack and is permanently housebound. He is completely dependent on his wife for washing, bathing, dressing, using the toilet, cutting his toenails and moving anywhere. He can feed himself only with help. This puts an enormous strain on his wife who has herself suffered two heart-attacks. She receives an attendance allowance, their only other personal income comes from the state pension, but the son is working full time. They had asked the district nurse who comes once a fortnight if she could help them get a telephone from social services but were told there was no point applying. Since then they have had one installed themselves. They have a car in the household but neither spouse drives.

Between them, Mr and Mrs Morgan, who have both been married before, have many children. Mr Morgan has fourteen ranging in age from 27 to 58. Apart from the son living with him, one of his daughters lives within 5 miles, the others further away. They are all married and the sons all working full time. However, one daughter and two sons come to see him more than once a week and two other sons two or three times a month. He would like to see more of some of his children. His eldest daughter cannot come to see him because she is ill and her own husband is also an invalid. He has seventeen grandchildren and sees at least one of them more than once a week. Mr Morgan also has a brother and three sisters. His brother lives within 5 miles and his sisters more than 15 miles away but he rarely sees any of them, and says his relationship with all of them is based more on duty than anything else. He sees two of his sons more frequently than any other relatives (including the one living at home) and although he cannot visit friends or relatives, friends from the village come to see him every day. He is also visited by neighbours and church members.

He says they get on very well with all their neighbours and rely very much on the people next door. Mr Morgan says they have a very close-knit community, 'where everybody knows each other'. Although he is visited every day Mr Morgan does not feel he meets enough people. However, he can ask his next-door neighbour to do favours for him and does feel he has real friends nearby. He confides not only in his wife but in a son and a friend and is lonely only sometimes.

He has belonged to the church all his life and three of his sons are clergymen, but he cannot attend services. However, he is visited by the vicar and members of the church also call from time to time. He still belongs to a pensioners' club but no longer attends meetings. His only spare-time activity now is watching television or listening to the radio. He used to do a lot of reading until his sight deteriorated and now he 'sleeps a lot in the armchair'.

Mr Morgan hardly ever goes out. A son does all their grocery shopping in the nearby village and they get greengroceries and meat from a mobile shop. Prescriptions are fetched from the next town, and he used to be taken there by car to see the doctor, chiropodist and optician and to change library books but had not been for over a year. The doctor now comes to the house. His wife does all the cooking, the laundry, the ironing, the fires, cuts wood and carries in fuel. The son living at home did not seem to feature large as a source of help but may, of course, do quite a lot, while Mrs Morgan is the primary source. His wife is also the one who takes care of him when ill, gives advice and talks to him when he feels 'down'. The son at home drives him if he needs to go anywhere – although it seemed unlikely that he could actually leave the house. The interviewer expressed concern about the burden being carried by Mrs Morgan. She said, 'He is a heavy person and Mrs Morgan has difficulty managing with him at times. If her health deteriorates, they won't be able to cope.' But she found them 'surprisingly bright and cheerful'.

Mr Morgan was identified as moderately isolated and moderately lonely with low morale. He has an average support network of seven, consisting of his wife, two sons and four friends who are also neighbours.

SUMMARY

The households described here exhibit a wide range of the types of support networks which occur. Some of these networks consist mainly of family, although very few are exclusively made up of family. Where there are members of the family nearby, most instrumental help comes from this source but friends are frequently still an important source of expressive support. Married couples rely heavily on each other, although, as Lipman and Longino (1981) have shown, women tend to receive mostly instrumental help from husbands and to turn to daughters or friends for emotional support. This tendency may go some way to explaining the higher level of loneliness among married women whose daughters do not live near. There is some indication in the cases discussed that emotional support in the form of someone to talk to is most frequently sought from a friend or relative of the same sex.

In most situations, it is quite apparent that the elderly person is mainly dependent upon one primary source of support. Usually this is a spouse or a child but it can be another relative or even a neighbour. This pattern is more common among those who have married, even if they have subsequently been widowed. For the single or childless widow, responsibilities tend to be more evenly distributed among the members of the network. Mrs Ivor is an example of this where her nieces share duties between them. There are examples of shared family support for the widowed too – Mr Ellis's and Mrs Fenwick's families follow this pattern; but with increasing dependency the indications are that one family member assumes, usually as a result of household composition and expediency, the largest part of care and support. Mrs Jones's and Mr Morgan's households follow this pattern. What these descriptions do not show is the support (or lack of it) which is available to the carers for the elderly. Without further study it is perhaps imprudent to generalise, but it would appear that heavier commitments are expected and made by spouses and children than those expected or made by more distant relatives. Other relatives appear to be more prepared to share responsibility if there is no 'obvious' person to take charge. The same seems to be true of neighbours where instrumental help is needed. When no apparently responsible member of the family is evident, those closest to the situation step into the breach. This phenomenon has been observed by Bytheway (1979) in urban South Wales.

One commonly voiced anxiety of social services is the concern that once statutory interventions take place, such as home helps or meals on wheels, informal help is undermined. This does not appear to happen. As noted in the previous chapter, people are more likely to receive instrumental help with gender-linked chores which are seen as appropriate for the opposite sex. It is likely that other constraints, not immediately explicit, operate in other areas. While instrumental help from non-relatives may be seen as appropriate in crises, some help may also be felt to be 'interfering' in other contexts. The same constraint does not apply to family who are in a way licensed to interfere! What the data from this study and a related study of social services clients (Black *et al.*, 1983) show is that involvement from relatives, friends and neighbours is not affected by social services support and, in fact, expressive support may be enhanced. Even when support networks are very small, as is the case with Miss Gwynne and Mrs Hughes, informal help *is* available.

Looking in more detail at actual networks also provides some insights into loneliness. It is clear that loneliness as a subjective state has very little to do with the actual amount of social contact. Some elderly people who have a high level of contact still feel lonely, while others who have little contact do not. The critical factor seems to be the state of health of the person involved. Those who are independent and living alone, such as Miss Probert or Mrs Hughes, are not lonely while their health is good. For others, there are indications that once their health fails, independence may be a constraint on seeking help. But for those living alone in poor or only fair health, loneliness is common despite relatively high levels of contact.

On the other hand, there appears to be a relatively high level of acceptance of objective isolation. Even those living in isolated places with high isolation scores, like Miss Probert or Mrs Hughes, are not without support and potential sources of help. Here again, health is a critical factor. However, hardly any whose health is fair or poor are very isolated and there appears to be a correlation between isolation and an independent nature.

The case studies clearly illustrate the correlation between low morale and loneliness and/or poor health. What is also clear is the overwhelming reliance of those in need of support on informal sources of care and the compensatory nature of statutory provision.

Part Five

---◆---

SIGNPOSTS

Chapter 10

INDEPENDENCE VERSUS DEPENDENCE

What this study has demonstrated is that overall the rural and the urban elderly are comparable populations which have similar levels of available family and intra-family contact. While migrants are more distant from close relatives their friendship networks are not affected. Relationships and contact with neighbours are marginally higher for all categories of the elderly in the rural context. There appears to be a higher level of community integration in rural communities as demonstrated by higher involvement in religious and voluntary associations, and it is felt that this goes some way in explaining the greater satisfaction expressed by the rural elderly with an equivalent level of contact with children and siblings. The overall pattern of social contact for the rural elderly may, therefore, be more autonomous than that of the urban elderly. This is possible because of the small scale of communities, which makes participation easier and also because of the generally higher value placed by rural populations on independence (Britton *et al.*, 1961a). They may be less dependent on their children for emotional support. This finding is confirmed by Walker (1975) who found that urban networks in the United States are more kin centred than comparable rural networks which include more neighbours and friends. But as Chapter 1 suggested, the evidence indicates that those without nearby family form relationships with others in both rural and urban contexts. In both environments, very few are found to have support networks of less than four (Stephens *et al.*, 1978).

It seems that the stereotype of the ailing, lonely, forlorn old person living on a subsistence income in poor housing has perhaps become far more widely accepted than it deserves (see Novak, 1979). While not denying the existence of elderly persons who fit the stereotype it is worthwhile questioning its validity. The findings indicate that for the most part the elderly and their families respond to the challenges of ageing through adaptive and coping strategies and the majority make creative changes in life-style to accommodate the inevitable losses which are part of the ageing process. Two of the major components of the negative image of old age relate directly to the potential for adaptation –

the reluctance of families to assume responsibility and the reluctance of the elderly to accept change. In the first place, in spite of evidence to the contrary, it has been asserted that families no longer care about their elderly relatives or are no longer in a position to help, and that growing numbers of old people, therefore, are denied the support of the family as a necessary resource (e.g. M. Abrams, 1980; Field, 1972).

Part of the reason for this may be that such evaluations are often based on the availability and proximate involvement of adult children. The childless and their relationships have received less attention. However, the data show that both the childless and those without proximate kin form close relationships with brothers, sisters, nieces, nephews, or cousins, and that those without relatives tend to develop similar close relationships with friends. Hunt's (1978) findings suggest that this is also true in urban areas.

The present elderly generation, freed in many countries from inevitable economic dependency on working children by the welfare state, value their physical independence and find pride in continued autonomy. The emphasis in the West on individualism, competition, independence and privacy as cherished values (Slater, 1970) reinforces this desire to be free of dependency on adult children. The elderly may turn to their children for help, but not without reluctance, and being dependent on children can lead to loneliness and demoralisation (Blau, 1973). By the same token, despite the general willingness and concern of families to care for their elderly members, daughters and daughters-in-law, who provide much of such care (Sussman, 1965), increasingly are employed full time and policies directed towards an increase in home care are in conflict with equal employment opportunities (Finch and Groves, 1980).

What seems to be absent from the negative stereotype of ageing is the effect of social change. The ideal image of the aged in the bosom of the family may be an anachronism. The majority of old people cherish their independence and frequently die at home or spend only a short spell in hospital during their terminal illness. Old people increasingly experience better health and place a high value on independence from children (Hellebrandt, 1980), which children respect. But, while respecting and reinforcing independence as a cherished part of the self-image of the elderly, the family remains the main source of help. The present ideal image of the aged is a healthy independence, supported by family, friends and community. The data presented in the preceding chapters suggest that this ideal *is* achieved by the majority of old people. Where family care is not available friends and neighbours help; statutory services fill gaps in the fabric of informal care for a minority.

The other important aspect of the negative stereotype of the old, as considered here, relates to the emphasis which has been placed on the rigidity of the elderly and their resistance to change. (See Tamir, 1979, for discussion.) However, the evidence is that the elderly can and do adapt to the changes that living longer presents.

Adaptive strategies of the elderly may be followed in anticipation of old age or as a response to increasing frailty and in both types of adaptation the family of the ageing person is likely to be involved. The nature of and the types of adjustments made and the strategies involved often make it impossible to identify the change as one made by the elderly person or by the family since in most cases both are involved. George and Maddox (1977) suggest retirement leads to 'a complex social process of adaptation'. At this age, the elderly plan for the future in terms of increased leisure and simplifying their living arrangements. Moves from one community to another or to a different residence are based on different considerations according to age. Retirement age is frequently marked by a move of residence, and more than a third of respondents had moved to a new community after the age of 60. Most of these moves were made at or about retirement age but for one-tenth a move had occurred after 70.

Recent moves from one community to another (within the last five years) were most common in the 65–75 age group (16 per cent moved), representing retirement moves; and after 85 (13 per cent), usually representing moves into a child's household or into sheltered or other housing designed for the elderly. Those who move at or near retirement appear chiefly to be affected by available housing, the environment of the receiving community and the proximity of relatives. Forty-two per cent of parents who had moved from one community to another within five years before being interviewed had moved to within 5 miles of a child, some into the same household. Those who *do* move at retirement, as the preceding chapters show, demonstrate their capacity for adaptation by getting to know their neighbours, making friends and joining voluntary groups in the new community. Contact with children is maintained by letter, telephone and visits in both directions. Some who received weekly visits from children lived more than 50 miles away.

Larger proportions, of course, change their residence without moving to another community. In this respect also, moves are most likely before 75. Moves of residence after 85 appear to be less likely to occur within the same community and only to reflect movement to be near relatives when this means a new community. However, for those who live alone, the experience of becoming alone (often widowhood) is frequently associated with a change of residence.

Household composition is also affected by increasing age, which sees a growing proportion of the elderly living *with* younger relatives. A quarter of the rural elderly share a household with younger relatives. In more urban areas, where the pressure for housing is greater, one-third live in households with younger members (Hunt, 1978). Since the younger relative is in most cases an adult child, single people are less

Table 10.1 *Proportions Living with Younger Relatives by Marital Status and Age (percentages)*

	Widowed	Married	Single
Age			
65–79	22	13	7
80+	49	19	17
All	32	13	10

likely to have younger relatives in the same household. Those who are still married are also less likely to live with younger relatives, but among the widowed and the single twice as many of the over-80s (as the under-80s) do have younger relatives in the household. In fact, half the widows over 80 were living in such a household. (See Table 10.1.)

The importance of children as supporters in old age becomes very clear when the proportions living with younger relatives are correlated with the number of children. The likelihood increases with the number of children. The proportions increase markedly after age 80, with more than half of parents over 80 living with a child, and four out of five parents of four or more children living with one of them. It seems apparent that the availability of supportive relatives is essential in keeping the majority of over-80s in the community. This fact is of special importance now that more and more are living into their eighties and will be discussed more fully in the final chapter.

What this seems to clearly demonstrate is the willingness of adult children to care for elderly parents, although it is impossible to tell from the data how well the elderly adjust to the situation. Not all these parents are moving into a child's household. Some have children who have not left home or who have returned. However, where the elderly person had moved into a child's home it was found that they were often very lonely.

Reliance on and contact with family or close friends appears, therefore, to intensify with increasing age and the majority of the elderly have support networks of five or more persons. What is reassuring is the apparent ability of the elderly to adjust to the emotional shock of the loss of spouse or other confidant and to overcome the initial loneliness of such loss. Qualitative data, however, indicate that loneliness which results from loss of friends and siblings through longevity seems to be harder to overcome.

Chapter 7 on Help and Helpers has shown that the elderly are as likely to help as be helped. The fact that one in ten is caring for a dependent relative and one in three helping out their neighbours in a regular way is convincing evidence. The younger middle-class elderly are known to provide more help for their children in terms of child care and financial help than they receive (Bell, 1968). In the rural areas grandparents continue to be a favourite holiday destination. Those older elderly who receive support from friends and neighbours are mostly receiving such help from other elderly people. At the same time, local adaptations to provide transport and other access to goods and services are further testimony to the interdependence which exists between the elderly and other segments of society. It is perhaps an artificial boundary which suggests we look at those over 65 separately from the community as a whole. The concepts of dependence, independence, interdependence and reciprocity are complex. Reciprocal relationships may never be entirely symmetrical as needs change over time. Most attention is paid to the instrumental aspects of such interactions but the expressive and latent aspects may be equally important. It has been suggested that those who are dependent on another may also be needed by the care-giver (Daatland, 1983). For instance, providing care may be our expression of affection or a reinforcement of self-image (as good husband, daughter, or niece, for instance) which is necessary for the self-esteem of the giver. The rewards of reciprocal affection, gratitude, advice, or merely well-being may be an important part of the carer's social reality. At the same time, while independence may be cherished, it may only be possible because it is reinforced and negotiated through significant others who are 'here if you need me', 'always ready to help', or comment 'you're marvellous for your age'.

While the elderly may rely predominantly on one relative, either in the same household or in another close by, this caring relationship may only survive because of others in the social network. Although most instrumental help comes from one source, well-being may be enhanced by brief visits, telephone calls, or letters from others, without which the dependent person could be more demanding than the carer could bear. At the same time, the carer is receiving support from her own social network. Such help may include instrumental help with transport or shopping, for instance, or expressive help such as listening to problems or merely acknowledging the input of care by asking, 'How is your mother today?' In many cases, however, carers are faced with demoralising burdens of care and receive little support.

In cases of high dependency, instrumental help from the health and social services plays a part. Support networks, therefore, do not exist in isolation from the social networks of others. Each member of the network has their own network which interlocks with the support network of the elderly person. Without this interlocking of networks the individual network would probably break down. The failure of the support network, therefore, may be the result of a breakdown in the ability or willingness of support from the network of the primary carer rather than in the elderly person's own network. Interdependence may, therefore, be seen as a chain of dependence and reciprocities.

The elderly, their families and other members of the community do adapt their living arrangements and behaviour to accommodate the changing needs of increasing dependency. Indeed, it would be more surprising if this were not so since the behaviour of the ageing individual is more likely to approximate earlier patterns than to develop new ones, and the developmental life cycle consists of a series of adjustments and adaptations.

However well prepared the individual may be, changes forced on the ageing person may be sudden as in the case of retirement, loss of a spouse (or other close relative), moving to a new community, or sudden failure of health; or they may be gradual, as with deterioration of mobility from arthritis and rheumatism, loss of energy, increasing reliance on others for help, failing hearing or vision. Sudden changes take longer to adapt to, but far from indicating a lack of adaptive response, the elderly for the most part demonstrate a resilience and determination at least equal to that of younger people, which belies the pathetic stereotype with which we have become familiar.

Far from resisting change, it is apparent that the old person not only adapts well but even initiates change in anticipation of or as a response to the ageing process. They move to more appealing locations or more convenient residences, they join voluntary associations, and more of the elderly are involved in caring for others or providing help to others than are receiving such help. Approximately one-fifth of the rural elderly, for instance, could name someone who *needed* them to take care of them. They are thus involved in both instrumental and expressive adaptations, which in turn probably aid physical and psychological well-being.

The evidence clearly shows that all but a very small minority of the elderly are in contact with relatives, friends and/or neighbours, including the childless and those who have never married. The implications of the social embeddedness of the elderly are obvious. Potential help and care exists and the ability of the elderly to adapt suggests that creative coping strategies will be employed by most old people to overcome difficulties as they occur. Discussion of the help received by the elderly demonstrates how non-familial helpers assume responsibilities where there are no obviously involved family members available. Despite commonly voiced anxieties about the withdrawal of informal care when social services become involved, the evidence is that even among customers of formal social services, the elderly continue to seek help in crises from informal sources and that such sources are available.

In considering the elderly as a category it can be seen that while much help comes from the family, the elderly themselves provide a substantial amount of the informal care of the community. The argument can be made for the recognition of a high level of interdependence amongst the elderly. Not only do they provide care for frailer spouses, siblings and in some cases parents, but the younger elderly, because they have more time available, frequently help out more elderly neighbours and friends and provide a high proportion of the volunteers who deliver meals on wheels. The type of reciprocity this form of interdependence represents is not symmetrical, although it could be argued that filling such caring roles compensates for other role losses and thus contributes to the self-esteem of helpers. It may make it easier subsequently to relinquish some independence and to accept help where needed.

The fact that family and friends care about and for the elderly does not, of course, mean that the growing proportions who live on into their eighties will not put pressure on the health and social services. The families of today's middle-aged cohort are smaller and thus when they become elderly there will be fewer adult children available to care. A side effect of this will be that there will be fewer people who can support elderly aunts and uncles who are childless. At the same time, while friends and neighbours do step in to give support to the elderly, the evidence suggests that they are less willing or able to make long-term commitments or to undertake the intimate personal care of advancing frailty. There comes a time when it is clear that a frail old person can no longer live alone. By the same token, caring relatives cannot always assume the full burden of care and should not be expected to continue to provide nursing services (medical or psychiatric) where the burden is such that the quality of their own lives and consequently those of their patient are unsatisfactory. When this point has been reached will obviously differ from one family to another and will depend on the dynamics and perceptions in each case. Where, for whatever reason, informal care is not available the responsibility devolves on to the health and social services.

With a growing proportion of the very old in the population, the importance of the contribution of informal support takes on a new significance. While the willingness to help exists, its durability and reliability will depend on the support that informal carers can rely upon from other sources. All the social services, therefore, have an investment in nurturing, supplementing and reinforcing informal support not as an alternative to residential care but as a necessary complement to it. Society depends more on informal care than on the health and social services, but for a healthy community, the interdependence of these two sources of help must be fully recognised and accepted.

Chapter 11

◆

POLICY IMPLICATIONS

The data presented in the preceding chapters should go some way towards making explicit the types of care, the sources of help available and the nature of support networks for the elderly who are the largest client group of the health and personal social services. While differences between areas may be expected, the fact that the elderly upon whom this study has been based compare in most important respects with Hunt's stratified (more urban) sample of the elderly at home (1978) and M. Abrams's urban study (1978, 1980), together with evidence of caring commitment in inner cities (Isaacs *et al.*, 1972) and in other communities (Bayley *et al.*, 1982), suggests that patterns of informal care are likely to demonstrate more similarity than differences. While the existence of support networks may be expected in most social contexts, the style of such networks may differ. It has been shown, for instance, that support networks in stable neighbourhoods (whether urban or rural) are more likely to be of the close-knit and self-supporting type while those in more transitional or unstable neighbourhoods are more diffuse. However, while close-knit networks are seen as better able to provide emotional support, they may inhibit help-seeking behaviour from professional sources even when such actions are dysfunctional, for instance in the case of mental illness. Diffuse networks, on the other hand, are likely to be less homogeneous and to offer a broader range of help-seeking pathways giving those looking for help more choice and flexibility but less direct help and moral support (Warren, 1981). It would seem, therefore, that different types of networks offer different types of help and have different implications for statutory services. Knowledge of local network patterns is thus essential in projecting needs and planning interventions.

The findings describe an active, competent and capable elderly population, a minority of whom need support and help to remain in their own homes. However, with succeeding generations a higher proportion can hope to live on past 80 and after this age a high proportion become dependent. It may be that increased longevity will mean better health for the very old but the medical evidence suggests that those who achieve greater age also suffer longer periods of final dependency

(Isaacs, 1982). This suggests that the numbers of dependent elderly in the community are likely to increase over the next decade. As we have seen, the burden of care falls on the family and family size is decreasing. The most dependent elderly living at home are cared for mainly by spouses or adult children who are usually daughters or daughters-in-law (Bayley *et al.*, 1982). Where the carer is a spouse, supplementary help from statutory services is least likely and with increased longevity caring spouses are older, and even adult children are more likely to be over 60 themselves and may be faced with the care of spouse and parent simultaneously. The family, however, will continue to be the primary source from which help is sought reflecting, as Shanas (1979) has pointed out, not so much need as mutual expectations.

However, as Chapter 7 has shown, there are significant sub-groups of old people who depend more on friends and neighbours than do other groups, including those who live alone, retirement migrants, those who have never married and the childless. Much of such help is regular, but non-family helpers are less likely to make long-term commitments to caring, particularly where this involves intimate personal care. It is not clear whether this reflects unwillingness to make commitments which may be demanding, or whether it reflects constraints on non-family intervention. It was also discovered that men, even single men, rely far more on family help than do women. Since most carers are women, this may reflect constraints on cross-sex non-family care provision in the same way. Most of the elderly manage with routine types of help and support but for a minority total care is needed, and in those cases the expectation is that such care will be provided by the family or the state. Non-family commitment is seen as unlikely. Warren (1981) has demonstrated that problems are more stressful if there is no perceived solution or help and crises make availability of help more critical.

Recent trends towards greater reliance on family and community sources of care have raised questions about the capacity of the family to cope in cases of extreme dependency, and Hobman (1981) has suggested that statutory help for the carer if it comes at all comes too late to repair the damage that long-term caring has done. The largest category of carers are spouses, and Fengler and Goodrich (1979), in a study of the wives of disabled elderly men, identified such women as 'hidden patients' and found that they are able to cope well only if supported by friends, sympathisers and children. They suggest that such women manage better and help their husbands more if treated by professionals as part of the care team, and urge training and better support for carers. Support via counselling, self-help groups, day care, short-term care, as well as through fiscal and housing policies has also been urged (Hobman, 1981; Tinker, 1980; Fengler and Goodrich, 1979). Where support groups for carers of spouses or parents exist, common problems emerge and a high level of participation has been experienced (Hausman,

1979), indicative of the need such support fills. On the other hand, where such care is reinforced by taxation and other legislated benefits, a higher proportion of the elderly are cared for at home (Maede, 1981).

Recent policy statements (DHSS, 1981; Shanas, 1977) have stressed the importance of keeping the elderly at home as long as possible, and independence from children is valued by the old people themselves. For subsequent cohorts this independence is likely to be even more salient. It would seem therefore that government policy which seeks to maintain the elderly at home must also seek to reinforce those adaptations which make this possible. Such reinforcement might include subsidies which make moves nearer to supportive kin possible, a shift in emphasis to preventive and rehabilitative health and social services provision and the provision of support services for carers (for example, counselling, relief nursing, incontinence laundry and compensation for work lost). It may also include services to those in an earlier phase of the life cycle. Maas and Kuypers (1974), for instance found that successful adaptations in young adulthood may predispose the individual to a poor adjustment to ageing. Thus they argue that mothers of more than two children who devote all their energies to bringing up a family may face old age with underdeveloped interests and social skills necessary for successful adaptation. They suggest that more adequate child care facilities would provide opportunity not only for employment but for the development of friendships and interests outside the home. At the same time, such facilities would also make it easier for parents of young children to support elderly relatives.

The publication of the Barclay Report (NISW, 1982), with its emphasis on community social work, has been heralded as being of major significance for the future of social work, but at the same time, its implicit assumptions about the extent and nature of informal care have been likened to 'an article of faith' (Bamford, 1982) and suggestions have been made that its extent has been exaggerated (Pinker, 1982). While the report urges 'a close working partnership with citizens focusing more closely on the community and its strengths' (para. 13.1) 'which takes full account of informal care' (13.13), it admits that 'we still know too little about what determines the shape and style of informal networks' (para. 13.70).

The natural helping networks described in this book have several identifiable characteristics which might be seen as pointers for an effective model of community-based social work. They are local; they consist of individuals known to one another; they are recognised by others outside the network. That is, they are relatively visible; they are flexible and responsive to changes in need; and they are accessible to those whom they serve. These principles appear to underlie the successful functioning of community care for the elderly.

First of all, it would seem that a collaborative approach to presenting problems might be adopted, with whenever possible the elderly person and, where appropriate, significant others in his or her network discussing potential solutions. The role of the helping professional could encourage the individual and the family or other potential carers to look at options, perhaps hitherto unconsidered. Such an approach would, of course, necessitate a change in perspectives. It becomes necessary to see the old person in most cases as potentially competent and as active in decisions about his or her future rather than as the passive recipient of resources. This type of approach would lead to renewed emphasis on problem identification and solving for and on the part of the elderly and to a greater educational input (planning, nutrition, mobility, cooking, and so on), and from the health services a greater emphasis on, and facilities for, prevention and rehabilitation. Certainly, the data suggest that the majority are able and willing to solve their own problems but that they may need support to do this.

A model of social services based on participative democracy and a consultative approach has already been urged (Hadley and Hatch, 1981). The present predominant pattern of social services provision for the elderly is, however, superimposed from above, designed to react to crisis and to ration specific resources. This is in contrast to natural informal help which provides a flexible and adaptive response based on resources inherent in the community. The findings, therefore, support the main thrust of the Barclay Report towards 'the development of flexible decentralized patterns of organization based upon a social care plan which takes full account of informal care, and mobilises voluntary and statutory provision in its support' (para. 13.3).

Secondly, if informal care is to be fostered, those who care for dependent others – many of whom are themselves elderly – need additional support. This applies not only to those who are caring for a totally dependent household member but also to those who provide regular support to elderly persons in a separate household. The evidence is that friends and relatives are prepared and happy to help but many children are employed full time, are parents or in some cases themselves retired and may be caring for other relatives or themselves in poor health. It is therefore imperative that possible solutions to the problems of ageing are sought with the total social network in mind, both in terms of resources available and potential strains and stress that must be avoided to ensure the continuance of the support network.

To maintain the elderly in their own homes greater support for the care-givers must be an integral part of the social care programme. At present such care is limited in most cases to those who form part of the same household as the elderly person. In order to provide help earlier, identification of carers is necessary. Supporters who may live in other households must also be recognised even when as the data demonstrate they are unrelated to the person needing support. Such interventions presuppose greater outreach into the community. Given that supportive others exist for most of the elderly, that the elderly themselves are capable of adaptation and adjustment but also given that the elderly value their independence, it appears that there are clear indications here for the treatment of old people, only a small proportion of whom need constant care.

Among those whose frailty requires that they live with younger members of the family (mostly children), loneliness is more common than among other sub-groups. Frequently, this is so even though the elderly person concerned is rarely left alone. When verbalised it seems such loneliness results from a lack of one's own friends and contacts. Sometimes this is one of the unavoidable losses associated with longevity as old friends die. However, for the old person without her own contacts, the demoralisation of role loss and the sense of being dependent and perhaps a burden is frequently exacerbated by her observation of the strain her care places on the caring relative. In this context, support for the relative in the form of relief caring can provide contact and relief from this anxiety, if only temporarily, for the old person involved and potentially extend the efficacy of the caring relationship. As the data show the old *are* able to establish new relationships, even those as intimate as confidant, and may have a need to do so. More than half turn to someone outside the family when they feel a need to talk, perhaps reflecting the genesis of tension within the household. For those who are housebound this outlet is often not available.

Thirdly, given the demonstrated capacity of the elderly for change and adaptation and the willingness of the family to help it seems that more attention could be given to public education on and preparation for the latter part of the life-cycle. The literature of both education and psychology emphasises the formative years of babyhood and youth to such a degree that most people assume that learning and growing are not for old people. Perhaps the time has come, with the increasing proportion of elderly people in the population, for this perspective to be re-evaluated and for a greater emphasis on self-help and self-development throughout life. The elderly can adapt and they jealously guard their independence. In this context it would seem to be self-evident that they would welcome the knowledge and demonstrate the ability to take an active role in preventive and rehabilitative strategies with regard to their own physical and mental health.

A trend towards more locally based service delivery systems has developed. These include such innovations as the Kent Community Care project and the Gofal schemes (Challis and Davies, 1980) where care is contracted from the local community; patch-based community-oriented models of organisation (Hadley and McGrath, 1980); and a variety of neighbourhood care or good neighbour schemes (P. Abrams *et al.*, 1981). All these systems provide a more local, visible, familiar and accessible service to the community. Indications are that neighbourhood care and patch schemes lead to earlier intervention (Hadley and McGrath, 1984 in press). In all three types of service natural carers are more easily identified and supported.

In all of these localised schemes self-help and mutual aid appear to be natural spin-offs which have implications for the extension of community resources. In the Gofal scheme husbands and children of contracted helpers have become involved in caring, and relatives who had withdrawn in the face of overwhelming demands have become re-involved when the burden can be shared with statutory helpers (Tarran, 1982). In the Normanton patch team co-operation between domiciliary services, residential establishments, voluntary agencies and doctors has been extended and higher visibility has resulted in more referrals, but because intervention is earlier this increased demand has been met without additional resources (Cooper, 1980).

There is, however, an intrinsic tension in a system which seeks to adapt itself more readily to local needs and at the same time provide a national service. Social services in many European countries have demonstrated a pendulum effect between centralism and localism, and this tendency has not yet been resolved (Wenger, 1979). The problems of management in a diffuse and flexible system seem to predispose policy-makers towards more accountability and control while strong centralist systems stifle innovation and lead to demands for the devolution of power. It is, therefore, difficult to assess current developments without considering whether we are witnessing yet another swing of the pendulum.

Professionals from most European countries, however, agree that domiciliary services for the elderly are best provided from the grass roots. Most of the needs of the dependent elderly are more practical than specialised, involving as they do problems concerning personal care and household routine. At the same time, those who care for frail old people have a need for emotional and practical support. What is necessary is a responsive generic service at the community level, with home helps, social workers, district nurses, health visitors and general practitioners functioning in collaboration to support existing care systems, supplemented by specialist consultants covering wider areas.

If the interdependence between informal and formal sources of support is to be appreciated, acknowledged and fostered, this presupposes a greater input into domiciliary services. Such services cannot be seen as an alternative to residential services for, as noted in Chapter 10, the proportions living into very old age are growing. In order to avoid a breakdown of existing provision, the logical steps would appear to be the provision of services which recognise and bolster existing informal care provision. Such a programme will not be cheap; it demands investment in improved domiciliary services but in the long run it is likely to prove less costly than the provision of residential beds in the same ratios as at present. Failure to make this investment is likely to result in a crisis in residential care provision which could lead to a total breakdown of care for the dependent elderly.

The necessary provision would stem from policies which specifically rewarded caring behaviour, including increased more broadly available tax benefits and other allowances for those caring for physically or mentally infirm relatives; greater provision of relief care (both day or night), holiday care, short stay residential care, incontinence laundry; and casework with caring families giving other relatives as well as the principal carer a chance to talk about and find solutions to problems arising not only in their caring role but also in family relationships (both nuclear and extended) as a result of that role. At lower levels of dependency, provision might be designed to identify persons needing help before a crisis developed by working closely with doctors, clergy and voluntary groups and through the use of volunteers as monitors of the less integrated elderly, that is, by being aware of potential problems. Help for those elderly living alone or with other elderly people might include a more facilitating approach, for instance in the case of men who cannot cook or women who do not understand financial management. A need for work with the recently bereaved is also indicated and a role exists for social services to liaise with and promote the development of voluntary self-help support groups in this area.

This approach calls for a more integrated perspective of service provision where the personnel of different agencies adopt a co-operative stance, sharing tasks and information in order to provide a cohesive support package. Depending on the problems existing, it would involve, for instance, social workers working through family networks to negotiate and bolster support; home helps, social workers, district nurses and doctors keeping one another informed and dovetailing visits; or housing, health and personal social services co-operating, to ensure that the carer's task is made less onerous. Bayley (1980) has called this model of working 'sensitive interweaving', consciously integrating as it does the formal and informal sources of care. Such interweaving should be possible at all levels, including, for instance, greater collaboration between domiciliary and residential services, between statutory agencies and voluntary, charitable and religious groups, and between professional and natural helpers. The interface between informal and formal help and between agencies is fraught with difficulties and conflicts (particularly over boundaries of responsibility and budgeting), which frequently go unacknowledged. A need exists for a local authority forum where health, housing and social services representatives might discuss and formulate co-operative plans for their area, and the indications are that more jointly funded projects could provide local innovations which would reinforce co-operation and improve care packages, the quality of life of recipients and the job satisfaction of practitioners. Social workers might play an important role in ensuring liaison between care-providers.

If interweaving of formal and informal care is successful, social workers will find themselves working with indigenous non-professionals like members of the family, neighbours and volunteers, but where does agency accountability fit into this picture? Although accountability to the social services agency will still be important to social workers, especially in statutory work, much social work with the elderly is non-statutory. This presents opportunities for some re-definition of accountability giving more weight to agreements reached between helpers, clients and social worker rather than strict responsibility to the agency. It may also need to include access to discretionary funds for social workers in order to make such negotiations practical.

The problem of confidentiality is one which is closely allied to accountability. For the professional attempting to work through natural support networks, ethical and statutory constraints may impede progress. Social workers are also members of the culture and while informal helpers act intuitively and discreetly, formal helpers must observe agency rules on confidentiality. Adaptations such as asking a client's permission to approach relatives or neighbours then become marked behaviour and some of the informality is lost. However, it may well be that anxieties about confidentiality are overstated. Some element of risk-taking cannot be avoided in drawing upon support within the informal care system but this may be the price of identifying and relying upon locally based care agents. As one social worker comments, 'they know everything about everybody anyway' (Black *et al.*, 1983).

Although neighbours may be willing to support old people in a day-to-day way the indications from the Gofal and neighbourhood care schemes are that outside the family financial inducements may make it possible to recruit and maintain carers who are not already involved in helping. At the same time, constraints may exist on neighbours entering the houses of the elderly to provide support. This is particularly likely in working-class neighbourhoods where the home is experienced more as a protected space against the outside world than as a form of self-expression as among middle-class persons (Klein, 1965). As we have noted, men rely more heavily on family help than do women, indicating a possible constraint operating on predominantly female carers. Where family are known to exist in the same community, neighbours may hang back or prefer to alert relatives when they are concerned for fear of being seen as interfering. It may also be assumed that elderly persons 'need' or 'want' family support in preference to neighbour help. Often people will feel inhibited from helping where an offer of help could be interpreted as a slur. It is easier to offer to cook a meal than to suggest cleaning up the house and unlikely that many feel confident enough to suggest washing or bathing a neighbour except in a crisis situation.

Nominal payments and co-operation with social services can overcome such constraints. Such payments may even make it possible for neighbours to accept caring responsibilities in lieu of other part-time employment. An immediate implication of this for good neighbour schemes would therefore be a need for greater financial backing. This may not amount to much since the proportion of very dependent elderly people who require intensive, regular and long-term help in any locality will be extremely small and in the long run may prove to be more cost-effective than expansion of Part III accommodation.

It must not be assumed that any one pattern of interweaving of the formal and informal sectors can be adopted. Rather the style of integration and co-operation will be determined by local needs and resources, and Bayley (1980) urges a creative relationship between the sectors, so that flexibility is maintained and with it the possibility for innovation. The pattern which develops in any one locality will reflect local strengths and weaknesses and expectations. In his study of helping networks Warren (1981) identified four levels of help provision: informal; quasi-formal, including self-help groups; professional; and interorganisational. Help-seeking behaviour is shaped by variations in the availability of help from these sources and by the nature of the need – in other words, by the social context. In working-class neighbourhoods there is more reliance on kin and neighbours while middle-class networks are more widespread, involving the wider society and better access to resources. He found that most people need encouragement to seek professional help and that working-class people delay longer before seeking such help. As a result, the use of professionals differs widely between neighbourhoods. Warren suggests that pathways to help (whether formal or informal) are related to different types of social network and are associated with reducing risk for the individual. He states: 'Effective neighbourhood contexts are those which either maximise choice and entry points [to help] or provide a consistent and secure cluster of helpers and well-trod pathways' (p. 195). The advantages of more localised social services provision are thus found in the opportunity to acquire knowledge of local networks and in the visibility of alternative pathways to help.

Interweaving the formal and informal support systems is a task requiring tact and diplomacy. Despite the need for adaptation and flexibility it is important to spell out quite clearly what is envisaged and particularly what interweaving is not. Interweaving is not about shifting responsibility from statutory services on to informal providers. Neither is it about co-opting and colonising informal systems (Froland, 1980) nor about superimposing existing packages of care on to the community. Formal agencies cannot provide, stimulate, or co-opt informal networks but must work with them, balancing informal and formal resources, in co-operation with natural helpers.

If interweaving is to work well it must start from a perspective of the community or locality as a care-giving system by seeking to reinforce and optimise existing resources and creating resources to fill gaps in provision. It requires familiarity with family and neighbourhood networks; consultation with network members as well as clients; development of partnerships with other social services such as doctors' practices, schools, churches and voluntary organisations; and, as Seebohm and Kilbrandon envisaged over a decade ago, and Barclay has reiterated, a requirement to view the entire community as both needing and offering support. This raises important questions about the training and skill requirements of social workers. It implies the need for social work education to include attention to the sociology of groups and communities and the whole area of community organisation as a central part of the social work role. More than that, it demands a greater commitment to the sharing of professional and administrative skills with clients, lay helpers and voluntary agencies. Communication, entrepreneurial, brokerage and organisational skills will then become essential attributes of the successful community-oriented social worker. If care is to be woven into the community fabric, the value of both informal and professional carers must be recognised for what each can do best and these two complementary groups become parts of the same helping networks.

APPENDIX 1 UNIVERSITY COLLEGE OF NORTH WALES, BANGOR, ELDERLY IN THE COMMUNITY: QUESTIONNAIRE

INTERVIEWER COMPLETE Name of Interviewer: _____
                       Community: _____
                       Time interview started: _____
                       Time interview finished: _____
                       Date: _____

1 Rating No.: _____
2 Name of Interviewee: _____
3 Address: _____
           _____
           _____   Code for community:
                                                   1
                                                   2
                                                   3
                                                   4
                                                   5
                                                   6
                                                   7
                                                   8
                                                   9

INTRODUCTION

TO BE USED AS A GUIDE ONLY:
Good morning. I'm ____(give name)____ , a research worker, from the University at Bangor. Last Autumn you may remember, we took a census of everyone who is 60 or older in ___(name the community)___ .

To help planners of services for the elderly in the future, we are now talking to many of the people over 65 whom we met then to find out something about their lives, their problems and how they cope with retirement and living in a rural area. IF PHASE I FORM DOES NOT INDICATE EXACT AGE AND YOU DO NOT KNOW IF RESPONDENT IS OVER 65, ASK AT THIS POINT: Are you over 65? IF YES, CONTINUE: IF NO, Well then I won't bother you, but I wanted to make sure you were given an opportunity to express your views if you were over 65.

Would it be convenient for me to talk to you for a while now or can I make an appointment to come back at a more suitable time? PRIOR TO STARTING

APPENDICES

APPENDIX 1 UNIVERSITY COLLEGE OF NORTH WALES, BANGOR, ELDERLY IN THE COMMUNITY: QUESTIONNAIRE

INTERVIEWER COMPLETE   Name of Interviewer: _____
Community: _____
Time interview started: _____
Time interview finished: _____
Date: _____

1 Rating No.: _____
2 Name of Interviewee: _____
3 Address: _____
_____
_____   Code for community:
1
2
3
4
5
6
7
8
9

INTRODUCTION

TO BE USED AS A GUIDE ONLY:
Good morning. I'm __(give name)__ , a research worker, from the University at Bangor. Last Autumn you may remember, we took a census of everyone who is 60 or older in __(name the community)__ .

To help planners of services for the elderly in the future, we are now talking to many of the people over 65 whom we met then to find out something about their lives, their problems and how they cope with retirement and living in a rural area. IF PHASE I FORM DOES NOT INDICATE EXACT AGE AND YOU DO NOT KNOW IF RESPONDENT IS OVER 65, ASK AT THIS POINT: Are you over 65? IF YES, CONTINUE: IF NO, Well then I won't bother you, but I wanted to make sure you were given an opportunity to express your views if you were over 65.

Would it be convenient for me to talk to you for a while now or can I make an appointment to come back at a more suitable time? PRIOR TO STARTING

INTERVIEW AFTER YOU ARE IN THE HOUSE AND READY TO START:

I want to reassure you that anything you tell me will be treated in strictest confidence. The main aim is to assist in improving the delivery and future planning of services, and the information will be used statistically.

RESIDENCE AND MIGRATION

I'd like to start by asking you something about your background.

* 1 Can you tell me where you were born?

_____ (place)

_____ (county)

Within 5 miles of here	1
More than 5 but less than 15	2
More than 15 but less than 50	3
More than 50 miles away	4

MAKE SURE PLACE CAN BE IDENTIFIED. IF A SMALL PLACE GIVE NEAREST TOWN AS WELL AS PLACE NAME AND COUNTY. SEE INSTRUCTIONS FOR CODING.

2 Are you married? IF YES: ASK

And where was your husband/ wife born?

_____ (place)

_____ (county)

Within 5 miles of here	1
More than 5 but less than 15	2
More than 15 but less than 50	3
More than 50 miles away	4

SEE INSTRUCTIONS FOR CODING.

IF INTERVIEWEE BORN ELSEWHERE, ASK:

* 3 How long have you lived in this community? ROUND UP TO NEAREST YEAR

_____ year arrived
(INTERVIEWER ASCERTAIN)

Less than 3 years	1
3–5 years	2
6–10 years	3
11–20 years	4
21–30 years	5
31 years or more	6

4 How old were you when you came to live in this community? IF INTERVIEWEE HAS LIVED AWAY FOR SOME YEARS AND RETURNED, RECORD THE DETAILS AND THE AGE AT RETURN.

Under 20	1
21–40	2
41–50	3

51–60	4
61–65	5
66–70	6
Over 70	7

5 How long have you lived in this house/flat/farm?
ROUND UP TO NEAREST YEAR

Less than 3 years	1
3–5 years	2
6–10 years	3
11–20 years	4
21–30 years	5
31 years or more	6

6 What were the main reasons for moving to this house/flat/farm?
IF RESPONDENT HAS ALWAYS LIVED HERE,
INDICATE ACCORDINGLY.

Size	1
Near children/relations	2
Convenient locations	3
One storey	4
Cost	5
Other (specify) _____	6
————————————————————	
Always lived here	7

* 7 IF APPLICABLE:
Where did you live directly before you came to this community?

_____ (place)   _____ (county)   ☐☐

Within 5 miles of here	1
More than 5 but less than 15	2
More than 15 but less than 50	3
More than 50 miles away	4

SEE INSTRUCTIONS FOR CODING.

8 IF INTERVIEWEE HAS LIVED ELSEWHERE:
Why did you decide to come to live in this community?
RECORD RESPONSE VERBATIM.

	Yes	No
Return to home area	1	2
Near relatives	1	2
Connections with area	1	2
Job	1	2
Country/seaside environment	1	2
Small town	1	2
Available housing	1	2
Other (specify) _____	1	2
————————————————————————————		

9 PROMPT: Anything else?

ACCOMMODATION

Now let's talk about your house/flat
* 10 Do you own your own home or rent it?

Owned outright	1
Mortgage	2
Council rent	3
Private rent	4
In relative's/friend's home	5
Other (specify) _____	6

* 11 INTERVIEWER RECORD TYPE OF HOUSING:

One storey bungalow/cottage	1
House/cottage more than one storey	2
Farm	3
OAP housing (without warden)	4
Sheltered housing (with warden)	5
Ground floor flat	6
Upper floor flat	7
Other (specify – caravan, maisonnette, etc.) _____	8

*(12) APPROXIMATE AGE OF HOUSING (in years)   ☐☐☐
       How old is this house/flat?

13 INTERVIEWER ASCERTAIN WHETHER HOUSEHOLD
    HAS SOLE OR SHARED USE OF THE FOLLOWING:

(a) Hot water – Sole	1	(b) Fixed bath – Sole	1	(c) Inside – Sole	1
Shared	2	or shower Shared	2	flush Shared	2
None	3	None	3	toilet None	3

14 IF SHARED OR NONE, DESCRIBE WHAT FACILITIES
    ARE AVAILABLE AND RECORD INTERVIEWEE'S
    STATEMENTS RE USE, CONVENIENCE, ETC.
    (*a*) Water facilities

    (*b*) Bathing facilities

    (*c*) Toilet facilities

* 15 Is your bedroom upstairs?   Yes 1
                                     No   2
* 16 Is your only toilet upstairs? Yes 1
                                     No   2

17 Are there any things about this house which make life difficult for
you? For instance:

	Yes	No
Steps/stairs	1	2
Heating/damp/condensation	1	2
Noise or other nuisance	1	2
Too large	1	2
Too small	1	2
Too isolated	1	2
Outside access difficult	1	2
Lack of any facilities	1	2
Other	1	2
Nothing	1	2

* 18 What is your main source of heat in the living room?

Coal or wood fire	1
Gas fire	2
Full central heating	
gas	3
oil	4
electric	5
solid fuel	6
Partial central heating	7
Storage heaters	8
Electric fire	9
Paraffin heater	10
Other (specify) _____	11

PROMPT AND RECORD INTERVIEWEE'S COMMENTS
RE ADEQUACY, COST OR PROBLEMS INVOLVED.

19 Do you have any heating in your bedroom?

Coal or wood fire	1
Gas fire	2
Full central heating	
gas	3
oil	4
electric	5
solid fuel	6
Partial central heating	7
Storage heaters	8
Electric fire	9
Paraffin heater	10
Other (specify) _____	11
No heat	12

PROMPT AND RECORD INTERVIEWEE'S COMMENTS
RE ADEQUACY, COST, OR PROBLEMS INVOLVED.

20 How satisfied would you say you are with this house/flat?

Very satisfied	1
Satisfied	2
Neutral	3

Dissatisfied	4
Very dissatisfied	5

HOUSEHOLD COMPOSITION

* 21 Can you tell me something about who else lives here with you?
INTERVIEWER TO ASCERTAIN THE FOLLOWING
INFORMATION FOR EACH MEMBER OF THE HOUSE-
HOLD. INDICATE HEAD OF HOUSEHOLD BY
ASTERISK.

First name and relationship to Respondent	Sex M. F.	Age	Marital status S M W D/S	Occupation (state FT/PT, retired, housewife, disabled, etc.)
(i) respondent	1 2	——	1 2 3 4	————
(ii) ————	1 2	——	1 2 3 4	————
(iii) ————	1 2	——	1 2 3 4	————
(iv) ————	1 2	——	1 2 3 4	————
(v) ————	1 2	——	1 2 3 4	————
(vi) ————	1 2	——	1 2 3 4	————

* 22 IF RESPONDENT IS NOT HEAD OF HOUSEHOLD,
ASCERTAIN WHETHER HEAD OF HOUSEHOLD IS
EMPLOYED/RETIRED/DISABLED/UNEMPLOYED/
HOUSEWIFE, ETC. AND RECORD.

Head of Household is Employed full time	1
Employed part time	2
Retired	3
Disabled	4
Unemployed	5
Housewife	6

_____ (Occupation).

(23) IF APPLICABLE: How long have you been/were you married?
_____ years.

(24) Have/had you been married before?

No	1
Yes, widowed	2
Yes, divorced	3

* 25 INTERVIEWER CODE WHETHER RESPONDENT

Lives alone	1 I.M. ☐
With spouse only	2
Alone with child(ren)	3
Elderly couple with child(ren) at home	4
In child's household	5
With other elderly relative(s) only	6

| | With other younger relative(s) present | 7 |
| | Other (specify) | 8 |

* 26 INTERVIEWER CODE IF:
(Specify relationship of
dependent person to
interviewee).

_____

Parent or older generation dependent* on interviewee	1
Spouse, brother or sister dependent on interviewee	2
Child or younger generation dependent on interviewee	3
No one dependent on interviewee	4

* Dependent = incapable of taking care of self.
Older generation = parent, aunt, uncle, etc.
Younger generation = niece, nephew, grandchild, etc.

CONTACT WITH COMMUNITY SERVICES

27 Let's move on now to talk about the various services that may have
called here. For instance:
(a) which of the following has called to see you during the past
six months?
ASK (b) WHEN PERSON IN QUESTION HAS CALLED,
THEN (c) and (d).
(b) How often does _____ call on you?

NOTE: VISITS IN A PERSONAL CATEGORY ARE TO BE
INCLUDED.

	(a) Has called		(b) How often?				(c) Is that often enough?		(d) Is visit long enough	
	Yes	No	more than once a week	once a week	once a fortnight	less often	Yes	No	Yes	No
Doctor	1	2	1	2	3	4	1	2	1	2
Health visitor	1	2	1	2	3	4	1	2	1	2
Community/district nurse (AHA)	1	2	1	2	3	4	1	2	1	2
LA home help	1	2	1	2	3	4	1	2	1	2
Council welfare officer/ social worker/ occupational therapist	1	2	1	2	3	4	1	2	1	2
Social security/ supplementary benefits officer	1	2	1	2	3	4	1	2	1	2

	(a) Has called		more than once a week	(b) How often? once a week	once a fortnight	less often	(c) Is that often enough?		(d) Is visit long enough?	
	Yes	No					Yes	No	Yes	No
Meals on wheels	1	2	1	2	3	4	1	2	1	2
Voluntary organisation	1	2	1	2	3	4	1	2	1	2
Insurance man	1	2	1	2	3	4	1	2	1	1
Minister of religion	1	2	1	2	3	4	1	2	1	2
Chiropodist	1	2	1	2	3	4	1	2	1	2
Private nurse	1	2	1	2	3	4	1	2	1	2
Private household help	1	2	1	2	3	4	1	2	1	2
Other visiting service (specify) _____	1	2	1	2	3	4	1	2	1	2
None of these	1	2								

*(29) Have you ever asked for help from the social services? For instance, for a home help, nursing, mobility aids, a telephone or meals on wheels? IF YES, what happened?

RECORD DESCRIPTION VERBATIM   Yes 1
                                     No   2

PROMPT IF NECESSARY FOR OUTCOME AND
FEELINGS ABOUT FAIRNESS OF DECISION IF
REFUSED.

                    Still receiving help   1
                    Received help once   2
                    No help   3

MORALE: NOT PROXIES

30 Now, I'd like to ask you a few questions about how you feel about life in general.
READ SLOWLY

	Yes	No	D/K	
Do things keep getting worse as you get older?	1	3	2	
Do you have as much energy as you did last year?	3	1	2	
Do you feel lonely much?	1	3	2	L.M. ☐
Do you see enough of your friends and relatives?	3	1	2	L.M. ☐
Do little things bother you more this year?	1	3	2	

As you get older do you feel less useful?	1	3	2
Do you sometimes worry so much you can't sleep?	1	3	2
As you get older are things better than expected?	3	1	2
Do you sometimes feel life isn't worth living?	1	3	2
Are you as happy now as when you were younger?	3	1	2
Do you have a lot to be sad about?	1	3	2
Are you afraid of a lot of things?	1	3	2
Do you get angry more than you used to?	1	3	2
Is life hard for you most of the time?	1	3	2
Are you satisfied with your life today?	3	1	2
Do you take things hard?	1	3	2
Do you get upset easily?	1	3	2

FAMILY, FRIENDS AND NEIGHBOURS

I'd like to ask you about your family and friends now if I may.
ASK THOSE WHO LIVE ALONE IF NO CLOSE RELATIVES
ALREADY MENTIONED. THIS WILL HELP TO SCREEN
SUBSEQUENT QUESTIONS.
CODE FOR ALL RESPONDENTS.

31 Do you have any living close relatives?   Yes   1
                                                   No   2   I.M. ☐

IF LIVING ALONE:

32 How long have you lived alone?   _____ years (ROUND UP)

IF WIDOWED:

(33) May I ask how long you have been a widow?   _____ years (ROUND UP)

IF NOT WIDOWED BUT ALONE:

(34) Who did you live with before that?
RECORD REASONS FOR BEING ALONE (e.g. parent died,
brothers and sisters moved away, etc.)

Parent	1
Child(ren)	2
Sibling	3
Other relative	4
Friend	5
Other _____	6

IF APPROPRIATE:

*(35) How many children have you got?   ☐☐

36 Can you tell me something about your children. Where are they
now, what are they doing, how often you see them and things
like that?

PROMPT AS NECESSARY. IF MORE THAN SIX
CHILDREN, RECORD DETAILS OF SIX SEEN MOST
OFTEN.

			(Children)					
			1	2	3	4	5	6
(a)	Sex	Male	1	1	1	1	1	1
		Female	2	2	2	2	2	2
(b)	Age							
(c)	Where living: code for each child							
	Within 5 miles of here		1	1	1	1	1	1
	More than 5 but less than 15		2	2	2	2	2	2
	More than 15 but less than 50		3	3	3	3	3	3
	More than 50 miles away		4	4	4	4	4	4
(d)	Marital status:							
	single		1	1	1	1	1	1
	married		2	2	2	2	2	2
	widowed		3	3	3	3	3	3
	div/sep		4	4	4	4	4	4
(e)	How often do you usually see them or their spouse?							
	more than once a week		1	1	1	1	1	1
	weekly		2	2	2	2	2	2
	2–3 times monthly		3	3	3	3	3	3
	6–12 times a year		4	4	4	4	4	4
	rarely		5	5	5	5	5	5
	never		6	6	6	6	6	6
(f)	Would you like to see more or less of them or are you quite happy with the frequency of visits?							
	more		1	1	1	1	1	1
	less		2	2	2	2	2	2
	satisfied		3	3	3	3	3	3
(g)	How would you describe your relationship with them? (WAIT)							

ASK QUESTION ONLY: USE CATEGORIES ONLY AS
VERIFICATION.

			1	2	3	4	5	6
	very close and friendly		1	1	1	1	1	1
	based on duty/responsibility		2	2	2	2	2	2
	superficial or out of habit		3	3	3	3	3	3
	contact by letter only		4	4	4	4	4	4
	no contact		5	5	5	5	5	5
(h)	Is he/she working?							
	full time		1	1	1	1	1	1
	part time		2	2	2	2	2	2
	retired		3	3	3	3	3	3
	housewife		4	4	4	4	4	4
	does not work		5	5	5	5	5	5

* 37 How many *grandchildren* do you have?   [|]

  38 How often do you see any of them?

More than once a week	1
Weekly	2
2–3 times monthly	3
6–12 times yearly	4
Rarely	5
Never	6
No grandchildren	7

  39 Do you feel you would like to see more or less of them or are you
     satisfied with the contact you have with them?
     TRY TO RECORD VERBATIM COMMENTS.

More	1
Less	2
Satisfied	3

* 40 How many brothers and sisters do/did you have?   Living   Deceased

                                                       [|]   [|]

  Can you tell me something about them. Are they nearby, do you see
  them often?
  BE SURE TO RECORD NUMBERS OF DECEASED AS WELL AS
  LIVING. TRY TO GET AS MUCH INFORMATION FROM
  CONVERSATION. PROMPT AS NECESSARY.

		(Brothers and sisters)				
		1	2	3	4	5
(a)	Sex Male	1	1	1	1	1
	Female	2	2	2	2	2
(b)	Age					
(c)	Where living?					
	Within 5 miles of here	1	1	1	1	1
	More than 5 miles but less than 15	2	2	2	2	2
	More than 15 but less than 50	3	3	3	3	3
	More than 50 miles away	4	4	4	4	4
(d)	How often do you usually see them?					
	More than once a week	1	1	1	1	1
	weekly	2	2	2	2	2
	2–3 times monthly	3	3	3	3	3
	6–12 times yearly	4	4	4	4	4
	rarely	5	5	5	5	5
	never	6	6	6	6	6
(e)	Would you like to see more or less of them or are you satisfied with the frequency of visits?					
	more	1	1	1	1	1
	less	2	2	2	2	2
	satisfied	3	3	3	3	3

(*f*) How would you describe your relationship
with them? (WAIT). ASK QUESTION
ONLY: USE CATEGORIES ONLY AS
VERIFICATION.

very close and friendly	1	1	1	1	1
based on duty/responsibility	2	2	2	2	2
superficial or out of habit	3	3	3	3	3
contact by letter only	4	4	4	4	4
no contact	5	5	5	5	5

(41) Do you have other relatives or friends and neighbours with whom
you are in contact? PROMPT: COUSINS, NEPHEWS/NIECES,
FRIENDS IN NEIGHBOURHOOD, ETC.
GIVE DETAILS OF *WHO*, *WHERE* THEY LIVE, *HOW
OFTEN SEEN*.

(42) How often do you see any of your children or other relatives to
talk to?

Every day/same household	1
Every day/different household	2
2–3 times a week	3
Once a week	4
2–3 times a month	5
Once a month	6
Every 3 months	7
3 months–1 year	8
About once a year	9
Never	10
No living relatives	11

(43) IF APPLICABLE. Of your relatives, who do you see *most* often?
FIRST NAMES:

Child	1
Brother/sister	2
Parent	3
Uncle/aunt	4
Nephew/niece	5
Cousin	6
Grandchild	7
Other (specify) _____	8

44 Do you ever go to see relatives or friends? Yes 1
INCLUDE BOTH DAY VISITS AND No 2
OVERNIGHT STAYS
How often?

More than once a week	1
Weekly	2
2–3 times a month	3
6–12 times a year	4
Rarely	5

Never   6⎞
No relatives   7⎠ I.M. ☐

45 Apart from the people we have already mentioned, who else do
   you see to talk to regularly? (e.g. church members, village shop,
   milkman, neighbours, etc.)   *Yes   No*
   Neighbours   1   2
   Church members   1   2
   Milkman   1   2
   Local shops   1   2
   Postman   1   2
   Other members of
      community   1   2
   Other (specify) _____   1   2
   No one   1   I.M. ☐

46 In general how do you get on with your neighbours?
   RECORD COMMENTS FULLY AND THEN ASK
   QUESTION BELOW.

47 Would you say you get on very well with all of them, very well with
   most of them, not very well with most, or not very well with any of
   them, or do you have no real contact with them?
   Very well (all)   1
   Very well (most)   2
   Not very well (most)   3
   Not very well (any)   4
   No contact   5⎞
   No neighbours   6⎠ I.M. ☐

48 Do you help any of your neighbours out in any way?   Yes 1
                                                         No   2
   Specify: *Yes   No*
      Shopping   1   2
      Gardening   1   2
      Fuel   1   2
      Cleaning   1   2
      Cooking   1   2
      Other (specify)
      _____   1   2

49 Do you meet as many people as you would like to?   Yes 1
   RECORD COMMENTS.   No   2 L.M. ☐

   LONELINESS/ISOLATION

* 50 Do you have a telephone?   Yes 1
                                                        No   2 I.M. ☐

(51) IF NO: Where do you go to use a telephone?
GIVE ADDRESS OR LOCATION AND DISTANCE FROM
INTERVIEWEE'S HOUSE.

(52) IF NO: Have you tried to get a telephone installed?   Yes 1
RECORD COMMENTS VERBATIM.   No 2

(53) Are you satisfied with your access to a telephone?
RECORD COMMENTS.

Very satisfied	1
Satisfied	2
Neutral	3
Dissatisfied	4
Very dissatisfied	5

* 54 Do you or does a member of your household have a car?

No car	1
Has car	2
H/H member has car	3

* 55 What kind of public transport do you use?

	Yes	No
Bus	1	2
Train	1	2
Taxi	1	2
Other (specify)	1	2
None	1	

(56) Do you find any problems with using public transport?
RECORD COMMENTS FULLY

	Yes	No
Mobility	1	2
Fares	1	2
Timetables	1	2
Other (specify)	1	2

57 In general, how satisfied are you with local public transport?

Very satisfied	1
Satisfied	2
Neutral	3
Dissatisfied	4
Very dissatisfied	5
Never use	0

* 58 Do you *ever* feel rather lonely?
RECORD RESPONSE, THEN ASK WHICH
CATEGORY BEST FITS: RARELY, SOMETIMES,
OFTEN, MOST OF THE TIME.

Never	1	
Rarely	2	
Sometimes	3	
Often	4	
Most of the time	5	

59 IF YES: Are there any particular times when you feel specially like this?
RECORD COMMENTS.

	Yes	*No*
Evening	1	2
Weekends	1	2
Special holidays	1	2
Winter	1	2
Other (specify)		
_____	1	2
No special time	1	2

60 How many hours a day are you usually in the house/flat alone?

0–3	1
3–6	2
6–9	3
9+	4

I.M. ☐

* 61 Are you usually alone in the house/flat all night? Yes 1 / No 2

*(62) Is there anyone in particular you can confide in or talk to about yourself or your problems?

IF YES: Who is it?

First name: _____

No	1
Spouse	2
Brother/sister	3
Child	4
Other relative	5
Friend	6
Neighbour	7
Other	8
More than one	9

L.M. ☐

(63) How long have you known this person? No. of years (ROUND UP)

☐☐

64 IF SPOUSE: Is there anyone else?

No	1
Brother/sister	2
Child	3
Other relative	4
Friend	5
Neighbour	6
Other	7
More than one	8

* 65 Do you wish you had more friends? Yes 1 / No 2

66 Are there people around from whom you can ask small
favours? Who?

PROMPT. Anyone else?	Yes	1	
FIRST NAMES: _____	No	2	L.M. ☐
_____	Never ask favours	3	

67 Is there someone who needs you to take care of them?

	Yes	1
FIRST NAMES: _____	No	2

68 Are there people in this area who you can call real
friends?

RECORD COMMENTS	Yes	1	
VERBATIM.	No	2	L.M. ☐

Can you tell me their first names?
LIST UP TO FIVE FIRST NAMES.

69 Is there someone who particularly depends on your
friendship?

FIRST NAME: _____	Yes	1
	No	2

*(70) Do you have a pet of any kind?

		Yes	No
	Dog	1	2
	Cat	1	2
	Bird	1	2
	Fish	1	2
	Other (specify)		
	_____	1	2
	More than one	1	1
	None	1	

* 71 Where does your nearest permanent neighbour live?
INTERVIEWER: DESCRIBE SITUATION IF
ATYPICAL:

Next door/attached	1	
Next door/detached	2	
Across road	3	
50–100 yards away	4	
100 yards–$\frac{1}{4}$ mile away	5	I.M. ☐
More isolated (estimate		
distance) _____	6	

MOBILITY/DEPENDENCY

* 72 We are interested to find out about how easily people can get around the house. I hope you don't mind my asking a few questions about this.
INTERVIEWER NOTE: SOME OF THESE QUESTIONS MAY SEEM MILDLY OFFENSIVE TO ABLE-BODIED PERSONS: OMIT IF THEY ARE OBVIOUSLY REDUNDANT. ONLY ASK (*a*) AND (*b*) IF TASK REQUIRES HELP OR PRESENTS DIFFICULTY.
Do you generally have difficulty in:

			Can do			(a)	(b)	
		Without diffi-culty on own	On own with diffi-culty	Only with help	Not at all	Who helps? (see codes below)	Is help enough Yes	No
(i)	Having all-over wash or bathing self	1	2	3	4		1	2
(ii)	Washing hands and face	1	2	3	4		1	2
(iii)	Putting on shoes or stockings yourself	1	2	3	4		1	2
(iv)	Doing up buttons and zips yourself	1	2	3	4		1	2
(v)	Dressing self other than above	1	2	3	4		1	2
(vi)	Getting to and using the W.C.	1	2	3	4		1	2
(vii)	Getting in or out of bed	1	2	3	4		1	2
(viii)	Feeding self	1	2	3	4		1	2
(ix)	Shaving (men) Brushing and combing hair (women)	1	2	3	4		1	2
(x)	Cutting own toenails	1	2	3	4		1	2
(xi)	Getting up and down steps	1	2	3	4		1	2

	Without diffi-culty on own	Can do On own with diffi-culty	Only with help	Not at all	(a) Who helps? (see codes below)	(b) Is help enough Yes No
(xii) Getting around the house	1	2	3	4		1 2
(xiii) Getting out of doors on own	1	2	3	4		1 2

Code list for (a)
Spouse 1
Someone else in household 2
Relative outside household 3
Friend/neighbour 4
Voluntary visitor 5
Home help 6
District nurse 7
Other (specify)
———————————— 8

LIST FIRST NAMES OF HELPERS:
————————————————
————————————————
————————————————
————————————————

* 73 INTERVIEWER:
ESTABLISH WHETHER
INTERVIEWEE:

bedfast permanently 1 ⎫
bedfast temporarily, usually
    housebound 2 ⎬ I.M. ☐
housebound permanently 3 ⎭
able to get out only with
    help 4
able to get out unassisted 5

* 74 How long is it since you were last up/went out?

	(a) Got up	(b) Went out
One month or less	1	1
Over 1 month–3 months	2	2
Over 3 months–6 months	3	3
Over 6 months–12 months	4	4
Over 1 year–3 years	5	5
Over 3 years–5 years	6	6
5 years plus	7	7
Vague	8	8
Not applicable	9	9

ASK BEDFAST BOTH PARTS.
ASK HOUSEBOUND (b)
ONLY

HEALTH

* 75 Now, just a few short questions about your health.
Do you suffer from any condition which limits your
activities in any way?
IF YES: SPECIFY: Yes   1
_____   No   2

* 76 In general, how would you describe your state of health?
NOT PROXIES
                              good or excellent   1
                              all right for age   2
                              fair   3
                              poor   4
                              other (specify) _____
                              _____   5

HELP WITH COMMON PROBLEMS AND CRISES

77 One of the things that we are interested in is the kinds of local help
available to people. Can you tell me who you would have turned to?

                                                    FIRST NAMES
(a) If you were ill and could not leave the house   _____
(b) If you wanted advice about money problems   _____
(c) If you were worried about a personal problem   _____
(d) If you were feeling 'down' and just wanted
    someone to talk to   _____
(e) If you needed a lift somewhere   _____
(f) If you needed to borrow something (e.g. food,
    tools, etc.)   _____

CODE FROM: Spouse   1
                       Someone else in household   2
                       Relative outside household   3
                       Friend/neighbour   4
                       Voluntary visitor   5
                       Home help   6
                       District nurse   7
                       Social worker   8
                       Other (specify) _____   9

78 Do you receive help from anyone with any of the following?
ASK (a), (b) AND (c) FOR ALL TASKS.

	Never	Occasionally	Regularly	Daily	(a) Who helps? First Names:	(b) Is help paid?		(c) Need for extra help?	
						Yes	No	Yes	No
Shopping	1	2	3	4		1	2	1	2
Cooking	1	2	3	4		1	2	1	2

	Never	Occasionally	Regularly	Daily	(a) Who helps? First Names:	(b) Is help paid? Yes No		(c) Need for extra help? Yes No	
Laundry	1	2	3	4		1	2	1	2
Ironing	1	2	3	4		1	2	1	2
Making fires	1	2	3	4		1	2	1	2
Cutting/ gathering firewood	1	2	3	4		1	2	1	2
Bringing in fuel	1	2	3	4		1	2	1	2
Gardening	1	2	3	4		1	2	1	2
Household decoration	1	2	3	4		1	2	1	2
Household repairs	1	2	3	4		1	2	1	2
Other (specify)	1	2	3	4		1	2	1	2

(79) INTERVIEWER: ESTABLISH SIZE OF GARDEN:

No garden	1
small	2
average	3
large	4

(80) IF GARDEN: How do you feel about the garden?
Would you say you

Wouldn't be without it	1
Are glad to have it	2
Would rather be without it	3

(81) IF WIDOWED: When your husband/wife died, who did you turn to for help?
RECORD COMMENTS AND GIVE AS MUCH DETAIL AS POSSIBLE.

Someone else in household	1
Relative outside	2
Friend/neighbour	3
Voluntary visitor	4
Home help	5
District nurse	6
Minister of religion	7
Other (specify)	
_____	8

82 One of the things we are interested in is how people manage to get various goods and services, knowing that some people live in very remote places, so I'd like to ask you, for instance:

Where do you do your/get your/ get to your	Local village	Mobile visiting service	Nearby town	Goods delivered/ house call	Other	Not available	Not needed	(a) Are you satisfied with _____ (see codes below)	(b) How do you usually obtain this service/ goods (see codes below)	(c) When did you last obtain this service (see codes below)
grocery shopping	1	2	3	4	5	6	7			
greengroceries	1	2	3	4	5	6	7			
fresh meat	1	2	3	4	5	6	7			
prescriptions	1	2	3	4	5	6	7			
post office	1	2	3	4	5	6	7			
doctor's surgery	1	2	3	4	5	6	7			
chiropodist	1	2	3	4	5	6	7			
optician	1	2	3	4	5	6	7			
library	1	2	3	4	5	6	7			

INTERVIEWER N.B.

CODES FOR (a)

very satisfied	1
satisfied	2
neutral	3
dissatisfied	4
very dissatisfied	5
not applicable	0

CODES FOR (b)

someone else goes	1
goods delivered/house call	2
walk	3
drive hh. car	4
taxi	5
lift	6
public transport	7
more than one of above	8
other (specify)	
	9

CODES FOR (c)

never see/use	1
within last week	2
within last month	3
within last 6 months	4
up to a year ago	5
more than a year ago	6

83 In general, how satisfied would you say you are with services in this community?

very satisfied	1
satisfied	2
neutral	3
dissatisfied	4
very dissatisfied	5

84 Is there anything that you miss living in this community? PROMPT IF NECESSARY: that you might appreciate if you lived somewhere else? OR That you enjoyed before you moved here?

(85) Changing the subject a bit again, could you tell me how you spent last Christmas? INTERVIEWER: IN ADDITION TO WHAT RESPONDENT DID, WE ARE INTERESTED IN THEIR FEELINGS ABOUT IT. SOME, FOR INSTANCE, MAY CHOOSE TO BE ALONE, OTHERS MAY FEEL UNHAPPY ABOUT IT. PROMPT IF NECESSARY: THIS MAY BE A DIFFICULT SUBJECT FOR THE LONELY. I RELY ON YOUR INTUITION AND SENSITIVITY. RECORD VERBATIM COMMENTS. CODE AS APPROPRIATE.

Stayed at home	1
Went away	2
With child(ren)	1
With brothers/sisters	2
With other relatives	3
With friends	4
Alone by choice	5
Alone and lonely	6 L.M.
In hospital	7
Other (specify)	
_____	8

(86) FOR THOSE WHO LIVE ALONE: If you were taken ill or had a bad fall, how would you get help? RECORD COMMENTS FULLY.

Call/shout	1
Bang or knock	2
Telephone	3
Wait for someone to come	4
Prearranged signal	5
Prearranged monitoring	6
Don't know	7 I.M.

(87) FOR THOSE WHO LIVE ALONE: Have you ever needed to get help in an emergency like that in the past? What did you do? RECORD COMMENTS AND DESCRIPTION OF EMERGENCY.

Called/shouted	1
Banged	2
Telephoned	3
Waited for help	4
Used signal	5
Other (specify)	
_____	6
No emergency	7

VOLUNTARY ORGANISATIONS

*(88) Do you belong to a chapel, church, or other religious group?

Yes	1
No	2
No longer	3

(89) IF YES, how long have you been going there?

All life	1
More than 20 years	2
10–19 years	3
5–9 years	4
Less than 5 years	5

*(90) IF YES, how often do you go?

Every week	1
Less than every week but at least once a month	2
2–3 times a year	3
Occasionally	4
Only for weddings/ funerals, etc.	5

(91) Other than the minister/rector, does anyone else from the chapel/church come to see you?
RECORD DETAILS AND COMMENTS.

Yes	1
No	2

(92) Are you a member of any organisations, clubs, societies or voluntary bodies?
LIST:

None	0
One	1
2–3	2
4–5	3
More than 5	4

	Yes	No
OAP organisation	1	2
British Legion	1	2
Women's Institute	1	2
Merched y Wawr	1	2
Trade union	1	2

Political organisation	1	2
Professional organisation	1	2
Red Cross	1	2
WRVS	1	2
Hobby group (gardening, etc.)	1	2
Charity organisation	1	2
Other (specify)		
_____	1	2

(93) IF YES, do you attend meetings?

Yes, regularly	1
Yes, irregularly	2
No	3

(94) IF NO: Why do you not attend meetings?

	Yes	No
Ill health	1	2
Eyesight poor	1	2
Hearing poor	1	2
Too far	1	2
No transport	1	2
Difficult time	1	2
Other (specify)		
_____	1	2

*(95) Do you have any sparetime hobbies, activities or interests? RECORD COMMENTS WITHOUT PROMPT. IF EXTENSIVE ASK: which four take up most time? CODE SUBSEQUENTLY.

	Yes	No
TV/radio	1	2
Gardening	1	2
Needlework/knitting	1	2
Reading	1	2
Other crafts	1	2
Walking	1	2
Playing cards/bingo/ games, etc.	1	2
Other (specify)		
_____	1	2

ETHNICITY

* 96 Do you think of yourself as English or Welsh or some other nationality?

English	1
Welsh	2
$\frac{1}{2}$ and $\frac{1}{2}$	3
British	4
Other	5

* 97 Can you speak Welsh fluently?

Yes	1
No	2

98 IF SPEAKS WELSH: Do you speak Welsh

Most of the time	1
sometimes	2
rarely	3

99 IF SPEAKS WELSH SOMETIMES OR RARELY, ASK:

When would you use Welsh then?

EMPLOYMENT

Now I'd like to ask a few questions about your working life.

(100) Do you have any kind of job now? ASK ABOUT VOLUNTARY WORK.	Not working	1
	employed full time	2
	employed part time	3
	unpaid voluntary work	4

*101 During your years of employment before retirement age, what was the occupation you had longest?
INTERVIEWER: DESCRIBE ACTUAL WORK DONE AND POSITION HELD.

(102) IF WORKING, INCLUDING VOLUNTARY WORK:

How many hours a week do you work?	Occasional/as needed	1
	Up to 5	2
	6–10	3
	11–20	4
	19–40	5
	40+	6

(103) IF IN PAID EMPLOYMENT:

Is your job one you had before retirement age or a new job since you retired?	New job	1
	Same job	2
	Return to earlier job	3

IF EMPLOYED, INCLUDING VOLUNTARY WORK:

(104) What do you do? _____

(105) What was the main reason for leaving your main job?	Compulsory retirement	1
	Voluntary retirement	2
	Disability/injury	3
	Ill health	4
	Redundancy	5
	Other (specify)	
	_____	6

(106) How old were you when you   Age ☐☐
      retired?
      IF NOT RETIRED CODE 99.

(107) IF NOT WORKING:
      Have you looked for a job   Yes   1
      since retirement?   No   2
      IF WORKING AFTER RETIREMENT OR IF THEY HAVE
      LOOKED FOR A JOB AFTER RETIREMENT, ASK:

(108) Why did you decide you   Needed to supplement
      wanted a job after retirement?   pension   1
                                    Wanted to feel useful   2
                                    Wanted something to do   3
                                    The job gives satisfaction 4
                                    For contact with other people 5
                                    Didn't feel ready to retire 6
                                    Other (specify) _____
                                    _____   7

*(109) ASK ALL WOMEN: What was your husband's job for most of
       his working life?
       INTERVIEWER: DESCRIBE ACTUAL WORK DONE
       AND POSITION HELD.

INCOME

Of course you know that this information will be kept quite confidential.
I am reminding you of that because I want to ask you some questions
about your income. The answers will be helpful in understanding what
financial problems elderly people may experience.

(110) Can you tell me whether you or your husband/wife have income from any
      of the following sources?
      INTERVIEWER: INCLUDE COMMON LAW HUSBANDS OR
      WIVES AND INCLUDE SPOUSE'S INCOME EVEN IF THEY ARE
      NOT ELDERLY.

	Yes	No
Wages or salary from employment	1	2
Income from business, practice, etc. if self-employed	1	2
Pension(s) from former employer(s) or spouse's employer	1	2
Any kind of state widow's pension or widow's allowance	1	2
Old age pension or National Insurance Retirement Pension	1	2
Supplementary pension, supplementary allowance	1	2
Attendance allowance	1	2
Other state payments (e.g. war disability pension, war dependant's pension, unemployment, sickness or invalidity benefits, family allowance, FIS, industrial disablement pension)	1	2
Other kinds of regular allowances from organisations, relatives, or friends outside the household (e.g.		

maintenance for self or children from ex-spouse, income
from TU, friendly society or charitable organisation)   1   2
Annuity, income from property, shares, rents
(including boarders, lodgers, bank accounts, bonds,
building societies, i.e. interest)   1   2
Do you receive a rent or rate rebate?   1   2

*(111) Could you show me into which of these groups the Total Net income of
yourself and your spouse combined comes?
INTERVIEWER: SHOW CARD AND READ OUT *WEEKLY*
SCALE (Annual scale matches weekly scale)

Weekly	*Annual*	*Code*
£ 0– 9.99	£ 0– 519	1
£ 10–14.99	£ 520– 779	2
£ 15–19.99	£ 780–1039	3
£ 20–29.99	£1040–1559	4
£ 30–39.99	£1560–2079	5
£ 40–49.99	£2080–2599	6
£ 50–59.99	£2600–3119	7
£ 60–69.99	£3120–3639	8
£ 70–79.99	£3640–4159	9
£ 80–89.99	£4160–4579	10
£ 90–99.99	£4680–5199	11
£100+	£5200+	12

* 112 Do you find this adequate or is   Adequate   1
it difficult to manage on that   Difficulty   2
income?
RECORD INTERVIEWEE'S COMMENTS

113 Do you ever find yourself   No   1
worrying about how to meet   Sometimes   2
your bills and other expenses? Always   3
RECORD COMMENTS

114 IF SOMETIMES OR ALWAYS: *Yes No*
What expenses do you find   Rent   1   2
particularly hard to meet?   Rates   1   2
PROMPT BY READING   Coal   1   2
LIST.   Electric   1   2
ASK: Anything else?   Oil   1   2
Gas   1   2
Food   1   2

Petrol	1	2
Other (specify)	1	2
_____	1	2

INTERVIEWER: INDICATE THIS IS THE END OF INTERVIEW.
THANK INTERVIEWEE: THEN ASK:

(115) Now, would you like to make any suggestions for things that could be done to help elderly people, not just yourself, but elderly people in general? RECORD COMMENTS AS FULLY AS POSSIBLE.

INTERVIEWER REPORT

Reception of interview by respondent:

co-operative	1
rather uninterested	2
unco-operative	3

Comments:

Disabilities impeding interview:

none	1
hearing	2
speech	3
confusion	4
illness/sickness	5
other (specify)	
_____	6

General impression of respondent: (Outstanding needs, problems, health, etc.)

General impression of house (cleanliness, heating, comfort, etc.)

Interview conducted:	Wholly or mainly in English	1
	Wholly or mainly in Welsh	2
	Both	3
Proxy:	Yes	1
	No	2
	Part	3
Indicate if other persons present during interview:	No	1
	Part of time	2
	All of time	3
Full or short interview form:	Full form	1
	Short form	2
	Incomplete	3

Brief resumé of household and respondent's situation. (Continue overleaf if necessary.)

CODING ONLY:

I.M.   (Qs 25, 31, 44, 45, 47, 50, 60, 71, 73, 86)

TOTAL SCORE: ☐☐

L.M.   (Qs 30 × 2, 49, 62, 65, 66, 68, 85)

TOTAL SCORE: ☐☐

Network: List all first names:
            (Qs 21, 43, 62, 66, 67, 68, 69, 72, 77)

TOTAL NUMBER OF
INDIVIDUALS IN
NETWORK: ☐☐

APPENDIX 2 PHILADELPHIA GERIATRIC CENTER MORALE SCALE

The subjective feelings which old people have about their lives have been a focal point of social gerontology. Measurement of subjective states has coalesced around three major scales: the Life Satisfaction Index (LSI) (Neugarten *et al.*, 1961); the Affect Balance Scale (ABS) (Bradburn and Caplovitz, 1965) and the Philadelphia Geriatric Center Morale Scale (PGC) (Lawton, 1972). The LSI scale has been shown to have a high correlation with the judgements of clinical psychologists and all three scales have high inter-correlation scores (Challis, 1982).

The Philadelphia Geriatric Center Morale Scale, used in this study, was designed to take account of the multi-faceted nature of morale. In his choice of items Lawton (1972) focused on three aspects of the life of the elderly person: self-acceptance, a positive attitude to the environment and an acceptance of the unchangeable nature of one's former life. The PGC scale was chosen because it has been shown to be reliable with the very old, with rural populations and because it is the only one to include social relationships among its items (Lawton, 1975).

The original twenty-two-item scale was subsequently refined by Morris and Sherwood (1975) and the resulting seventeen-item scale was adapted for use in this survey. The original method was to ask subjects to agree or disagree with statements about themselves, for example: As I get older, things keep getting worse. It was found during pilot work that elderly subjects had difficulty in understanding this procedure and thus statements were modified to question form. In order to arrive at an aggregate measure positive responses were scored 3, negative responses 1 and neutral (don't know) responses 2. These were subsequently averaged and aggregate responses ranged from a possible high of 3 down to 1·2. Those with scores higher than 2·5 were assessed as having high morale, 2·5–2·1 as having moderate morale and 2·0 and below as having low morale.

The items used in this survey were as follows:

Do things keep getting worse as you get older?
Do you have as much energy as you did last year?
Do you feel lonely much?
Do you see enough of your friends and relatives?
Do little things bother you more this year?
As you get older do you feel less useful?
Do you sometimes worry so much that you can't sleep?
As you get older are things better than expected?
Do you sometimes feel that life isn't worth living?

Are you as happy now as when you were younger?
Do you have a lot to be sad about?
Are you afraid of a lot of things?
Do you get angry more than you used to?
Is life hard for you most of the time?
Are you satisfied with your life today?
Do you take things hard?
Do you get upset easily?

The PGC has been demonstrated to have a high correlation with the LSI (Lohmann, 1977) and a high level of comparability with various depression scales (Morris and Sherwood, 1975). While low morale and depression may sometimes be equivalent, however, it is possible for low morale to occur in the absence of clinical depression, and caution is urged in interpreting the scale in this way (Challis, 1982).

REFERENCES

Abrams, M. (1978), *Beyond Three Score and Ten: A First Report on a Survey of the Elderly* (London: Age Concern).

Abrams, M. (1980), *Beyond Three Score and Ten: A Second Report on a Survey of the Elderly* (London: Age Concern).

Abrams, P. (1978). 'Evaluating soft findings from non-experiments', PSSC/PSSRU conference on Evaluating Interventions for the Elderly.

Abrams, P. (1980), 'Community care: who cares?', introductory address, annual conference of British Society of Gerontology.

Abrams, P., Abrams, S., Humphrey, R., and Snaith, R. (1981), *Action for Care: A Review of Good Neighbour Schemes in England* (London: Volunteer Centre).

Adams, G. (1967), *Kinship in an Urban Setting* (Chicago: Markham).

Age Concern (1977), *Profiles of the Elderly: Their Health and the Health Services* (London: Age Concern).

Allan, G. (1977), 'Class variation in friendship patterns', *British Journal of Sociology*, vol. 28, no. 3, pp. 389–93.

Anderson, W. Ferguson, and Judge, T. (eds) (1974), *Geriatric Medicine* (London: Academic Press).

Andrews, F. M., and Withey, S. B. (1974), 'Developing measures of perceived life quality: results from several national surveys', *Social Indicators Research*, Part 1, pp. 1–26.

Arensburg, Conrad (1937), *The Irish Countryman* (London: Macmillan).

Aughney, H. (1963), 'Aged solitary rural dwellers in County Wexford. Part I – a survey of fifty rural dwellers', *British Journal of Geriatric Practice*, vol. 2, pp. 105–11.

Back, K. W. (1965), 'A social psychologist looks at social structure', in E. Shanas and G. F. Streib (eds), *Social Structure and the Family: Generational Relations* (Englewood Cliffs, NJ: Prentice-Hall), pp. 326–40.

Bailey, F. G. (ed.) (1971), *Gifts and Poison* (Oxford: Blackwell).

Bamford, T. (1982), 'The debate begins', *Social Work Today*. vol. 13, no. 33 (4 May), p. 1.

Bayley, M. (1980), 'Neighbourhood care and community care: a response to Philip Abrams', *Social Work Service*, vol. 26, pp. 4–9.

Bayley, M., Seyd, R., Tennant, A., and Simons, K. (1982), 'What resources does the informal sector require to fulfil its role?', *The Barclay Report: Papers from a Consultation Day*, NISW Paper No. 15 (London: National Institute of Social Work), pp. 5–45.

Bell, B. (1974), 'Cognitive dissonance and the life satisfaction of old adults', *Journal of Gerontology*, vol. 29, pp. 564–71.

Bell, C. (1968), *Middle Class Families: Social and Geographical Mobility* (London: Routledge & Kegan Paul).

Bennet, J., and Despres, L. (1960), 'Kinship structure and instrumental activities: a theoretical inquiry', *American Anthropologist*, vol. LXII (April 1960), pp. 254–67.

Bennett, R. (1973), 'Living conditions and everyday needs of the elderly with particular reference to social integration', *International Journal of Ageing and Human Development*, vol. 4, pp. 179–98.

Black, J. A. (1981), 'Social workers' perceptions of practice', part 1, Working Paper no. 17 (Bangor: Social Theory and Institutions, University College of North Wales).

Black, J. A., Bowl, R., Burns, D., Critcher, C., Grant, G. W. B., and Stockford, R. (1983), *Social Work in Context: A Comparative Study of Three Area Social Work Teams* (London: Tavistock Publications).

Blau, Z. S. (1973), *Old Age in a Changing Society* (New York: Franklin Watts).

Blenkner, M. (1965), 'Social work and family relationships in later life with some thoughts on filial maturity', in E. Shanas and G. F. Streib (eds), *Social Structure and the Family: Generational Relations* (Englewood Cliffs, NJ: Prentice-Hall).

Bollman, S. R., Moxley, V. M., and Elliott, N. O. (1975), 'Family and community activities of rural nonfarm families with children', *Journal of Leisure*, vol. 7, no. 1, pp. 53–62.

Bolton, C. R., and Dignum-Scott, J. (1979), 'Peer-group advocacy counselling for the elderly', *Journal of Gerontological Social Work*, vol. 1, no. 4, pp. 321–31.

Bott, E. (1957), *Family and Social Network* (London: Tavistock Institute of Human Relations).

Bradburn, N. M., and Caplovitz, D. (1965), *Reports on Happiness: A Pilot Study of Behaviour Related to Mental Health* (Chicago: Aldine).

Britton, J. H., Mather, W. G., and Lansing, A. K. (1961a), 'Expectations for older persons in a rural community: living arrangements and family relationships', *Journal of Gerontology*, vol. 16, pp. 156–62.

Britton, J. H., Williams, G., Mather, W. G., and Lansing, A. K. (1961b), 'Expectations for older persons in a rural community: work and retirement', *Geriatrics*, vol. 16, pp. 664–71.

Brody, H. (1974), *Inishkillane: Change and Decline in the West of Ireland* (New York: Schocken Books).

Bull, C. N., and Aucoin, J. B. (1975), 'Voluntary association participation and life satisfaction: a replication note', *Journal of Gerontology*, vol. 30, no. 1, pp. 73–6.

Butler, R. N. (1964), 'The life review: an interpretation of reminiscence in the aged', in E. Kastenbaum (ed.), *New Thoughts on Old Age* (New York: Springer).

Butler, R. N., Gertman, J. S., Oberlander, D. L., and Schlindler, L. (1979–80), 'Self-care, self-help and the elderly', *International Journal of Ageing and Human Development*, vol. 10, no. 1, pp. 95–117.

Bytheway, W. R. (1979), *Care in the Street* (Swansea: University College).

Central Statistical Office (1978), *Family Expenditure Survey* (FES), 1978 (London: HMSO).

Central Statistical Office (1976), *Regional Statistics*, no. 12 (London: HMSO).

Central Statistical Office (1979), *Regional Satistics*, no. 14 (London: HMSO).

Challis, D. J. (1981), 'The measurement of outcome in social care of the elderly', *Journal of Social Policy*, vol. 10, no. 1, pp. 179–208.

Challis, D., and Davies, B. (1980), 'A new approach to community care of the elderly', *British Journal of Social Work*, vol. 10, pp. 1–18.

Chatfield, W. F. (1977), 'Economic sociological factors influencing life satisfaction of the aged', *Journal of Gerontology*, vol. 32, no. 5, pp. 593–9.

Cibulski, O. (1981), 'Instrumental support networks of the elderly', paper presented to the XII International Congress of Gerontology, Hamburg, 11–17 July.

Coles, O. (1978), 'Transport and rural deprivation', in *Rural Poverty: Poverty, Deprivation and Planning in Rural Areas* (London: Child Poverty Action Group).

Collier, K. (1977), 'Rural social work: theory and practice', mimeographed paper presented to the Canadian Association of Schools of Social Work, 10th Annual Conference, Fredericton, New Brunswick, 6–9 June.

Collins, A. H., and Pancoast, D. L. (1976), *Natural Helping Networks: A Strategy for Prevention* (Washington, DC: National Association of Social Workers).

Cooper, M. (1980), 'Normanton: interweaving social work and the community', in R. Hadley and M. McGrath (eds), *Going Local* (London: National Council of Voluntary Organisations).

Craven, P., and Wellman, B. (1973), 'The network city', *Sociological Inquiry*, vol. 43, nos 3 and 4, pp. 57–88.

Creecy, R. F. (1976), 'Environmental and structural effects on the friendships, social integration and morale of the aged', doctoral dissertation, University of Wisconsin, Madison.

Cutler, S. G. (1973), 'Voluntary association participation and life satisfaction: a cautionary note', *Journal of Gerontology*, vol. 28, pp. 96–100.

Cutler, S. G. (1977), 'Ageing and voluntary association participation', *Journal of Gerontology*, vol. 32, no. 4, pp. 470–9.

Daatland, S. V. (1983), 'Care systems', *Ageing and Society*, vol. 3, pt 1, pp. 1–21.

Davies, E. R. Ll. (1978), *New Ways Forward: Public Transport in Clwyd* (Mold: Clwyd County Council).

Department of Employment and Productivity (1978), *Family Expenditure Survey* (London: HMSO).

Department of Health and Social Security (1981), *Growing Older*, Government White Paper (London: HMSO).

Dunnell, Karen, and Dobbs, Joy (1982), *Nurses Working in the Community*, OPCS, Social Survey Division, on behalf of the DHSS (London: HMSO).

Elder, G. H., and Rockwell, R. C. (1979), 'The life course and human development: an ecological perspective', *International Journal of Behavioural Development*, vol. 2, pp. 1–21.

Family Expenditure Survey (FES), see Central Statistical Office.

Fengler, A. P., Danigelis, N., and Little, V. (1981), 'Rural–urban differences among the elderly in subjective evaluations of unfavourable objective states', paper presented to the XIIth International Congress of Gerontology, Hamburg, 11–17 July.

Fengler, A. P., and Goodrich, N. (1979), 'Wives of elderly disabled men: the hidden patients', *The Gerontologist*, vol. 19, no. 2, pp. 175–83.

Field, M. (1972), *The Aged, the Family and the Community* (London: Columbia University Press).

Finch, J., and Groves, D. (1980), 'Community care and the family: a case for equal opportunities?', *Journal of Social Policy*, vol. 9, pt 4, October, pp. 487–511.

Firth, R., *et al.* (1969), *Families and Relatives* (London: Routledge & Kegan Paul).

Fooken, I. (1981), 'Women in old age: the need for a differentiated view', paper presented to XIIth International Congress of Gerontology, Hamburg, 11–17 July.

Frankeberg, R. (1957), *Village on the Border* (London: Cohen & West).

Froland, C. (1980), 'Formal and informal care: discontinuities in a continuum', *Social Service Review*, vol. 54, pp. 572–87.

Froland, C., Pancoast, D., Chapman, N., and Kimboko, P. (1979), 'Professional partnerships with informal helpers', paper presented to the annual convention of the American Psychological Association, New York, 4 September.

Gans, H. (1968), 'Urbanism and suburbanism as ways of life', in R. E. Pahl (ed.), *Readings in Urban Sociology* (New York: Pergamon).

Garrison, J. E., and Howe, J. A. (1976), 'Community intervention with the elderly: social network approach', *Journal of American Gerontological Sociology*, vol. 24, no. 7, pp. 329–33.

George, L. N., and Maddox, G. L. (1977), 'Subjective adaptation to loss of the work role: a longitudinal study', *Journal of Gerontology*, vol. 32, no. 4, pp. 456–62.

Gifford, A., and Golde, P. (1978), 'Self-esteem in an ageing population', *Journal of Gerontological Social Work*, vol. 1, no. 1, pp. 69–80.

Goffman, E. (1959), *The Presentation of Self in Everyday Life* (New York: Doubleday).

Golant, S. M. (ed.) (1979), *Location and Environment of Elderly Populations* (New York: Halsted).

Goldfarb, A. I. (1965), 'Psychodynamics and the three-generational family', in E. Shanas and G. F. Streib (eds), *Social Structure and the Family* (Englewood Cliffs, NJ: Prentice-Hall).

Goldstein, B., and Eichhorn, R. L. (1961), 'The changing Protestant ethic: rural-patterns in health, work and leisure', *American Sociological Review*, vol. 26, pp. 556–65.

Grant, G. W. B. (1981a), 'Monitoring social services delivery in rural areas: intake cases in two contrasting area teams', Working Paper no. 14 (Bangor: Social Services in Rural Areas Research Project, University College of North Wales).

Grant, G. W. B. (1981b), 'Monitoring social services delivery in rural areas: long-term work in two contrasting area teams', Working Paper no. 15 (Bangor: Social Services in Rural Areas Research Project, University College of North Wales).

Gross-Andrew, S., and Zimmer, A. H. (1980), 'Incentives to families caring for disabled elderly: research and demonstration project to strengthen the natural supports system', *Journal of Gerontological Social Work*, no. 2, pp. 119–33.

Hadley, R., and Hatch, S. (1981), *Social Welfare and the Failure of the State* (London: Allen & Unwin).

Hadley, R., and McGrath, M. (1980), *Going Local: Neighbourhood Social Services* (London: National Council for Voluntary Organisations).

Hadley, R., and McGrath, M. (1984 in press) *When Social Services Are Local: The Normanton Experience*, NISW series (London: Allen & Unwin).

Hadley, R., and Webb, A. (1974), *Loneliness, Social Isolation and Old People* (London: Age Concern).

Hadley, R., Webb, A., and Farrell, C. (1975), *Across the Generations: Old People and Young Volunteers* (London: Allen & Unwin).

Hannan, D. (1972), 'Kinship, neighbourhood and social change in Irish rural communities', *Economic and Social Review*, vol. 3, no. 2, pp. 163–88.

Harp, J., and Gagan, R. (1969), 'Changes in rural social organisations: comparative data from three studies', *Rural Sociology*, vol. 341, pp. 80–5.

Harris, A. I. (1971), *Handicapped and Impaired in Great Britain* (London: OPCS).

Harris, L. (1975), *The Myth and Reality of Ageing in America* (Washington, DC: The National Council on the Ageing).

Hausman, C. P. (1979), 'Short-term counselling groups for people with elderly parents', *The Gerontologist*, vol. 19, no. 3, pp. 102–7.

Hazan, H. (1980), *The Limbo People: A Study of the Constitution of the Time Universe among the Aged* (London: Routledge & Kegan Paul).

Hellebrandt, F. A. (1980), 'Ageing among the advantaged: a new look at the stereotype of the elderly', *The Gerontologist*, vol. 20, no. 4, pp. 404–17.

Help the Aged (1977), *Cry and You Cry Alone* (London: Help the Aged).

Hobman, D. (1981), 'Caring for the caregivers of the elderly', paper presented to the International Congress of Gerontology, Hamburg, 11–17 July (London: Age Concern).

Hörl, J., and Rosenmayr, L. (1981), 'Assistance to the elderly as a common task of the family and social service organisations', paper presented at the International Congress of Gerontology, Hamburg, 11–17 July.

Hunt, A. (1978), 'The elderly at home: a study of people aged sixty-five and over living in the community in England in 1976', Social Survey Division, OPCS.

Isaacs, B. (1982), 'The process of ageing II', paper delivered at DHSS seminar on support for elderly people living in the community, Norwich, University of East Anglia.

Isaacs, B., Livingstone, M., and Neville, Y. (1972), *Survival of the Unfittest: A Study of Geriatric Patients in Glasgow* (London: Routledge & Kegan Paul).

Jandetti, D. V., and Gelfand, D. E. (1976), 'Care of the aged: attitudes of white ethnic families', *The Gerontologist*, vol. 16, no. 6, pp. 544–9.

Jenkins, D. (1971), *The Agricultural Community in South West Wales at the Turn of the Twentieth Century* (Cardiff: University of Wales Press).

Jerrome, D. (1981), 'The significance of friendship for women in later life', *Ageing and Society*, vol. 1, pt 2, pp. 175–97.

Karn, V. (1977), *Retiring to the Seaside* (London: Routledge & Kegan Paul).

Kent, D. (1976), 'Can they go home again?', *Social and Rehabilitation Record*, vol. 3, no. 4, pp. 20–1.

Kivett, V. R. (1979), 'Discriminators of loneliness among the rural elderly: implications for intervention', *The Gerontologist*, vol. 19, no. 1, pp. 108–15.

Kivett, V. R., and Maxheamver, R. (1980), 'Perspectives on the childless rural elderly: a comparative analysis', *The Gerontologist*, vol. 20, no. 6, p. 708.

Klein, J. F. (1965), *Samples from English Culture* (London: Routledge & Kegan Paul).

Knapp, M. R. J. (1977), 'The activity theory of ageing: an examination in the English context', *The Gerontologist*, vol. 17, no. 6, pp. 553–9.

Knight, B., and Hayes, R. (1981), *Self Help in the Inner City* (Plymouth: McDonald & Evans).

Knox, A. B. (1977), *Adult Development and Learning* (London: Jossey-Bass).

Kutner, B. (1962), 'The social nature of ageing', *The Gerontologist*, vol. 2, no. 2, pp. 5–8.

Lake, T. (1980), *Loneliness: Why it Happens and How to Overcome it* (London: Sheldon Press).

Laslett, P. (1965), *The World We Have Lost* (London: Matthew).

Laslett, P. (1981), Response to Chairman's Report at British Society of Gerontology Annual Conference, Hull, September.

Law, C. M., and Warnes, A. M. (1973), 'The movement of retired people to seaside resorts: a study of Morecambe and Llandudno', *Town Planning Review*, vol. 44, no. 4, pp. 372–90.

Lawton, M. P. (1972), 'Dimensions of morale', in D. P. Kent *et al.*, *Research, Planning and Action for the Elderly* (New York: Behavioural Publications).

Lawton, M. P. (1975), 'The Philadelphia Geriatric Center morale scale: a revision', *Journal of Gerontology*, vol. 30, pp. 85–9.

Lawton, M. P. (1980), *Environment and Ageing* (Monterrey, Calif.: Brooks/Cole Publishing Co.).

Lebowitz, B. D. (1980), 'Old age and family functioning', *Journal of Gerontological Social Work*, vol. 1, no. 2, pp. 111–18.

Lee, G. R., and Ihinger-Tallman, M. (1980), 'Sibling interaction and morale: the effects of family relations on older people', *Research on Ageing*, vol. 2, no. 8, September, pp. 367–91.

Lehr, U. M. (1981), 'Consistency and change in family role activity and satisfaction in old age', paper presented to the International Congress of Gerontology, Hamburg, 11–17 July.

Lemon, A. (1973), 'Retirement and its effect on small towns: the example of Norfolk and Suffolk', *Town Planning Review*, vol. 44, no. 3, pp. 254–62.

Levin, S. (1964), 'Depression in the aged: the importance of external factors', in E. Kastenbaum, *New Thoughts on Old Age* (New York: Springer).

Leyton, E. H. (1975), *The One Blood: Kinship and Class in an Irish Village* (Newfoundland: Institute of Social and Economic Research, Memorial University).

Lipman, A., and Longino, C. F. (1981), 'Family support networks in two life care communities', paper presented at the International Congress of Gerontology, Hamburg, 11–17 July.

Littlejohn, J. (1964), *Westrigg: The Sociology of a Cheviot Parish* (London: Routledge & Kegan Paul).

Litwak, F., and Szelenyi, I. (1969), 'Primary group structures and their functioning: kin, neighbours, and friends', *American Social Review*, vol. 34, pp. 465–81.

Lohmann, N. (1977), 'Correlations of life satisfaction, morale and adjustment measures', *Journal of Gerontology*, vol. 32, no. 1, pp. 73–5.

Luders, I. (1981), 'Social work for the aged and family support', paper presented to the International Congress of Gerontology, Hamburg, 11–17 July.

Luft, H. S., Hershey, J. C., and Morrell, J. (1976), 'Factors affecting the use of physician services in a rural community', *American Journal of Public Health*, vol. 66, no. 9, pp. 865–71.

McAllister, L., and Fischer, C. S. (1978), 'A procedure for surveying personal networks', *Sociological Methods and Research*, vol. 7, no. 2, November, pp. 131–48.

Maclean, M. J. (1976), *Major Life Events, Life Satisfaction and Retirement Reactions*, unpublished PhD thesis, Bedford College, University of London.

Maas, H. S., and Kuypers, J. A. (1974), *From Thirty to Seventy: A Forty-Year Longitudinal Study of Adult Life Styles and Personality* (San Francisco: Jossey-Bass).

Maede, D. (1981), 'A study of the attitude towards old people and the sense of responsibility for the aged parents', paper presented to International Congress of Gerontology, Hamburg, 11–17 July.

Mauss, M. (1954), *The Gift*, trans. Ian Cunnison (London: Cohen & West).

Mellor, M. W. (1962), 'Retirement to the coast', *Town Planning Review*, vol. 33, no. 1, pp. 40–3.

Morris, J. N., and Sherwood, S. (1975), 'A retesting and modification of the Philadelphia Geriatric Center morale scale', *Journal of Gerontology*, vol. 30, pp. 77–84.

Moseley, M. J., Hannan, R. G., Coles, O. B., and Spencer, M. B. (1977), *Rural Transport and Accessibility*, Vols I and II (Norwich: University of East Anglia).

Moyes, A. (1976), 'Accessibility to general practitioners services on Anglesey: some trip-making implications', mimeographed paper (Aberystwyth: Department of Geography, University College of Wales).

Mulligan, M. A., and Bennett, R. (1977), 'Assessment of mental health and social problems during multiple friendly visits: the development and evaluation of a friendly visiting programme for the isolated elderly', *International Journal of Ageing and Human Development*, vol. 8, no. 1, pp. 43 ff.

National Council for the Single Woman and Her Dependants (1979), *The Loving Trap: Report of a Research Study of 700 Single Women with Elderly Dependants* (London: National Council for the Single Woman and Her Dependants).

National Institute for Social Work (1982), *Social Workers: Their Role and Tasks* (the Barclay Report) (London: Bedford Square Press).

Neugarten, B. L., Havighurst, R. J., and Tobin, S. S. (1961), 'Measurement of life satisfaction', *Journal of Gerontology*, vol. 16, pp. 134–43.

Novak, M. (1979), 'Thinking about ageing: a critique of liberal social gerontology', *Age and Ageing*, vol. 8, no. 4, pp. 209–15.

Office of Populations Censuses and Surveys (OPCS) (1980), *Social Trends No. 10* (London: HMSO).

Pahl, R. E. (1965), 'Class and community in English commuter villages', *Rural Sociology*, vol. 30, no. 1, pp. 5–22.

Palmore, R. (1976), 'Total chance of institutionalisation among the aged', *The Gerontologist*, vol. 16, no. 6, pp. 504–7.

Parsloe, P. (1981), *Social Services Area Teams* (London: Allen & Unwin).

Patterson, S. L. (1977), 'Towards a conceptualisation of natural helping', *Arete*, vol. 4, no. 3, pp. 161–71 (Lawrence, Kansas: University of Kansas).

Pinker, R. A. (1982), 'An alternative view', in National Institute for Social Work, *Social Workers: Their Role and Tasks* (London: Bedford Square Press).

Pope, P. J. (1978), *Emergency Admissions into Old People's Homes* Version 2 (Cardiff: Mid-Glamorgan County Council Social Services Department).

Power, B. (1980), *Old and Alone in Ireland* (Dublin: Society of St Vincent de Paul).

Power, M. J. and Kelly, S. (1981), 'Evaluating domiciliary volunteer care of the very old', in E. M. Goldberg and N. Connelly (eds), *Evaluative Research in Social Care* (London: Heinemann), pp. 214–34.

Redfield, R. (1956), *The Little Community* (Chicago: University of Chicago Press).

Rees, A. D. (1950), *Life in a Welsh Countryside* (Cardiff: University of Wales Press).

Regional Statistics, see Central Statistical Office.

Rieger, J. H., and Beegle, J. A. (1974), 'Integration of rural migrants in new settings', *Rural Sociology*, vol. 39, no. 1, pp. 42–55.

Robinson, F., and Abrams, P. (1978). *What We Know about the Neighbours*, a working paper (Durham: Rowntree Research Unit, University of Durham).

Rosenmayr, L. (1968), 'Family relations of the elderly', *Journal of Marriage and the Family*, vol. 30, pp. 672–80.

Rosow, I. (1965), 'Intergenerational relationships: problems and proposals', in E. Shanas and G. F. Streib, *Social Structure and the Family: Generational Relations* (Englewood Cliffs, NJ: Prentice-Hall).

Rosow, I. (1967), *Social Integration of the Aged* (New York: Free Press).

Rosser, C., and Harris, C. (1965), *The Family and Social Change* (London: Routledge & Kegan Paul).

Rueveni, U. (1979), *Networking Families in Crisis* (New York: Human Services Press).

Russell, A. J. (1975), *The Village in Myth and Reality* (The Charles Coulson lecture delivered in October at Luton Industrial College) (London: Chester House Publications).

Savitsky, E., and Sharkey, H. (1972). 'The geriatric patient and his family: study of family interaction in the aged', *Journal of Geriatric Psychiatry*, vol. 5, pp. 3–19.

Schooler, K. (1975), 'A comparison of rural and non-rural elderly on selected variables', in R. Q. Atchley (ed.), *Rural Environments and Ageing* (Washington, DC: Gerontological Society), pp. 27–42.

Scott, J. P., and Kivett, V. R. (1981), 'Differences in the subjective well-being of older widows and widowers', paper presented at the International Congress of Gerontology, Hamburg, 11–17 July.

Shanas, E. (1968), 'The family and social class', in E. Shanas *et al*., *Old People in Three Industrial Societies* (London: Routledge & Kegan Paul).

Shanas, E. (1977), 'The elderly: family, bureaucracy and family help patterns', paper presented Vichy, France – referred to by Mark Abrams, 1980.

Shanas, E. (1979), 'The family as a social support system in old age', *The Gerontologist*, vol. 19, no. 2, pp. 169–74.

Shanas, E. (1981), 'Old parents: middle aged children', paper presented to the International Congress of Gerontology, Hamburg, 11–17 July.

Shanas, E., and Streib, G. F. (1965), *Social Structure and the Family: Generational Relations* (Englewood Cliffs, NJ: Prentice-Hall).

Shapiro, J. (1969), 'Dominant leaders among slum hotel residents', *American Journal of Orthopsychiatry*, vol. 39, pp. 644–50.

Sheldon, J. H. (1948), *The Social Medicine of Old Age: Report of an Inquiry in Wolverhampton* (London: Oxford University Press).

Slater, P. E. (1970), *The Pursuit of Loneliness: American Culture at Breaking Point* (Boston: Beacon Press).

Smith, C. J. (1978), 'Self-help and social networks in the urban community', *Ekistics*, vol. 45, no. 268.

Snow, D. L., and Gordon, J. (1980), 'Social network analysis and intervention with the elderly', *The Gerontologist*, vol. 20, no. 4, August, pp. 463–7.

Spakes, P. R. (1979), 'Family, friendship and community interaction as related to life satisfaction of the elderly', *Journal of Gerontological Social Work*, vol. 1, no. 4, Summer, pp. 279–93.

Stephens, R. C., Blau, Z., Oser, G., and Millar, M. (1978), 'Ageing, social support systems and social policy', *Journal of Gerontological Social Work*, vol. 1, no. 1, pp. 33–45.

Stevenson, O. (1980), 'A special relationship', *New Age*, Summer, pp. 18–22.

Sussman, M. B. (1965), 'Relationships of adult children with their parents in the United States', in E. Shanas and G. F. Streib (eds), *Social Structure and the Family: Intergenerational Relationships* (Englewood Cliffs, NJ: Prentice-Hall).

Szalai, A., and Andrews, F. (1980), *The Quality of Life*, Sage Studies in International Sociology, Vol. 20 (London: Sage Publications).

Tamir, L. M. (1979), *Communication and the Ageing Process: Interaction throughout the Life Cycle* (Oxford: Pergamon).

Tarran, E. (1981), 'Caring for dependent elderly people in rural areas by means of enhanced forms of community support', interim report of a community care project on Anglesey, Working Paper no. 20 (Bangor: Social Services in Rural Areas Research Project, University College of North Wales).

Tarran, E. (1982), 'First impressions on helpers in the Anglesey community care project', Working Paper no. 28 (Bangor: Social Services in Rural Areas Research Project, University College of North Wales).

Thomas, C., and Winyard, S. (1979), 'Rural incomes', in J. Martin-Shaw (ed.), *Deprivation and Planning* (Norwich: Geo. Abstracts).

Tinker, A. (1980), *Housing the Elderly: Near Relatives, Moving and Other Options*, Housing Development Directorate, Occasional Paper 1/80 (London: HMSO).

Tinker, A. (1981), *The Elderly in Modern Society* (London: Longman).

Todd, H., and Taylor, H. (1981), 'Social gerontology in Britain: from research to policy', paper presented to the International Congress of Gerontology, Hamburg, 11–17 July.

Tönnies, F. (1957), *Gemeinschaft und Gessellschaft* (New York: Harper).

Toseland, R., and Rosch, J. (1979–80), 'Correlates of life satisfaction: and aid analysis', *International Journal of Ageing and Human Development*, vol. 10, no. 2, pp. 203–11.

Townsend, P. (1957), *The Family Life of Old People* (London: Routledge & Kegan Paul).

Townsend, P. (1965), 'The effects of family structure on the likelihood of admission to an institution in old age: the application of a general theory', in E. Shanas and G. F. Streib (eds), *Social Structure and the Family: Generational Relations* (Englewood Cliffs, NJ: Prentice-Hall).

Treas, J. (1977), 'Family support systems for the aged: some sociological and demographical considerations', *The Gerontologist*, vol. 17, no. 6, pp. 486–91.

Walker, G. (1975), 'Social networks in rural space: a comparison of two southern Ontario localities', *East Lakes Geographer*, vol. 10, pp. 68–77.

Warren, D. I. (1980), 'Support systems in different types of neighbourhoods', in J. Garbarino and H. Stocking, *Protecting Children from Abuse and Neglect* (San Francisco: Jossey-Bass).

Warren, D. I. (1981), *Helping Networks: How People Cope with Problems in the Urban Community* (Notre Dame, Ind: University of Notre Dame).

Weihl, H. (1981), 'Cultural differences and situational constraints on the interactions between aged parents and their adult children', paper presented to the International Congress of Gerontology, Hamburg, 11–17 July.

Weiss, R. S. (1973), *Loneliness: The Experience of Emotional and Social Isolation* (Boston, Mass.: Massachusetts Institute of Technology).

Wenger, G. C. (1979), *Report to DHSS on European Symposium on the Elderly and the Care System*, Jadwisin, Poland, 21–25 May (Bangor: Social Services in Rural Areas Research Project, University College of North Wales).

Wenger, G. C. (1980), *Mid-Wales: Deprivation or Development: A Study of Patterns of Employment in Selected Communities*, Board of Celtic Studies Social Science Monographs no. 5 (Cardiff: University of Wales Press).

Wenger, G. C. (1982), 'Ageing in rural communities: family contacts and community integration', *Ageing and Society*, vol. 2, no. 2, pp. 211–29.

White, D. (1974), 'The village life', *New Society*, vol. 29, pp. 790–4.

Whittington, H. J. (1977), 'Widowhood in a seaside resort: a study of the situation of some elderly widows and their response to bereavement', M. Litt thesis, Department of Social Administration, University of Lancaster.

Wilkes, R. (1978), 'General philosophy and attitudes to ageing', paper delivered at BASW Conference on Ageing, *Social Work Today*, vol. 9, no. 45, pp. 14–16.

Williams, W. M. (1956), *The Sociology of an English Village: Gosforth* (London: Routledge & Kegan Paul).

Williamson, J. W., Stoke, I. H., *et al.* (1964), 'Old people at home: their unreported needs', *The Lancet*, vol. 1, pp. 117–20.

Windley, P. (1977), 'Environmental intervention: case studies in independent living among the rural elderly', Gerontological Society Summer Research Fellowship Programme, Washington, DC.

Wood, V., and Robertson, J. F. (1978), 'Friendship and kinship interaction: differential effect on the morale of the elderly', *Journal of Marriage and the Family*, vol. 40, no. 2, pp. 369–75.

Wood, V., Wylie, M., and Sheafor, B. (1969), 'An analysis of a short self-report measure of life satisfaction: correlations with rater judgements', *Journal of Gerontology*, vol. 24, pp. 465–9.

Worach-Karolas, A. (1979), 'Family and neighbourly relations: their role for the elderly', in G. Dooghe and Y. Helander (eds), *Family Life in Old Age* (London: Martinus Nihoff).

World Health Organisation (1959), *Mental Health Problems of the Ageing and the Aged*, Technical Report Series no. 171 (Geneva: World Health Organisation).

Youmans, E. G. (1977), 'The rural aged', *Annals American Academy Social Science*, vol. 429, pp. 81–90.

Young, M., and Willmott, P. (1957), *Family and Kinship in East London* (London: Penguin Books).

INDEX